Caring is Sharing?

Caring is Sharing?
Couples navigating parental leave at the transition to parenthood

Katherine Twamley

First published in 2024 by
UCL Press
University College London
Gower Street
London WC1E 6BT

Available to download free: www.uclpress.co.uk

Text © Author, 2024
Images © Author, 2024

The author has asserted her rights under the Copyright, Designs and Patents Act 1988 to be identified as the author of this work.

A CIP catalogue record for this book is available from The British Library.

Any third-party material in this book is not covered by the book's Creative Commons licence. Details of the copyright ownership and permitted use of third-party material is given in the image (or extract) credit lines. If you would like to reuse any third-party material not covered by the book's Creative Commons licence, you will need to obtain permission directly from the copyright owner.

This book is published under a Creative Commons Attribution-Non-Commercial 4.0 International licence (CC BY-NC 4.0), https://creativecommons.org/licenses/by-nc/4.0/. This licence allows you to share and adapt the work for non-commercial use providing attribution is made to the author and publisher (but not in any way that suggests that they endorse you or your use of the work) and any changes are indicated. Attribution should include the following information:

Twamley, K. 2024. *Caring is Sharing? Couples navigating parental leave at the transition to parenthood*. London: UCL Press. https://doi.org/10.14324/111.9781800087439

Further details about Creative Commons licences are available at https://creativecommons.org/licenses/

ISBN: 978-1-80008-740-8 (Hbk.)
ISBN: 978-1-80008-741-5 (Pbk.)
ISBN: 978-1-80008-743-9 (PDF)
ISBN: 978-1-80008-744-6 (epub)
DOI: https://doi.org/10.14324/111.9781800087439

This one is for you, Mila

Contents

Figure and tables ix
Acknowledgements xi
Key terms xiii
Notes on transcription xv

1. The promise of shared parental leave: introduction to the study   1

Part I: Decisions about parental leave

2. Encountering barriers to the take-up of shared parental leave: 'non-sharers'   31

3. Why and how some couples decide to share leave: 'sharers'   53

Part II: Experiences of the leave period

4. Non-sharers' experiences and practices during the first year after their child is born   79

5. Leave sharers' experiences and practices during the first year after their child is born   105

Part III: After the leave is over

6. Breadwinning fathers and primary care mothers   131

7. Mothers as family managers   153

8. Parents sharing responsibilities of paid and unpaid work   179

9. Does shared parental leave live up to its promise? Concluding thoughts   195

Appendix: analysis methods   221
References   225
Index   239

Figure and tables

Figure

1.1	Emily and Edward's household portrait	18

Tables

0.1	The participants and their characteristics	xvi
1.1	Emily and Edward's household portrait	19

Acknowledgements

As any parent knows, the birth of a first child is a very hectic and disorienting period in a person's life. I have been very fortunate that 42 such new parents agreed to spend time with me and write regular diaries documenting their experiences and feelings during this time. I hope they will feel that I have done justice to their stories: this has been my primary concern in the pages that follow. I am very grateful for their time and trust.

I would also like to say thanks to the many colleagues who have supported me as I have developed this work. Thank you to Heejung Chung, Ann Oakley (as ever!), Margaret O'Brien and Eva-Maria Schmidt for reading drafts of this book. Your comments and suggestions sharpened the analyses and arguments and ultimately made this a much better book. I am also grateful to Andrea Doucet, Jacqui Gabb, Francine Hudson, Peter Moss, Jonathan Swan and Jo Swinson for their advice and inspiration as I developed the project and findings. And to Pat Gordon-Smith for her helpful suggestions but most importantly her enthusiasm and kind words for the proposal and first draft. Any faults that remain are entirely my own.

Thank you to the Leverhulme Trust for funding the research and to colleagues at the Thomas Coram Research Unit at UCL for providing such a supportive atmosphere. Special thanks to Charlotte Faircloth who has buoyed me through many a WhatsApp conversation at all times of day and night. My thanks also to collaborators who demonstrated boundless levels of patience as I have moved deadlines in order to complete this book, as well as for the many provocative conversations on gender, intimacy, care and work: I am looking at you, Petteri Eerola, Henna Pirskanen, Pedro Romero and Jenny van Hoof.

But my greatest debt of gratitude goes to my husband. Thank you for the emotional, intellectual and practical support which makes juggling our lives possible. You are still my best reader. Finally, I dedicate this book to my daughter, Mila, whose birth (and later her brother's) threw my world upside down in the most impossibly unexpected and joyful ways. Being your mother is an honour.

Key terms

Maternity leave: This leave is reserved for the mother (or primary parent) and is often seen as a health and welfare provision. It aims to safeguard the health of both the mother and the newborn, and is intended to be used shortly before, throughout and right after childbirth. In the UK, mothers can take up to 12 months of maternity leave, which starts usually around two weeks before her due date.

Paternity leave: Typically reserved for fathers, this leave is meant to be taken shortly following the birth of a child. Its purpose is to allow the father to spend time with his partner, the newborn and any older children they might have. In the UK, fathers can take up to two weeks' paternity leave.

Parental leave: This kind of leave is accessible to both parents. Generally, it is regarded as a caregiving measure, designed to provide both parents with an opportunity to care for a young child. It is typically available only after maternity leave concludes. Different countries configure this leave in different ways, in terms of how long each parent may take and whether one parent can take it all, or whether each parent is allocated a proportion of the leave. In this book, I use the term to refer to the gamut of leaves available to parents (maternity, paternity and so on).

Shared parental leave (SPL): In the UK, SPL allows the mother to transfer part of her maternity leave to the father of the child (or her partner).

These definitions were informed by the International Network on Leave Policies and Research: see https://www.leavenetwork.org/annual-review-reports/defining-policies/.

Notes on transcription

The book presents many quotations from interviews and extracts from diaries written by the participants. Words from interviews are presented as they were spoken, including grammatical errors, laughter and pauses, unless this impedes understanding. In the latter case, small changes were made to texts to make them more comprehensible for the reader.

Some conventions are used in the transcription of interview data. Long pauses are noted with the length of the silence recorded in square brackets [3 seconds]. Other non-verbal forms of communication are also indicated in square brackets, for example [laugh]. Parts of a quote edited out because they are not directly relevant to the discussion are indicated by [...]. When two people overlap in speech, a slash / is used to indicate the start of the overlap. For example:

A: I went to/the shop

B: /we go every day

where 'the shop' and 'we go' were spoken at the same time. When people speak directly after one another, = is used. Here's an example where 'not' and 'what' are spoken without any pause between them:

A: This is not=

B: =what it seems!

This approach to the presentation of data is used to allow the reader (and the researcher) to experience as far as possible the 'feel' of the diary entry or interview, and the flow of conversation between participants and between researcher and researched (see Sandelowski 1994).

Table 0.1 The participants and their characteristics

Name	Occupation at time of recruitment	Education	Shared leave?	Leave pattern	Part III Chapter (or care/work divisions after leave)	Paid work hours after leave
Anna	Set designer	University undergraduate (UG) degree	Yes	9 months' maternity leave	N/A (did not complete final interview/diary)	Full time
Adam	Medical doctor	University UG degree	Yes	2 weeks' paternity leave 3 months' SPL with Anna	N/A	Full time
Beth	Marketing executive	Postgraduate degree	No	9 months' maternity leave	8	Full time (condensed to 4-day week)
Bart	University postdoctoral researcher	Postgraduate degree	No	4 weeks' paternity leave (split across two time periods)	8	Full time (condensed to 4-day week)
Cara	Social worker	University UG degree	No	9 months' maternity leave	6	3 days a week
Chidi	Accountant	Postgraduate degree	No	1 week of paternity leave	6	Full time
Debbie	Nurse	University UG degree	No	12 months' maternity leave	7	Full time (condensed to 4-day week)
David	Physiotherapist	University UG degree	No	2 weeks' paternity leave	7	Full time (condensed to 4-day week)

Name	Occupation at time of recruitment	Education	Shared leave?	Leave pattern	Part III Chapter (or care/work divisions after leave)	Paid work hours after leave
Emily	Lawyer	University UG degree	Yes	10 months' maternity leave	8	Full time
Edward	Sales executive	University UG degree	Yes	2 weeks' paternity leave 2 months' SPL alone	8	Full time
Faria	Lawyer	University UG degree	Yes	12 months' maternity leave	7	Full time
Filip	Business consultant	University UG degree	Yes	6 months' paternity leave and SPL with Faria	7	Full time
Gina	Policy analyst	University UG degree	Yes	9 months' maternity leave and unpaid leave with Gerald	8	Full time (after the first 18 months)
Gerald	Website developer	University UG degree	Yes	9 months' paternity leave, SPL and unpaid leave with Gina	8	Full time (after the first 18 months)
Helen	Publishing editor	University UG degree	No, but unpaid parental leave	9 months' maternity leave	7	4 days a week

NOTES ON TRANSCRIPTION xvii

Name	Occupation at time of recruitment	Education	Shared leave?	Leave pattern	Part III Chapter (or care/work divisions after leave)	Paid work hours after leave
Henry	Transactions manager	University UG degree	No, but unpaid parental leave	2 weeks' paternity leave 2 months alone (unpaid parental leave and annual leave)	7	Full time
Ivy	Engineer	Postgraduate degree	No	12 months maternity leave	N/A	N/A
Ian	Company CEO	University UG degree	No	2 weeks' paternity leave	N/A	N/A
Judy	Administrator	University UG degree	No	12 months' maternity leave	6	Left paid work
John	IT manager	University UG degree	No	2 weeks' paternity leave	6	Full time
Kate	Pharmaceuticals salesperson	University UG degree	Yes	8 months' maternity leave	8	4 days a week
Keith	Business consultant	Postgraduate degree	Yes	4 weeks' paternity leave/SPL at time of birth 3 months' SPL alone	8	Full time

Name	Occupation at time of recruitment	Education	Shared leave?	Leave pattern	Part III Chapter (or care/work divisions after leave)	Paid work hours after leave
Linda	Care assistant/nurse	University UG degree	No	12 months' maternity leave	6	Left paid work
Larry	Waiter	A-levels	No	2 weeks' paternity leave	6	Full time
Mary	Charity officer	University UG degree	Yes	9 months' maternity leave	8	4 days a week
Mark	Civil servant	A-levels	Yes	6 weeks' paternity/SPL together at time of birth 10 weeks' SPL alone	8	4 days a week
Natasha	Data analyst	University UG degree	Yes	5 months' maternity leave	N/A	N/A
Nick	Journalist	University UG degree	Yes	7 months' SPL alone	N/A	N/A
Olivia	Accountant	University UG degree	No	12 months' maternity leave	7	Full time
Olly	Lawyer	University UG degree	No	2 weeks paternity leave	7	Full time
Pippa	Musician and administrator	University UG degree	No	12 months' maternity leave	6	3 days a week

Name	Occupation at time of recruitment	Education	Shared leave?	Leave pattern	Part III Chapter (or care/work divisions after leave)	Paid work hours after leave
Peter	Accountant	University UG degree	No	2 weeks' paternity leave	6	Full time
Rita	Advertising executive	University UG degree	No	12 months' maternity leave	6	4 days a week
Riley	Advertising executive	University UG degree	No	Interrupted paternity leave	6	Full time
Sarah	Lawyer	University UG degree	No	12 months' maternity leave	7	Full time
Sam	Surgeon	University UG degree	No	2 weeks' paternity leave	7	Full time
Tara	Screen writer	University UG degree	Yes	9 months' maternity leave	6	Left paid work
Tim	Communications manager	University UG degree	Yes	6 weeks' paternity/ SPL together at time of birth 6 weeks SPL alone	6	Full time
Vicki	Sports instructor	University UG degree	No	12 months' maternity leave	6	Left paid work
Victor	Mechanic	Diploma	No	2 weeks' paternity leave	6	Full time

Name	Occupation at time of recruitment	Education	Shared leave?	Leave pattern	Part III Chapter (or care/work divisions after leave)	Paid work hours after leave
Winnie	Scientist	University UG degree	Yes	10 months maternity leave	7	Full time
Weston	Scientist	University UG degree	Yes	2 weeks paternity leave 1 month SPL with Winnie and 1 SPL alone	7	Full time

Note: Some occupations have been changed slightly to ensure anonymity.

1
The promise of shared parental leave: introduction to the study

I first developed an interest in parental leave and how it might be shared when I became pregnant with my first child in 2012. At that time, additional paternity leave (APL), introduced in the UK in 2011, allowed mothers to give up to six months of their maternity leave to their partner from five months after the birth or adoption of a child. My husband and I were both in precarious positions at different universities, and I think it is fair to say that at that time he did not consider parental leave as high a priority as I did. Without much background knowledge on parental leave, I felt intuitively that it would be key to establishing equal parenting between us and an important precedent to set. I knew the birth of a child often heralds a more gendered pattern in divisions of labour within couples (Yavorsky et al., 2015) and wanted to avoid this outcome as best I could. Although I agreed that the career costs for my husband and financial costs for both of us were high (in that a longer period of leave overall would entail a longer period on low or no pay), I felt this was a price worth paying. Those negotiations were not easy. I felt aggrieved that he didn't immediately see things my way, sympathetic about his fears, but also ambivalent about 'giving up' part of my leave with my newborn child. I felt that if he 'really' cared for me, and our future child, he would share leave. It was, needless to say, not this simple. Later I was to hear similar (and other) stories from the participants in this book, including how *not* sharing leave may be conceived as care for a partner and child. These are the 'affective relational realities' (Lynch, 2007:555) in which we all live and love, reconciling personal preferences and goals with our commitments to others (Ball et al., 2004). In the end, like many couples faced with difficult choices, we compromised. I took six months of maternity leave and my husband, with considerable apprehension, took three months of APL, which (he now says) he does not regret taking.

Since that time, few other couples have taken APL, or its newer version, shared parental leave (SPL). Introduced in 2015 to replace APL, SPL enables the mother to transfer her leave to the father or her partner from two weeks after the birth or adoption of the child. It can also be taken in blocks of leave time or part-time (for example, alternating weeks at work and on leave over a period of weeks). Despite these updates to the leave, take-up has remained stubbornly low. In 2018, just 8 per cent of eligible parents reported an intention to take SPL (Twamley & Schober, 2019), and a more recent evaluation found that around 5 per cent of eligible fathers are taking SPL (Department for Business and Trade, 2023). There has been, therefore, a consistency in the (dis)engagement with the policy since its inception. This study contributes to a body of work which seeks to examine the potential of this leave, both why so few parents have taken it (and what may improve the take-up) and the ways in which such leave could shape parents' experiences of the transition to parenthood. The study is about shared parental leave, but SPL is also a lens through which I explore more generally parent couples' negotiations about caring and sharing labour.

Looking back at my experience of APL, I reflect that neither my husband nor I had a straightforward 'choice' around our leave take-up, at least in the individualised ways in which choice is frequently articulated (including in the APL and SPL policies as they are written). Our differing orientations to work and care, and moreover the gendered social pressures we felt in enacting motherhood and fatherhood, were driving our negotiations in whether to share or not to share leave. But our relationship with one another and the kind of family life we hoped to build *together* were also part of these considerations. Drawing on feminist care literature, and in particular the work of Marilyn Friedman (2014), Andrea Doucet argues that such a relational frame is often missing in studies on gendered divisions of labour, but it is vital to remember that 'people simultaneously respond relationally and autonomously to specific conditions, demands and contexts' (2023:12), and that to focus only on individual choices and circumstances is to miss an important part of the story in intimate and family life. Such considerations have been at the centre of this study's endeavour.

Previous research on the ways in which parents organise paid and unpaid work has tended to assume that each partner responds individually to defend their preferred division of labour (as discussed in chapter 3; see also Doucet, 2023). These assumed autonomous individuals are portrayed as reflexively making independent decisions which are moreover for themselves, with scholars failing to consider the relational matrices in which actions are negotiated. But as Phạm (2013:37) says:

> One's action is rarely one's own and rarely for one's own sake only, for it is pulled, pushed, harmonised, agitated, coaxed, pleaded ... by multiple bonds. In this sense, one could say it is always already co-authored.

A relational approach recognises that behaviour is often rooted not only in one's own preferences and constraints, but also by a concern to sustain intimate relationships with others (Smart, 2007). This is not to assume that all relationships are straightforwardly free of antagonism, but to highlight how different sets of emotions, including love and care, mean that 'we act according not only to our own needs and wishes but also to those of others' (Burkitt, 2016:335).

Such attention is particularly pertinent in research with couples, in which an intimate bond is the basis of the relational connection. As Wardlow and Hirsch argue, 'To think about couples only in terms of power ... is to miss the fact that men and women may also care for the conjugal partners with whom they are simultaneously involved in daily battles over bodies, power, and resources' (2006:3). Research which explores intersections of intimacy and gender in couples reveals a complex configuration of issues. While in the UK and other contexts the couple relationship is idealised as gender-equal (Jamieson, 2011; Twamley, 2012), empirical studies often uncover facets of inequality. For example, various researchers have observed unequal emotional expectations of men and women in relationships, with women often taking on the bulk of emotion work within couples and families (Fox, 2009; McQueen, 2023). This may translate to more care work being conducted by women, who are seen as more emotionally competent (Brooks & Hodkinson, 2020). Such discrepancies are sometimes explained by popular romantic and heteronormative 'scripts' which reify gendered differences and inequalities. For example, Ellen Lamont (2014) examines how women in the US continue to expect romantic courtship practices that are inherently sexist, positioning women as passive and dependent, and men as active breadwinners, such as the idea that men should pay for dinner, or hold the door open for a woman. The women in her research understand these practices as a means to demonstrate and recognise romance, even if they also recognise that they are highly gendered and sexist (see similar findings from the UK in relation to weddings, in Carter, 2022). Paul Johnson (2005) argues that heterosexuality works together with love, creating a normative ideal which draws on ideas of opposite characteristics as natural, thereby reifying gendered differences within couples (including same-sex couples). Feminist scholars note that women's material and status dependency on men and marriage/coupledom can tie them to relationships which may not live up to ideals of equality (Gunnarsson, 2016; Jackson, 1993), and indeed there is empirical evidence that women may accept inequality in their relationship if they feel 'loved' in other ways (Jamieson, 2011; Twamley, 2012). These studies highlight the importance of attending to understandings of intimacy and coupledom, as well as the gendered norms in which intimate relationships are navigated.

The failure to examine how intimacy with others shapes gendered participation in paid and unpaid work is also apparent in the lack of consideration of love and care between parents and their children. Division-of-labour studies often assume that the person with the most resources is more likely to 'bargain' their way out of unpaid care and domestic work (Brines, 1994; Evertsson & Nermo, 2004; Ross, 1987). These studies focus on what women lose by their greater care role – 'status, financial rewards, and work opportunities' – and give less attention to what they may gain: 'personal growth, relationships, and connection with their children' (Doucet, 1998:53, 54). For instance, a common theoretical explanation for unequal divisions of labour is that they are shaped by the relative resources of individuals in a couple, so that the person with lower earnings is less able to negotiate their way out of unpaid work. These studies also fail to take into account the different attractions of housework and childcare (Gabb, 2008; Oakley, 1974; Sullivan, 2013), often conflating them. Such an approach, focusing on intra-couple bargaining, is widely applied, but it has not been able to fully explain disparities in unpaid work, in particular childcare (e.g. Deutsch & Gaunt, 2020).

A relational and intimate approach to research, such as the one I have adopted, at its most basic level means attending to how connections with others may shape everyday practices. For instance, Jenny Alsarve's (2021) research with parents in Sweden who took parental leave demonstrated the ways in which decisions about care and work were embedded in negotiations with partners, grandparents and colleagues at work. Alsarve describes how her participants took into account advice from others on how to manage combining work and family, and how colleagues enabled or stood in the way of their preferred arrangements. A study such as this highlights how significant individuals in our lives may shape decision-making, as well as how behaviour may be motivated by a desire to sustain relations with such individuals (Smart, 2007). A 'stronger' relational frame (Roseneil & Ketokivi, 2016) goes further by not only attending to explicit or external negotiations with others, but also attempting to understand how negotiations of practices may occur between *and* within subjects. Such an approach recognises that our very identities are 'embedded within webs of relationships' (Mason, 2004:177) and that the 'concept of self (and self value) is tied into how they [people] behave towards significant others' (Smart, 2011:17). For example, in their investigation of divorce amongst British South Asian Muslims, Kaveri Qureshi and Zubaida Metlo (2021) chart the ways in which decisions to divorce are shaped by interpersonal and *intersubjective* relations with others. Focusing on the experiences of a woman they call Nusrat, they describe how at the interpersonal level she draws on her interactions with those around her as sounding boards and advisors as she considers whether to divorce her husband. At the intersubjective level, they show how she anticipates the responses of others in her decision-making processes, and that these anticipations influence how she interprets events. Ultimately, they explain, Nusrat's 'sense of what she wanted was tied to others' (p. 165), so that her very desires were shaped for and with others.

In attending to these emotional and relational matrices, I explore the narratives of first-time parents from the perspective of 'future building' (Holmes et al., 2021). This means examining how participants imagine couple and family life, and the ways in which they negotiate with relational others and structural forces (such as gendered norms and institutions) in making this future a reality. I thus attend to the interpersonal and intersubjective dialogic practices of participants, while also recognising that a 'sense of self' is 'constructed in relationships with others, and in relation to others and to social norms' (May & Nordqvist, 2019). These norms are upheld by hegemonic discourses about, for example, appropriate motherhood and fatherhood, as well as by institutional structures which embed them into the fabric of social life. The future-building approach weaves these together, with a particular attention to emotions. This chimes with my previous research, which demonstrated the ways in which emotional attachments to intimate others and intimate ideals shaped couples' divisions of labour (Twamley, 2012, 2014).

Holmes et al. (2021:735) argue that a future-building approach is particularly pertinent in 'a world where an array of differently gendered intimate futures seems possible' as people navigate possibilities through emotional reflexivity, guiding their actions through the ways they (and those around them) feel about different possibilities. This book focuses on how couples negotiate the sharing of parental leave at the transition to parenthood and its impact on paid and unpaid work divisions. Ann Oakley noted in the 1970s that 'having a first baby permanently alters the emotional interior of a couple's relationship' (2018 [1979]:223), with a sharp division of labour often at the root of these changes. This continues to be the case. The study of parental leave can be seen as a lens through which to explore negotiations of paid and unpaid work more generally, at this 'crossroads' (Hodkinson & Brooks, 2023) in couples' lives. This is the time when, typically, couples' divisions of labour become more gendered and we begin to see the gender pay gap magnify (Costa Dias et al., 2020). The ability to share leave opens up new possibilities in the ways in which couples can begin to imagine and practise their future family life, and thus I have found the future-building approach particularly relevant for this study.

I have also been inspired in this study by the work of scholars in the sociology of everyday life. Neal and Murji (2015:812) comment, 'Everyday life can be thought of as providing the sites and moments of translation and adaption. It is the landscape in which the social gets to be made – and unmade', and thus it is fitting to explore how divisions of leave are lived out and how they shape participants' experiences of the transition to parenthood. Attending to everyday practices of participants reveals the vibrancy and the temporal aspects of social interactions. We come to see 'moments of the repair and hope in which a livable life is made possible' (Back, 2015:832). Through applying this approach, I explore how participants sustain and manage their relationships with one another ('relationship work', as per Gabb & Fink, 2015) at a time of great change and often friction after the birth of a first child, as well as how these sustaining practices are helped or hindered by the social and political structures in which the participants navigate this transitional period in their lives. This guided me towards a longitudinal in-depth approach in which I solicited diaries from my participants that charted their everyday experiences of leave and the post-leave period, and couple interviews in which I could observe interactions between partners (methods are discussed in more depth on pages 15–23 of this chapter).

With a particular interest in gendered differences in the experiences of paid and unpaid work, I have focused on mixed-sex couples. I examine how lived experiences of different patterns of parental leave shape gendered parenting roles and participation in paid work. I do this by comparing the in-depth accounts of first-time parents who share leave and those who do not. In order to understand how prior expectations and values around gender, intimacy and family life shape decisions about parental leave, I follow couples from pregnancy to approximately 14–18 months after the baby is born, when the UK maternity/SPL leave period is over. I examine why parents take leave in the ways they do, how their individual and couple circumstances and negotiations shape their decisions and practices, what they do during the leave period, and how these practices shape their family life after the leave period is over. Within the relational and intimate frame of this study, I have attended to how understandings of intimacy with and care for partner and (future) child are linked to the sharing of leave, both in the decision to take leave and in the final practices of care and intimacy. In the following section I review the current evidence base concerning gendered divisions of paid and unpaid work, and consider how parental leave may make an intervention in gendered relations more widely and in family and couple life in particular.

Parental leave and its potential impact on gender equality

Different forms of leave for parents have different associated intentions. Maternity leave is primarily to allow the mother to recuperate from the birth and to support the early nurturing of the baby and breastfeeding (if she chooses to feed in that way) while she maintains her job. This kind of leave was introduced in the UK in 1973. Paternity leave is for the father or the mother's partner and is taken around the time of the birth. Usually it is a short leave – in the UK just two weeks long – and is primarily so that the father can support the mother at the time of birth. Men's access to leave is a much more recent policy development: paternity leave was introduced in 2003 in the UK.[1] Some countries also offer 'parental leave' that is available for either parent to take, usually after the maternity and paternity leave period is over. Its purpose is to allow parents to take time out of employment and care for their child(ren). Typically, women take the bulk of leave, whether that be maternity leave (which is usually longer than paternity leave) or parental leave (Chanfreau et al., 2011; Department for Business and Trade, 2023). I use the term 'parental leave' as a catch-all phrase in discussing the gamut of parent-related leaves.

Parental leave for fathers has been presented as a key policy area for promoting gender equality (Floro & Meurs, 2009; Gornick & Meyers, 2009). The International Labour Organization (Floro & Meurs, 2009), for example, passed a resolution on gender equality, calling for governments to develop policies that include paternity and parental leave, with incentives for men to use them. The aim is to encourage men to take on care work, thereby shifting gendered norms of who should care for a child, while enabling women's engagement in employment. This is in recognition of the fact that across the world women do more housework and childcare than men, and work fewer paid hours (Walthery & Chung, 2021; Wishart et al., 2018), though men's time spent on housework and childcare has been steadily increasing (Sullivan, 2019). It was widely hoped that the COVID pandemic, which occurred after the data collection for this book, would transform gendered divisions of domestic labour because of the increased presence of fathers in the home (Barker et al., 2021; Wojnicka, 2022), but these hopes were not borne out in empirical studies (Sevilla & Smith, 2020; Twamley et al., 2023).

Parenthood is a moment in which gendered divisions of paid and unpaid work in mixed-sex couples become most acute (Yavorsky et al., 2015). In the UK this is seen in the shift to part-time work amongst mothers, over half of whom work part-time; men are much more likely to work full-time (ONS, 2018b). These differences in paid and unpaid work contribute to the gender pay gap (Olsen et al., 2018), which in the UK stands at 8.6 per cent for full-time workers but jumps to 17.9 per cent when part-time employees are included (ONS, 2018a). These disparities lead to adverse impacts on women's careers, such as reduced earnings, restricted access to managerial positions, and biases in selection and evaluation processes (Budig & England, 2001; Cukrowska-Torzewska & Lovasz, 2020; Cukrowska-Torzewska & Matysiak, 2020; Goldin, 2021). A study conducted by the Equality and Human Rights Commission (2015) in the UK found that about 10 per cent of mothers reported that they were either dismissed or treated so poorly they felt they had to leave their job because of their pregnancy, while 20 per cent experienced harassment related to pregnancy or to requests for flexible working to provide childcare.

Time-use studies and employment figures give only a partial picture of gendered labour practices. More difficult to measure, but just as critical, are the allocation of *responsibilities* in care work and housework and the associated emotional and cognitive labour. Drawing on Sara Ruddick's (1995) tripartite framework of parental responsibilities, Andrea Doucet (2016) argued that there are three chief responsibilities which we should attend to as social researchers: emotional, community and moral responsibilities. More recently, she and her colleague Lindsay McKay added housework as a fourth parental responsibility, as a related but distinct form of care (Doucet & McKay,

2020). Emotional responsibilities involve being attentive and responsive towards those being cared for, informed by an understanding of others' needs. Community responsibilities encompass the organisation, management and upkeep of relationships within and between households and communities, tailored to children's evolving social and developmental requirements. Women are more likely to undertake the bulk of housework, emotional and community responsibilities than men (Christopher, 2021; Faircloth, 2021; Twamley, Faircloth & Iqbal, 2023), though some shifts have been observed in families with a primary care father in relation to emotional responsibilities (Brooks & Hodkinson, 2020). Moral responsibility is tied to emotional and community responsibilities, in that women more often *feel* they ought to take on these responsibilities in the care of their children. Research shows that women are more often charged with overall responsibility for the care of children, and men for economic provisioning (Duncan et al., 2003; Duncan, 2015; Faircloth, 2021; Schmidt, 2018). The organisational and emotional aspects of these responsibilities are sometimes referred to as the 'mental load' (Dean et al., 2022). This kind of work is 'boundaryless' and 'invisible' (Dean et al., 2022), which makes it difficult to quantify for both researchers and the individuals that are grappling with it. It also means that it can be experienced as overwhelming, since there are no limits to how much mental load one takes on. The importance of examining the mental load and the factors that underlie its uneven distribution is increased by its links with poorer career advancement for women, high stress levels and lower relationship satisfaction (Reich-Stiebert et al., 2023).

Parental leave, and specifically men's increased take-up of parental leave, is considered a potentially transformative policy measure for tackling these gendered inequalities (Gornick & Meyers, 2009). Men's participation in parental leave is associated with greater involvement in childcare, and to a lesser extent housework, after the leave period ends (Almqvist & Duvander, 2014; Eerola, Närvi & Lammi-Taskula, 2022; Haas & Hwang, 2008; Meil, 2013; Rehel, 2014; Schober, 2014; Seward et al., 2006). There are also observed benefits for women's career outcomes. These include a reduced household gender wage gap (Andersen, 2018; Druedahl et al., 2019) and an increased likelihood that women will be in paid work (Andysz et al., 2016; Corte Rodríguez, 2018). Parents report that sharing leave improves empathy and understanding within the couple (Almqvist et al., 2011), and research has observed an association between fathers' leave-taking and reported couple relationship quality up to five years after the birth of a child (Petts & Knoester, 2020).

Despite this impressive range of studies, there is a lack of more in-depth qualitative research about parents' understandings and experiences of fathers' leave or their views on the consequences of different forms of leave. Early work from Nordic countries, where fathers' access to extended leave alone has been established for much longer than in the UK, found that men on leave alone developed an increased awareness of their children's needs, experiencing a child-centred temporality that Brandth and Kvande (1998, 2002) call 'slow time'. Men also reported feeling more confident in their caring abilities and having a deeper relationship with their child because of the leave alone experience (Brandth & Kvande, 2001; Haas, 1992). However, it wasn't clear that leave alone challenged hegemonic forms of masculinity (Connell, 1995). For example, these fathers did not often report sharing housework. But a central tenet of bringing men into care is the hope that it will lead to what Elliott calls caring masculinities, which involve the 'rejection of domination' as well as the 'integration of values of care, such as positive emotion, interdependence, and relationality' (Elliott, 2016:241). That is, the hope is that men's participation in care will lead to transformative practices and perspectives concerning masculinity with impacts beyond the couple dyad.

More recently, Margaret O'Brien and Karin Wall (O'Brien & Wall, 2017) edited a book which charted the experiences of fathers on leave alone in 11 different countries. Basing their research on in-depth interviews with fathers after they had taken parental leave, they reported that men who took leave alone learned to take responsibility for their children, in particular emotional responsibility, as well as meeting the day-to-day care needs of their children while they were on leave. Some of the men became more independent carers for their children after the leave period, assuming levels of overall responsibility for the children similar to their partners'. There was also evidence of an increase in men's participation in housework. This was not consistent across the country case studies, however. The editors note that 'context, conjugal relations and agency are all important shaping factors of what fathers "do" and experience while taking full-time parental leave' (K. Wall & O'Brien, 2017:263). It is important therefore to consider local cultural factors, as well as the situation of the parents themselves, when examining parental leave and its outcomes.

These studies of the impact fathers on leave have on gendered relations are often cross-sectional in nature, relying on retrospective individual accounts from fathers or mothers (rarely the couple). This makes it difficult to pull apart the contributions of the leave and of previously held attitudes towards gender equality which prompt the sharing of leave (K. Wall & O'Brien, 2017). Other research shows that attitudes towards gender roles are key in shaping parents' divisions of labour and decisions about sharing leave (Banister & Kerrane, 2022; Kaufman et al., 2024; Leshchenko & Chung, 2023; McMunn et al., 2020; Schmidt, Zartler & Vogl, 2019). Sometimes it appears that the actual leave had little impact. For example, an interview study undertaken with fathers who had taken extended parental leave in the UK found that their *intention* to take leave (rather than necessarily the leave itself) was key in establishing more gender-equal parenting practices after the leave was over (Banister & Kerrane, 2022). This points to the complexity involved in drawing causal links between men's take-up of parental leave and the apparent outcomes, and therefore to the necessity of longitudinal qualitative research if we are to understand more fully the lived experience of leave and its implications for men and women. This book attempts to fill these gaps.

Parental leave and its take-up in the UK

The UK is an example of a 'late liberal' welfare state (Povinelli, 2011): it combines a neoliberal economic approach with historical state welfare provision for the most in need. In line with this approach, the state parental leave system is minimal in its offer but facilitates the 'choice' to take longer leave for those that can afford it (Baird & O'Brien, 2015). Since 2003, mothers have been able to access up to 12 months of maternity leave, which internationally is considered a long period; many countries offer six months or less (Blum et al., 2023). The first six weeks of maternity leave in the UK are paid at 90 per cent of earnings, followed by a flat-rate payment of around £170 per week for the next 26 weeks (at the time of writing), with the final 13 weeks unpaid. This statutory flat rate is less than half of the estimated 'living wage' in the UK (TUC, 2017) (potentially even less since the cost-of-living crisis). Women typically take 39 weeks of this leave, with nearly half utilising the full 12 months (Chanfreau et al., 2011). Fathers (or partners of mothers) receive just two weeks of paternity leave, paid at the same statutory flat rate that mothers receive after their first six weeks of maternity leave.

Such low statutory pay impacts on leave take-up. Parents in higher-income households take more leave after a child's birth than parents in lower-income households (Koslowski & Kadar-Satat, 2019). Higher-earning parents are also more likely to receive leave pay enhancements from their employers (Koslowski & Kadar-Satat, 2019). The last comprehensive survey on maternity and paternity leave in the UK found that about 28 per cent of employers top up maternity leave pay, and 20 per cent paternity leave pay (Chanfreau et al., 2011). On the other hand, around a quarter (28 per cent) of men and women in employment did not even have access to statutory paid paternity or maternity leave in 2016 (O'Brien, Aldrich et al., 2017). Most ineligibility for leave is due to respondents being self-employed or not having been in employment for the qualifying period. While the UK was still a member of the European Union, 18 weeks of non-transferable, unpaid leave was introduced (for more details see O'Brien & Uzunalioglu, 2022). This can be taken in blocks until the child turns 18. However, awareness and uptake of it have been very low (O'Brien & Koslowski, 2017), and participants in this study reported no prior knowledge of the leave.

Since 2011, UK mothers have been able to transfer their maternity leave to partners, initially through APL, and from 2015 by its replacement, SPL. Fathers on SPL access the same low level of maternity pay from the sixth week at a flat rate until the 39th week. SPL can be taken simultaneously with the mother or in phases over 52 weeks (for example, the mother could take one month, then the father, then the mother and so on). Both parents must meet criteria for eligibility to this leave: mothers must be eligible for maternity allowance (the minimum statutory payment) and fathers for paternity leave. For mothers, the criteria include 26 weeks of continuous work before the due date and a minimum-earnings threshold. Fathers must be related to the child or be a partner to the mother, be expected to share child-rearing responsibilities, and have continuous employment by the same employer for at least 26 weeks by the end of the 15th week before the due date, and be employed at the time of the birth. These rather limiting and complicated eligibility criteria mean that, in practice, up to a third of parents are estimated to be ineligible for SPL (Twamley & Schober, 2019). Eligibility is associated with being white, university-educated and a home owner, and the take-up profile is similar (Department for Business and Trade, 2023).

The preamble to the Bill which introduced SPL emphasises how this policy opens up choice for parents in the ways in which they arrange paid and unpaid work: 'Legislating to give parents access to flexible parental leave; so that where they want to, mothers and fathers can share caring' (Department for Education & Department for Business, Innovation and Skills, 2013). But the leave transfer mechanism appears to contradict the (neoliberal) emphasis on individual autonomy. This policy design emanates from a cultural emphasis on the mother as primary carer and is a reflection of the prevalence of the modified male breadwinner household, where mothers work part-time while fathers work full-time (Baird & O'Brien, 2015; OECD, 2017; ONS, 2021). SPL gives parents the option to share leave or to maintain the status quo of extended maternity leave alone. In general, research from other countries shows that where leave is constructed in this way, as ostensibly 'gender-neutral', mothers tend to take all of it or most of it (Blum et al., 2023). In contrast, the fathers' quota policies favoured in Nordic countries are more encouraging of men's leave, since parents must forgo paid leave if the father does not take it. Such 'daddy quotas' have been observed to be much more effective in promoting men's take-up of leave than gender-neutral parenting leaves (Brandth & Kvande, 2020; Deven & Moss, 2002; Kaufman, 2020).

Qualitative research into UK parents' decision-making regarding sharing leave and other flexible working mechanisms indicates that there is a common concern that fathers may suffer greater career repercussions than mothers for taking leave (Kaufman, 2018; Kelland et al., 2022). Kelland et al. (2022) found that fathers were sometimes discouraged from taking SPL by their employers, in what they conceptualise as organisational 'fatherhood forfeits' for men who attempt to take a more active role in caring than is the norm. Fathers may attempt to mitigate employers' negative responses by taking SPL in ways perceived as convenient for their employers (Atkinson, 2023) or by avoiding SPL entirely (Kaufman, 2018; Kaufman & Almqvist, 2017; Koslowski & Kadar-Satat, 2019). This may be the case even when the father's employer has supportive policies on leave in place, such as enhanced pay (Koslowski & Kadar-Satat, 2019). Employers may have poor understanding of SPL, leaving parents confused and unsure of how to organise their leave and whether they even have a right to such leave (Birkett & Forbes, 2019; Gheyoh Ndzi, 2021; Uzunalioglu & Twamley, 2023).

Other studies have revealed women's reluctance to transfer part of their maternity leave to their partners (Twamley, 2019; Stovell, 2021) and men's discomfort in 'taking' their partner's leave (Banister & Kerrane, 2022). These studies show how the transfer mechanism of SPL may inhibit wider take-up, as well as the influence of gendered ideas about appropriate caring roles in shaping parental leave divisions. Despite shifting ideas about fathers' involvement in the care of children (Brannen et al., 2023), women are still widely understood to be ultimately responsible for and more able to care for (young) children (Lee et al., 2023; Schmidt, Décieux et al., 2023). Scholars argue that the differences in moral responsibilities between mothers and fathers have intensified over the last 30 years, even as more women have entered paid work and expectations of fathers' involvement in care have increased (Hays, 1996; Lee et al., 2023; Miller, 2023). They note the increasingly prescriptive nature of parenting, with an emphasis on the 'right' ways to raise children, often leading to heightened anxieties and pressures on parents (Furedi, 2001; Gillies et al., 2017; Lee et al., 2023). Despite the use of the gender-neutral term 'parenting', it is apparent that mothers are under much more pressure to conform to idealised notions of intensive parenting than men (Faircloth, 2023; Shirani et al., 2012b). Contemporary fatherhood in the UK has been characterised as more 'intimate' than 'intense' (Dermott, 2008). Such understandings of fatherhood prioritise an emotionally close relationship between father and child, but not necessarily one that is time-intensive. This may help explain why we continue to see disparities in fathers' and mothers' participation in parental leave and childcare more generally. It should be noted here that these scholars are referring to hegemonic understandings of motherhood and fatherhood, which not everyone may aspire to (Gillies, 2009) or be able to live up to, but via which they may nonetheless be judged (Dermott & Pomati, 2016; Gillies, 2008; Hamilton, 2023; Jensen, 2010).

Research, mostly from other country contexts, suggests that employment status and earnings can disrupt these gendered assumptions, though to a limited degree (Beglaubter, 2017; Bygren & Duvander, 2006; Geisler & Kreyenfeld, 2011; Reich, 2011; Yarwood & Locke, 2016). For example, in Canada Beglaubter (2017) found that when men's parental leave was well paid, or when women expressed strong attachment to their careers, these factors could prompt negotiations within couples for men's increased participation in parental leave. However, other research has revealed that women may plan their work lives in anticipation of being primary carers, which means they may be in a better position to take leave from work than their partners (for example by being in a workplace with better parental leave pay or by choosing a job which will better facilitate taking time out) (Daminger, 2020; Grunow & Evertsson, 2016). These studies demonstrate that decisions about leave are not entirely individual but may be tied to a partner's situation and preferences.

Thus, most research in the UK and abroad has focused on barriers and facilitators to leave. Given the low rates of take-up of SPL, this is an important area of research. However, how negotiations between parents shape these decisions and their later experiences on leave is less understood, since most studies take an individualised and often retrospective approach to leave decisions and experiences (McKay & Doucet, 2010; Schmidt, Zartler & Vogl, 2019). In addressing these gaps, I have conducted an in-depth, longitudinal and comparative research project, which I now detail.

The study

In order to understand how couples make decisions about care and work at the transition to parenthood, and how SPL shaped these negotiations, I planned a longitudinal study in which I could follow first-time parents from pregnancy through to after the leave period, up to 10 years after their first child is born. In this book I focus on data collected in the first 18 months of the child's life. Given the limited nature of the research on SPL, I started with a survey of expectant parents in National Health Service (NHS)[2] antenatal clinics in England in 2017 (one in central London and one on the outskirts of London). To recruit these participants, I approached expectant parents in the clinic waiting rooms with an iPad for participants to fill in a questionnaire. Most of the attendees at the clinic were women; this is reflected in the final survey sample. Participants were asked about their parental leave plans, and asked various questions intended to help me understand their eligibility for leave. They were also asked how they thought they might behave under different parental leave policy conditions. A total of 856 expectant parents responded to the survey, the results of which have been reported elsewhere (Twamley & Schober, 2019). Overall finances and worries about fathers' careers were the primary barriers reported to the take-up of SPL, while an individual entitlement for fathers, and knowing others who took SPL, increased individuals' reported intention to take SPL in hypothetical scenario questions. The latter case, in which participants reported that they would be more likely to take SPL if lots of their friends and colleagues were taking it, suggests the importance of the normative and relational context in shaping parents' decisions around SPL, as is discussed in more detail in chapters 2 and 3.

At the end of the survey, participants were asked if they would like to participate in the qualitative part of this study. A sample of 21 mixed-sex couples (42 parents) were recruited in this way. As I wished to understand decision-making about leave, I recruited only parents who reported themselves to be eligible for SPL;[3] therefore all the participating couples were dual earners at the time of recruitment. I also focused on first-time parents to explore the transition to parenthood and how this is shaped (if at all) by sharing parental leave. The participants are mostly university-educated and in white-collar occupations (see table 0.1). Most of the participants are white; only four self-identified as belonging to a minoritised ethnic group: Faria is of South Asian descent but born and brought up in East Asia; Chidi is Black African and migrated to the UK as an adolescent; Larry is British Indian (born in the UK) and Linda is Indian and moved to the UK upon marrying Larry. One couple, Pippa and Peter, have twins. As the survey results show, white university-educated parents are the most likely to know about, be eligible for and intend to take SPL (Twamley & Schober, 2019). Salaries varied across the sample, but no individual earned less than the UK median wage, and many earned significantly more.[4] This study, then, focuses on a relatively homogeneous and privileged set of parents, meaning that the findings should not be assumed to be similar for parents from more diverse backgrounds. On the other hand, such privileged parents frequently exhibit the most influential and visibly prominent models of family life, which are articulated in public discourse and policy; others are compared with them and may attempt to emulate them (M. Lamont, 1992; Strathern, 1992). Moreover, as noted by Shani Orgad (2019) in her study of university-educated professional women who had left paid work after becoming mothers, identifying barriers to more gender-equal relations amongst the most privileged may help identify the most entrenched impediments to change, which those with fewer resources are likely to find even more difficult to overcome. I return to this point in the final chapter.

I also made sure to recruit a sample in which half of the couples were intending to use SPL and half were not. Of those taking SPL, in all but two cases the mother took more leave, with men taking an average of 3.5 months and women 8.5. I included parents who were eligible for SPL, but ultimately did and did not take it up, to unpack the various factors which encourage and discourage take-up, and to explore whether and how SPL shapes parents' experiences of the transition to parenthood, which is a gap in the literature. These differences come out most forcefully in the ways in which sharing and non-sharing parents describe the leave period, giving an in-depth understanding into the *mechanisms* through which leave practices shape the formation of parents.

The parents were interviewed together as a couple when the mothers were eight months pregnant. At the end of this interview, each parent was asked to individually fill in a short qualitative survey reflecting on their experience of the interview and their expectations for the coming year. These interviews took place in 2017 or 2018, depending on the mother's due date. I conducted a second couple interview when the babies were 6 months old, and then an individual interview with each parent when the babies were approximately 14–18 months old, that is, when the maternity leave/SPL period was over. Additionally, the parents were asked to keep individual weeklong diaries at four different time points over the study period: when the baby was 1 month old, 6 months old, 9 months old and just over a year old. This is the first wave of data collection. The second wave is planned for when the children turn 10 years old and the parents will be preparing them for secondary school entry (this wave is due to take place in 2027/28 and therefore not reported in this book). All participants have been given a pseudonym; each member of a couple is given a name starting with the same letter so that their connection to one another is clear for the reader.

Each data collection method was used for a different reason. Couple interviews gave me an opportunity to observe interactions and negotiations between partners, which allowed an examination of both 'narratives of practice and practices of narrative' (Heaphy & Einarsdottir, 2013). This was particularly important in the first interview, during pregnancy, as I wanted to understand the negotiation processes and decision-making factors which fed into couples' parental leave practices, what I call their intimate negotiations. While explanations for taking particular leave patterns may shift over time, as parents' experiences influence their assessment of the leave (O'Brien & Twamley, 2017), plans are rarely changed. In that first interview, the couples were asked to describe their family story, including: how they got together as a couple; their pregnancy experiences so far; decisions about leave; current division of household tasks; future expectations of division of care; and their understandings of feminism and gender equality. The last of these questions followed on from their responses to the survey, in which participants were asked 'Do you consider yourself a feminist?' with the following three options available: yes; no; I believe in gender equality but do not consider myself a 'feminist'. These data fed into discussions about whether and how gender equality was important to them and the ways in which they understood 'equality' in their everyday lives.

Discussions around how household and care labour were divided within the couples were conducted using the Household Portrait, a qualitative visual tool devised by Andrea Doucet (Doucet, 2015, 2018; Doucet & Klostermann, 2024). The Household Portrait consists of a large table with five columns, headed Person A always does it, Person A mostly does it, Persons A and B do it equally, Person B mostly does it, and Person B always does it, where each person is a member of the couple. The participants are given stickers with a different household task or responsibility on each one and asked to decide together in which column to place the sticker. (For example, see Figure 1.1 from Emily and Edward's first interview, and Table 1.1, into which I have copied their responses for the benefit of the reader.) The aim for the researcher is not to determine who does what, but to understand how couples feel about and account for their divisions of household labour, as well as to observe the ways in which they negotiate the shared account of their divisions. The advantage of this method is that through couple discussions about where to place stickers, the researcher is exposed to the shared and contested meanings of different kinds of household and care work and couples' accounts of why they organise them in the ways they do. The Household Portrait also 'makes visible complex differences between partners in how domestic

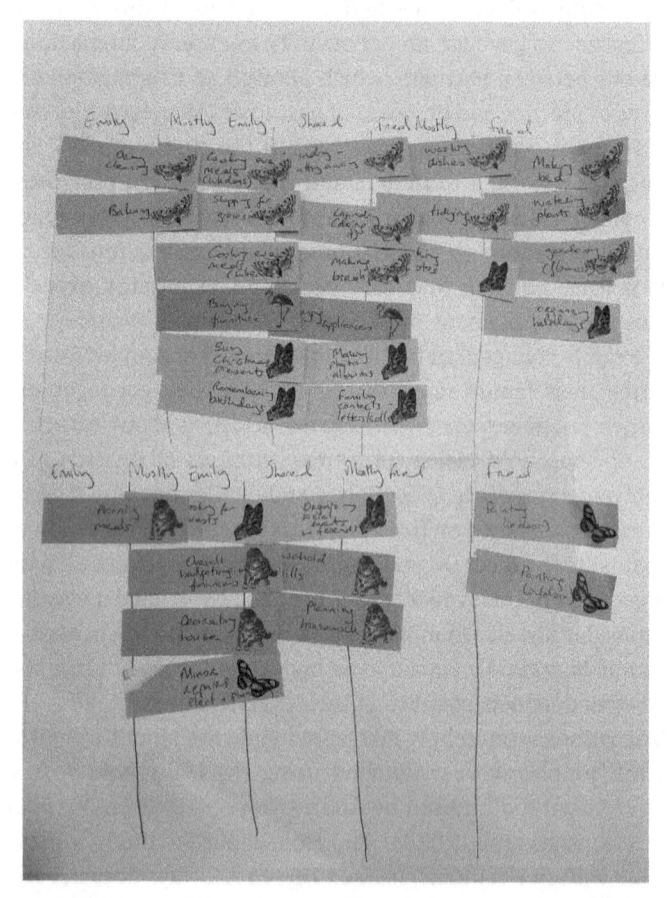

Figure 1.1 Emily and Edward's household portrait. Source: Author. Note: Edward was originally given the pseudonym 'Fred' but was later changed to 'Edward'.

Table 1.1 Emily and Edward's household portrait

Emily always does it	Emily mostly does it	Shared	Edward mostly does it	Edward always does it
Planning meals	Cooking evening meals (weekdays)	Laundry (putting it away)	Washing dishes	Making bed
Baking	Shopping for groceries	Laundry (doing it)	Tidying	Watering plants
Dry cleaning	Cooking evening meals (weekends)	Making breakfast	Taking photos	Gardening
	Buying furniture	Buying appliances		Organising holidays
	Buying Christmas/holiday presents	Making photo albums		Painting (indoors)
	Remembering birthdays	Buying furniture		Painting (outdoors)
	Overall budgeting and finances	Family contact (emails/calls)		
	Decorating house	Organising social events		
	Minor house repairs	Household bills		
		Planning housework		

Source: Author

labour is conceptualised and measured' (Christopher, 2021:466), as well as the different ways in which couples negotiated these differences. I found that, without prompting, participants often 'explained' to me why they divided things in the ways they did, and moreover that they reflected on changes they would like to see and on barriers to such changes. Some participants photographed their portraits and later told me that they had shared them with friends or family in discussions about different ways of managing household work. In the second couple interview, when the baby was 6 months old, I revisited their Household Portrait and couples discussed whether and how it had shifted since their baby (or babies) had been born, and their expectations of any shifts before the third interview.

The final individual interview, when the maternity leave/SPL period was over, gave the participants space to reflect separately on their experiences over the previous year. The focus here was less on the negotiated couple account; these interviews offered individual parents more room to offer a different account of their experience from the one their partner might give. I also asked all participants in their final interview to consider what their lives might look like in nine years' time, when their child is 10; at that time I will return to interview the parents again. This interview, of course, was also important to explore how they felt about their experiences of leave and their practices during it now that it was over.

The individual diaries elicited data which focused on the everyday practices and feelings of the participants during the period of the study. I chose four different time points to capture experiences both during and after the maternity/SPL leave period. I asked participants to write daily entries for a week each time, detailing the high point and the low point of each day, and describing any care they conducted for their partner or child. Participants were given either a notebook and a Polaroid camera or a smart device with which to record their entries. They were thus encouraged to include both text and images in their accounts. This multimodal approach allowed participants to express themselves in different ways, thus potentially evoking different elements of experience and narrative that could be unpacked later in individual interviews (Harper, 2002). Diaries encourage participants to record their thoughts and feelings and to provide information on the experiences and events of their daily lives (Alaszewski, 2006). They can capture sensitive or private accounts that might not be shared during interviews (Bytheway, 2012). Diaries also facilitate the collection of 'real-time' or near real-time data (Boase & Humphreys, 2018; Twamley, Iqbal & Faircloth, 2023), encouraging participants to record data that might seem obvious or banal in an interview. Given the literature to date on parents' experiences of leave, I was particularly keen to explore what they actually did while on leave and their feelings about these practices. The longitudinal nature of the diaries enabled me to examine how different forms of leave shape practices and to observe change over time through different phases of the project.

The study began with 21 couples, but along the way three couples took time out. Ivy and Ian and Nick and Natasha participated in their first interview, but, after a difficult birth experience, decided they did not feel able to complete later interviews or diaries. Anna and Adam completed their first and second interviews and diaries, but experienced a death in the family close to the third interview and decided to take a break while they grieved. Since these couples may return to the study when their child turns 10, and since they were happy to have their data contribute to the study, I have decided not to exclude their experiences from the analysis. In addition to these accounts which were cut short, not all parents completed all diaries, and some participants were more prolific in their diaries than others. I did not observe a systematic pattern though, and in any case this is reflective more broadly of varying participation in other forms of research, even one-off interviews (Brannen, 2013).

In the analysis, I followed Doucet's approach to the 'Listening Guide' (Doucet, 2006, 2018), combined with a process of coding to understand patterns across the data. The Listening Guide is a narrative form of analysis which was devised by Carol Gilligan and Lyn Mikel Brown in the early 1990s (Brown & Gilligan, 1992), and developed by Mauthner and Doucet, who both worked with Gilligan when they were doctoral students (Doucet & Mauthner, 2008; Mauthner & Doucet, 2003). 'Listening' refers to the directed attention of the researcher through multiple readings of the data 'each time listening in a different way' (Brown, 1999:33) and also (literal) *listening* to the recording of the interview. A key aspect of the approach entails being attentive to the relational underpinnings of the participants' narratives and to the co-construction of data between participant and researcher. To that end, in this opening chapter I have tried to outline my own particular interests and concerns in devising this study, in particular my interest in how understandings and experiences of intimacy in a couple shape gendered relations. This necessarily influences the kinds of data I have elicited from participants and the ways in which I have focused my analysis of these data. Throughout the findings I have attempted to make clear my own interventions in the data generation and interpretation. Readers will see some of the interactions I had with participants (in which I am referred to as 'Katherine'), and how my interpretations developed through listening/readings of the data and the literature. A more detailed overview of the analytical methods can be found in the appendix.

Interviewing couples together as well as apart presents some unique ethical challenges (Heaphy & Einarsdottir, 2013; D. L. Morgan et al., 2013; Twamley, 2012). Joint interviews may unsettle assumptions previously held by individuals about their relationships and bring up topics which had not been previously addressed within the couple. For example, in some of the discussions, particularly those based on the Household Portrait, there were heated debates about who did what and how various tasks should be defined or included, though I did get the sense that these were generally oft-rehearsed conversations. Other participants had clearly not discussed parental leave in any great depth before the first interview and were seen to work out their leave narrative in my presence. These interviews were critical for the scope they offered for analysis of how couples 'co-produced' knowledge, and because they allowed me to witness couples' interactions in confirming or contradicting accounts. I tried to offset potential issues arising for couples by ensuring that they understood what would be discussed in the interviews before consenting to participate (with a list of topics given in the information sheet). This might have meant that couples with heightened tensions around divisions of labour excluded themselves from the study (though tensions were certainly observed in some interviews). The individual interviews and diaries offered participants the opportunity to give a different account, but these were not entirely anonymous, since participants will likely recognise accounts from their partner in disseminated findings: while external confidentiality can be assured (by using a pseudonym and changing or anonymising other personal details, which I did), internal confidentiality cannot (Tolich, 2004). Participants were reminded of this at the time of giving consent and before individual interviews, and also of their right to withdraw from the study at any time, and were given the opportunity for debriefing or asking for particular sections of interviews to be excluded from publications or not attributed to their pseudonym. I also followed up some participants about quotes from individual accounts which I felt might be received negatively by their partner, to see whether they wanted them removed or anonymised. None took up this option. But as an extra precaution I edited out some phrases which I viewed as particularly laden with resentment or ire (which were few). I have also written up the findings in the past tense and given as much detail as possible about the contexts of the participants' accounts. I hope this will emphasise to the reader the time- and context-bound nature of these narrations: the participants and their relationships are not fixed or defined by this particularly difficult time as they transition to parenthood.

Outline of chapters

I have set out the findings in chronological order to take the reader on a journey with the participants as they experience the different phases of the transition to parenthood. This layout facilitates an analysis of how each phase (decisions about leave and the actual experience of different types of leave) impacts on the final practices as reported when this leave period is over.

In Part I I focus on participants' accounts of how they came to share leave or not. Chapter 2 unpacks the narratives of the 11 couples in this study that did not share leave, and considers the various factors which prompted their initial decisions. Drawing on the 'future building' framework (Holmes et al., 2021), I examine how participants make sense of their own and others' emotions as they negotiate parental leave options and the constraints which they perceive to its take-up. I show how the social context in the UK – where there is a historical norm of mothers' long maternity leave and very low numbers of fathers taking SPL – coupled with the policy construction of SPL, shapes their decision-making and their emotional rejection of SPL. Building on previous literature, I explore how ideals and understandings of paid work – in particular the ideal worker norm (Acker, 1990) and a context of 'greedy work' (Goldin, 2021) – and mothering and fathering norms shape participants' decisions. I then explain how understandings and practices of couple intimacy, including how intimacy intersects with understandings of gender equality, cut across these factors to discourage couples from taking SPL, exploring in depth both how participants talk about their couple relationship and the interactions which I observed during the interviews.

In chapter 3 I explore the motivations and the facilitating factors which led 10 of the study couples to share leave, in contrast to the non-sharers discussed in chapter 2. As was to be expected, 'sharers' observe and react to similar norms to non-sharers, such as the ideal worker norm or normative expectations of the roles of mothers and fathers, and this strongly shapes their experiences of and feelings about taking SPL (and later their experiences during the leave period). For example, some fathers reported being deterred from taking longer periods of SPL for similar reasons to why non-sharers do not take any SPL at all. There are important differences in why they ultimately do choose to take SPL, however. First, most sharers reported an extra catalyst for sharing leave, such as generous SPL pay from the father's employer, or a large potential loss of family income if the mother took all the leave, because her salary was higher than the father's. Second, amongst sharers fewer distinctions were made between mothers' and fathers' roles (though the distinctions still lingered), meaning that the sharers had less emotional attachment to the idea of mothers' long and uninterrupted maternity leave. Third, for some participants, their social networks supported and encouraged a non-normative sharing of leave, even though sharers are in the minority in the UK. In terms of family ideals, sharers drew on understandings of couple equality which favoured symmetry in men's and women's paid and unpaid work, and expressed strong support for the idea that inequality would disrupt couple intimacy. This belief shaped not only their visions of future parenting practices, but also their interactions and negotiations concerning leave. This chapter highlights the importance of personal circumstances and relational networks in shaping leave take-up and the imagining of shared futures with intimate others.

Part II draws primarily on diary data to explore participants' experiences while on leave. The accounts of non-sharers in chapter 4 demonstrate how strongly leave take-up shapes men's and women's differing experiences of the first year of their child's life, on top of the physical differences which already emanate from women's experiences of pregnancy and birth. In most cases women report high levels of anxiety about caring 'correctly' for their babies, struggles with breastfeeding, and feeling lonely. This was particularly acute in cases where fathers worked long hours and where there was a lack of other support (such as from extended family). Non-sharing men reported that, in contrast to women's, their lives had not radically changed. Beyond exploring 'who does what', I discuss the different meanings attached to care work, housework and paid work and how these shape participants' experiences of the leave period. Drawing on Hochschild's writing on the 'gift economy' of couples (2003), I explore how participants reacted to these different experiences of the transition to parenthood and the varying impacts on their intimate relationship and their understandings and practices of 'relationship work'.

In chapter 5 I draw out how different leave patterns (such as both parents taking leave at the same time or parents individually taking leave in two different chunks), as well as the timings of leave, influenced participants' divisions of labour during leave. For example, mothers' experiences of leave all occurred in the immediate aftermath of the birth and were focused on establishing sleep and feeding their babies. Just like non-sharing women, sharing women described their maternity leave alone as very difficult as they got to grips with caring for their newborn. In contrast, couples where fathers took four or more weeks of leave at the time of the birth (using paternity leave and SPL) gave very different accounts of this time. The presence of the father during this period helped mothers to establish their preferred method of feeding and gave them a sense of parenting as a 'shared endeavour', which was a key priority for sharing parents. But leave together, even when extended for longer periods, was not seen to destabilise gendered parenting norms. When fathers took leave alone, the babies had been weaned (at around 9 months), and sleep routines were generally established. This meant there was a much greater focus on 'having fun' in men's accounts of their leave alone and much less focus on anxieties like those reported by women on leave alone. Nonetheless, fathers were able to foster a sense of themselves as primary carers, even if just for a short time, thus counteracting popular discourses about the primacy of the mother for young babies.

In Part III I explore the experiences of couples after the leave period. This part is divided into three chapters according to the couples' described patterns of dividing paid and unpaid responsibilities, since whether a couple took leave or not did not map neatly onto their post-leave practices of paid and unpaid work. The accounts demonstrate the importance of considering factors beyond leave, including other family policies such as flexible working (Chung, 2022; de Laat et al., 2023). In the chapters in this part, I also explore parents' visions of the future for the final planned period of data collection when the child is 10 years old. Applying a 'sociology of the future' lens (Cantó-Milà & Seebach, 2015), I examine how participants anticipate constraints on, and opportunities to shape, their preferred family life.

In chapter 6 I describe the practices of couples who follow a largely traditional pattern of parenting, with the father as the breadwinner and the mother as the primary carer. Now and in the future, the families' finances are seen as dependent on men's incomes, while women's engagement in paid work is positioned as contingent on multiple factors. These gendered divisions of labour are strongly influenced by decisions made in pregnancy about leave (in all cases except one, these couples had not taken SPL), by the experience of leave itself and by the assumed impact maternity leave would have on women's career progression. The women in this chapter that continued in paid work struggled with the demands of combining it with unpaid work, while those who had left paid work struggled with long days with little company from other adults. Men reported working long hours, influenced by masculine norms in professional jobs and in an effort to make up for their partners' reduced pay. Empathy and appreciation between partners played a key role in the management of these challenges, which in one case was prompted by a father's SPL experience.

In chapter 7, I chart the experiences of couples who largely share paid and unpaid work but where the mother takes on the bulk of the management role in care and domestic work, the 'mental load'. Most of these parents had either not shared leave or had taken SPL at the same time as one another. I found that fathers in this group had greater, though still limited, opportunities to care for their child independently than the fathers in chapter 6. For example, they had taken leave together with their partner or had used some form of flexible working arrangements that meant they regularly took solo care of their children after the leave period ended. These experiences were enough to establish the sharing of everyday housework and care, but not enough to shift mothers' position as the person *responsible* for care and housework overall. Men and women struggled to maintain full-time care and paid work, but family-managing mothers struggled the most since they also took on the bulk of the mental load. These struggles shaped their visions for the future, in which both women and men envisaged the women stepping back from paid work in order to meet these multiple demands more effectively.

In chapter 8, I detail the experiences of parents who described largely sharing responsibilities for paid and unpaid work, that is, both the everyday practical tasks and the 'mental load' associated with these tasks. In all but one case the fathers had taken extensive leave alone, clearly shaping this final pattern of paid and unpaid labour divisions. I argue that fathers' leave alone was an important factor in destabilising the moral responsibilities of motherhood and fatherhood in this group. Men's long experiences of caring alone meant that they built up an individual relationship with their child that was not mediated by the mother. They and their partners described how their confidence grew while they were on leave and that they learned to care for their children 'in their own way'. One couple in this group did not share leave. Their shared perspective on care and work, as well as the father's access to flexible working, shaped their final shared responsibilities, demonstrating that men's participation in parental leave is not necessarily 'indispensable' for more equal gendered relations (see also O'Brien & Wall, 2017) and that shared ideology and access to other work–care reconciliation policies can also play a role.

In the final chapter I bring together the key strands from across the book, drawing empirical and conceptual conclusions as well as developing practical and policy recommendations. Overall, I argue that the study shows that men's and women's visions and practices of parenting are relational, as they reflect on real and imagined reactions from peers, wider family, and colleagues. They are also deeply emotional, tied to meanings of and attachments to intimacy as an ideal and a practice. These relational and intimate negotiations shape how parents navigate the wider institutional and structural context of the UK, and ultimately their divisions of paid and unpaid work. Parents may demonstrate 'care' for one another and for their children, through both sharing and not sharing leave, which impacts on the ways in which they care and share after the leave period and in their imagined futures. I connect this with recent scholarship in 'relational agency' (Burkitt, 2016) and consider how it can inform research on parental leave more broadly. In thinking about the specific context of the UK, it is clear that sharing leave has the potential to transform gendered practices, but SPL alone is in no way sufficient and in its current configuration is unlikely ever to lead to societal transformations. I therefore propose changes to UK leave policy and outline other factors which could support a reconfigured leave policy to affect change.

Notes

1. Adoption leave is similarly constructed, with one parent (usually the mother) getting access to a level of leave and pay comparable to maternity leave, and the second parent or partner (usually the father) able to access paternity leave. In this book I focus on biological mixed-sex parents and thus will not be discussing adoption leave in any depth.
2. The universal healthcare system available to all UK residents. Private healthcare accounts for a very small proportion of maternity care provision in the UK: the vast majority of mothers give birth in an NHS hospital.
3. One couple, Helen and Henry, appeared from their responses to be eligible and were in fact planning to take SPL, but later discovered that they were not, as Henry had changed jobs too late into Helen's pregnancy. They continued to participate in the study and I followed their experiences of trying to 'make up' for this loss of eligibility in other ways.
4. The median household income of an average-sized family (two parents and two children) in the UK was approximately £42,000 a year after tax in 2020; at the time of writing (2024) it has risen to around £50,000. See 'Your household's income: Where do you fit in?', https://ifs.org.uk/tools_and_resources/where_do_you_fit_in (last accessed 13 June 2024).

Part I
Decisions about parental leave

In this part I focus on data from the first set of couple interviews, when the women were approximately eight months pregnant. I draw on participants' accounts of their decisions concerning leave, as well as on my observations of their interactions and negotiations during the interview. As outlined in chapter 1, I apply the framework of 'future building' developed by Mary Holmes and colleagues (2021) in interpreting the narratives of the participant couples. This is a relational approach which draws on understandings of emotional reflexivity to examine how individuals navigate social structures. In applying this theoretical approach, I pay attention to the participants' ideals of couple and family life, to their emotional attachment to such ideals, and to how they negotiate these visions with real and imagined others, as well as to the various structural forces which may impede their making this future a reality. This lays the groundwork for the following chapters, in which I examine what happened during the leave period, and how these experiences shaped the transition to parenthood and parents' divisions of paid and unpaid work.

2
Encountering barriers to the take-up of shared parental leave: 'non-sharers'

> We don't know what the pregnancy's going to be like so, based on us not knowing anything, a gut feel decision that we took was that, you know, Rita probably wants to stay home for nine months and then we'll see what happens.
>
> Riley, Interview 1

As detailed in chapter 1, to date few parents have taken SPL – only around 5 per cent of eligible parents (Department of Business and Trade, 2023). More commonly, women take 9–12 months of maternity leave, and fathers take two weeks of paternity leave (Chanfreau et al., 2011). This context of low uptake of SPL strongly shapes how parents make a decision about SPL – if they make a 'decision' at all – as well as how they *feel* about taking SPL. In this chapter, I discuss the 11 couples who did not share their leave and consider the various factors which prompted their decisions. Five main themes shaped the non-sharers' decisions.

'I just assumed I'd take all my maternity leave'

It's clear that with a lack of knowledge or familiarity with SPL, many parents don't even consider taking it. In this study, five of the non-sharing couples told me they just assumed that the mother would take all the maternity leave she could afford or that it was a 'gut feeling' about how they should arrange the leave. My questions about leave plans to these parents often simply prompted the mother to discuss her thoughts on the length of her maternity leave (usually related to affordability), which indicates a lack of consideration of SPL. These findings challenge prevailing assumptions in work–family research (as seen in Blood & Hamblin, 1957; Lundberg & Pollak, 1996), that couples engage in bargaining or rational evaluations of the costs and benefits of dividing household duties and leave, and, rather, point to how individuals often simply follow patterns of behaviour they observe around them.

This perceived norm, of mothers taking all the maternity leave available, is reinforced in multiple ways. For example, when I discussed their leave plans with Ivy (engineer) and Ian (company CEO), Ivy told me that her line manager said they would 'put her down for a year' of maternity leave when she announced that she was pregnant, and she never really considered changing that. In no case (including amongst the sharers) did a line manager or human resources colleague suggest or enquire about SPL. Mostly, SPL was simply never mentioned as an option in their workplaces. Moreover, in many cases participants noted that employers did not enhance SPL statutory pay, while they did enhance maternity pay, signaling institutional support for women's leave and not men's. This is important. Research on the take-up of paternity leave (the two weeks available to UK fathers/partners at the time of birth) shows that when employers provide additional compensation on top of the statutory pay, men are more likely to take the full two weeks (Hobson et al., 2002). Such remuneration both improves the affordability of the leave *and* indicates organisational support for fathers' leave.

The affordability of SPL did arise amongst the participants as a barrier to taking SPL, as in John and Judy's case, where John (IT manager) earned substantially more than Judy (administrator) and therefore his leave would come at a greater financial cost to the family as a whole. Given the enduring gender pay gap in the UK and the low numbers of employers enhancing SPL pay (Chambraud & Chanrai, 2018), this is likely to be a common scenario. Amongst the non-sharers, in seven couples the fathers earned substantially more than the mothers, and in the other four couples both partners earned a similar amount. On the other hand, sometimes affordability was mentioned as a barrier even though the actual pay loss was similar whoever took the leave period, as for example in the case of Cara and Chidi discussed in the following section. Gayle Kaufman uncovered similar findings in her research on barriers to British fathers' uptake of SPL, concluding that economic rationalisations for men's lack of leave could be used no matter what the salary difference, or even if there was none at all (Kaufman, 2018). Clearly, there is something more going on.

The norm of mothers taking all or most of their maternity leave is embedded within parents' visions of appropriate motherhood, and mothers express a long-held expectation of and an emotional attachment to this vision:

> I always sort of assumed I would take my full entitlement at my work, I guess, even before meeting Sam and knowing if and when I'd have children and with whom.
>
> Sarah, Interview 1

> Because I've always known I've wanted to have, have children I've always known there was going to come a time in my life where, you know, I'm going to hopefully be a mum and therefore I'm willing to obviously compromise my career [and take leave], because I'm going to be a mum. I don't expect to do everything in life. So no, I don't feel like bitter or anything like that, you know, I feel quite lucky really.
>
> Pippa, Interview 1

It's clear that, for Pippa, taking the full length of her maternity leave represents ideologically what good motherhood looks like. This long-held expectation, or even *preparation*, has a powerful impact on how differently men and women approach the transition to parenthood. For one thing, it may trigger career choices which make mothers' leave more tenable or more affordable than men's leave. For example, long before Sarah (lawyer) met her husband Sam (surgeon) she was working towards becoming a partner in a large firm, but decided to step back into an in-house position on the assumption that this would ultimately be more compatible with having a family. In this new role she works fewer hours and is more easily covered by her colleagues when on leave, but she is paid a lower salary than she would be as a partner (though her salary is similar to her husband's). This is consistent with research on young people's visions of the future: women are likely to imagine combining care and paid work, while men focus on their imagined career progression (Cantó-Milà & Seebach, 2015; Patterson & Forbes, 2012).

Tied to mothers' expectation of taking all the maternity leave, however, is a sense that the leave belongs to mothers and that mothers are more deserving of it, as Sarah explains later in her third (individual) interview:

> I also felt like I sort of deserved it, having done the pregnancy, and, you know, I'd be the one getting up most of the time in the middle of the night, I was the one who, you know, wanted to kind of get back in shape and get back to my physical normalness. Um, so I wanted the most time and also, from Sam's perspective, I don't think he particularly had it on his radar as something he wanted to do. I don't think either of us were that aware of our legal right to do it, to be honest.
>
> Sarah, Interview 3

This sense that a long leave is due to a mother emerged as the case even for those parents that did share leave, no doubt shaped by the transfer mechanism of SPL (see also Brooks & Hodkinson, 2020; Kaufman & Almqvist, 2017; O'Brien & Twamley, 2017). The 12 months of available leave are essentially earmarked for the mother, and it takes a bureaucratic process and joint eligibility criteria to transfer it, which embeds a potential for so-called 'maternal gatekeeping' into the make-up of the leave.

For some couples, then, the leave 'belonged' to the mother, both legally and morally. Thus, some mothers were reluctant to give it up and their partners to take it from them, as hinted in Sarah's reference to Sam not having leave 'on his radar' as something for him. In the case of another couple, David told me in his first interview that he was planning to take six weeks' SPL at the same time as his wife Debbie, but even though Debbie had been strongly encouraging him to take this leave, he had doubts. He told me he worried about 'taking' this formative experience from Debbie (since she will have fewer weeks of maternity leave overall if he takes more leave with her). 'What if she is really enjoying being with the baby?', he asked me, when his turn for SPL came around. These accounts reflect how intimate connections, both present and imagined, shape negotiations. They also destabilise straightforward interpretations of 'maternal gatekeeping' which underestimate the role men may themselves play in determining their involvement in leave. It is not necessarily that David was trying to 'get out of' care work, but rather that he, and men like him, negotiate with the perceived needs and wishes of their partners (Burkitt, 2016), as well as with what he understands to be the role of a good partner in supporting Debbie. David's anticipation of Debbie's possible regret at missing out shapes how he interpreted SPL. These feelings about who properly 'owns' the leave sometimes translated into increased efforts amongst men to earn a higher salary, so that women could take longer maternity leave and later return to paid work part-time.

Greedy work and risky leave

Riley and Rita are advertising executives, working in the same company and at the same level at the time of Rita's pregnancy. On the face of it, they would seem to be in an ideal situation to share leave. However, as discussed above, they pretty quickly decided that Rita would take all her leave, in a 'gut decision'. When I probed them a bit further on their reasoning, Riley told me the following:

> I would love to take some time off but again, it's a very tough decision to take, not least because Rita will have already taken time off, and as a woman, they [employers] have patience for you to take that time off. But that does impact your career. If we have another child, Rita will probably have to take off a couple of months, so somehow it makes sense that one of us stays more career-focused than the other one, who will be more child-focused. That sounds awful but ...
>
> Riley, Interview 1

For Riley, only one person can take leave, because of the expected impact on career earnings and progression. That women's maternity leave impacts on their careers is well evidenced (Cukrowska-Torzewska & Matysiak, 2020). Since Rita will 'obviously' want to take several months' leave, and moreover to recover from the pregnancy and birth, the impact on her career is taken for granted. From his perspective, it 'makes sense' that all career penalties be focused on one career – Rita's. It is interesting nonetheless that he added 'That sounds awful but ...', indicating a recognition that traditional divisions of paid and unpaid work go against popular discourses of gender equality within couple relationships (Faircloth, 2021; Jamieson, 2011; Twamley, 2014). Here we see how parental leave decisions are negotiated in dialogue with real and imagined others and their expected reactions to couples' leave plans (Burkitt, 2012; Holmes et al., 2021), but in concert with (perceived) structural constraints. Fear of repercussions for men's careers was one of the most common responses in the survey on the question of why participants were not sharing leave; it has moreover been observed in multiple contexts beyond the UK, which indicates the pervasive nature of such concerns (Samtleben et al., 2019).

This idea that 'role specialisation' is necessary was not uncommon; it actually emerged most forcefully in later interviews as participants began to consider how to manage the demands of paid and unpaid work after the leave period (we will return to this in chapter 6). Fundamental to this perspective is a view of paid work as precarious and very demanding (as much as the intensive demands of parenting, which I discuss in the next section). Participants described working in high-pressure contexts which necessitated long working hours to keep on top of their workloads and especially for career progression. Goldin (2021) argues that such 'greedy work' is a key driver in the role specialisation of earner and carer within couples. Greedy work is embedded in cultural ideals which value professional achievements over personal needs; it is most commonly found in white-collar jobs and professions, and it is at its 'greediest' in high-stress, high-demand sectors such as finance, law and technology. The glorification of overwork, the pressure to conform to high-performance expectations and the lack of institutional support for work–life balance contribute to the prevalence of this phenomenon (Goldin, 2021; T. A. Sullivan, 2014).

The 'patience' that Riley said employers show as regards women's take-up of leave underlies an understanding of personal and family life as a hindrance to employers, who 'patiently' accept limited incursions into the work sphere. In this context, SPL is felt as risky for Riley and other participants, conscious of the potential repercussions on their career. Riley appeared to internalise what Acker calls the ideal worker norm here: a hypothetical worker 'who exists only for the job' without allowing any other commitments to intrude on their work (1990:149). Such workers typically perceive long work hours as *legitimate* (Byun & Won, 2020; Williams et al., 2013) and therefore place indirect limits on fathers' leave take-up (their own and other's) (Haas & Hwang, 2019). This was the case with Riley, not only in his avoidance of SPL, but also in his take-up of paternity leave. When Rita went into labour, Riley explained, he was asked to forgo his paternity leave until a later time as his manager didn't want him to take 10 days off in a row; the manager suggested Riley took annual leave instead – two days a week for three weeks – and delayed his paternity leave until work was more settled:

> He [Riley's manager] didn't directly say 'Don't take paternity leave', but he did say that it would be better if I took it later. I get on really well with him, so I could have said 'No, I want to take it now', but I'm lucky how well we get on and we had this difficult project so I agreed and it was fine. I'll take the paternity leave maybe later in the year.
>
> Riley, Interview 2

It is striking that Riley describes himself as 'lucky' despite the pressure from his manager not to take paternity leave. Such seeming gratitude to employers was observed in other fathers, who also told me that they were 'lucky' their employers facilitated time off during their partner's pregnancy, for example, or in the generally positive reaction to the request for paternity leave, despite the fact that it is a legal right for fathers. The gratitude signals a socio-political narrative of individual responsibility for care and family (rather than a shared societal one).

This gratitude also works in tandem with the ideal worker norm. Here Bart, a university postdoctoral researcher, explained to me why he felt he couldn't take SPL and will, moreover, work during his two-week paternity leave:

> And the projects that I follow somehow are, ah a little bit like in your case, but I feel like are *my* projects so I can't say I will stop working on this, or I could but I don't feel like to say like ah 'I don't work on it for a year and then let's see' because ah there are students who are working on that who depend on these projects.
>
> Bart, Interview 1

Bart went on to praise the flexibility of his work, which allowed him to keep up with his colleagues and students during non-normative hours. In fact, he told me that this flexibility was a key deterrent to taking SPL, since it was 'not necessary' for his involvement with his new baby:

> As you know it's different work from going to [an] office and work[ing] nine to five so it's, it's super-flexible, so I don't feel the need of officially taking something, because I can go [to the office] or I can keep working from, from home.
>
> Bart, Interview 1

For Bart, this reluctance to take leave was compounded by the fact that his contract with his university was temporary, thus underlining the significance of job insecurity in upholding ideal worker norms. Indeed, other research has found that less stable employment decreases men's likelihood of taking parental leave (Geisler & Kreyenfeld, 2011).

Sam (a medical doctor in a secure position) and Ian (a company CEO) expressed similar sentiments to Bart: the inherent flexibility in their schedules made the idea of SPL redundant. This chimes with the work of Heejung Chung, who argues in *The Flexibility Paradox* (2022) that having more freedom to control one's work schedule may, ironically, lead one to work longer hours, well beyond one's contracted time, in a bid to keep up with the ideal worker norm (see also Wynn & Rao, 2020). Here we see how such flexibility may impact on men's take-up of parental leave.

Riley also suggested that employers are more tolerant (or 'patient') of women taking leave than of men, which he elaborated on thus:

> I will get more of a brand on me as a man for taking maternity leave than Rita does as a woman. That is expected and accepted – if Rita took two years off, that would be equivalent to me taking two months off, or three months off.
>
> Riley, Interview 1

The idea that men suffer greater career penalties by taking leave than women do was not uncommon amongst male participants, though it often appeared to be based on a perception rather than any concrete evidence, and was discussed even in the face of what appeared to be strong organisational support for men's leave. For instance, in his first interview with me, David told me he was planning to take six weeks of SPL with his wife Debbie, but because of his doubts he had not yet actually requested it from his line manager. He had recently moved to compressed hours – meaning that he was working four long days rather than five regular work-hour days – and told me that his colleagues and boss were generally very supportive. Nonetheless, he felt that requesting leave would be a step too far:

> It was a big thing for me to say 'Can I compress my days?' and the reaction was very positive from my manager at the time. In the new team, they thought that maybe I couldn't do that, but the boss was fine about it. Said it was no problem. My friends and peers say 'It's a statutory thing, you have a right to it, it shouldn't matter what gender you are, you should take it if you want to'. But I am worried about how it will be perceived. [...] I liken it, myself – if I am unwell, I will go to work unless really unwell, or I feel like people will think I am slacking off. I just feel like the perception will be, 'You've just joined this team, why are you asking for time off work?' I am worried that, even if not said overtly, I can feel like behind the scenes certain people will be saying 'Why are you doing that?' But lots of the senior people at work are women who work compressed hours. When I am feeling anxious I do try to think about their situation and think, I would hate for someone to say that about them. So I try not to think about that, but I guess I am actively worried.
>
> David, Interview 1

For David, women taking leave or moving to compressed hours is understood differently than when men do it. His anxieties are potent. We can see that he discussed his options with multiple others, and considered their views and related them to me in the interview. His friends and peers tried to convince him that 'it shouldn't matter what gender you are' in taking up flexible working arrangements, but he continued to worry. Ultimately, he did not take any SPL, saying that he was not ready to be a 'trailblazer' (interview 3). Despite her initial suggestion that they share the leave period equally, which was later reduced to a suggestion that he could take six weeks, Debbie eventually supported David's decision to forgo any period of SPL. She told me that she was disappointed, but did not want to see him suffer unduly; his peace of mind was of greater importance than her desire to share leave.

While men spoke long and often of their worries about the impact of leave on their careers, this concern barely figured in women's accounts. As discussed above, women had long anticipated taking leave from work (as those around them anticipated they would), so any impact on their career was a taken-for-granted aspect of being a mother, as is apparent in this discussion between Olivia (accountant) and Olly (lawyer):

> Olivia: Yeah, it probably does probably affect my career progression in terms of promotion to the next level, it probably puts you back. I don't know if I would get through anyway, but, um, it has that impact, but I think you just accept that.
>
> Olly: Well I wouldn't! Well it depends what your ambitions are, doesn't it? I sort of think, and what you want, and you just make life=.
>
> Olivia: =Yeah, I'm not in a huge hurry / like it doesn't really bother me hugely.
>
> Olly: / fit around it.
>
> Olivia: But um, I think it does impact but it doesn't, for me the priori-, it doesn't, for me my priority obviously is family, so I, it doesn't really, I don't feel angry [short laugh] about it.
>
> Olivia and Olly, Interview 1

Here we see Olivia say that it doesn't 'bother her' that her decisions have that impact on her career, but Olly, hearing her, said, 'I wouldn't!'. This is not to say that Olivia and other women do not worry about their careers:

in fact later, in chapter 7, I will discuss in more depth Olivia's ambivalence in regards to her career progress. But it demonstrates that women's worries about their careers are not an available narrative for mothers in the way that this narrative is for fathers. Beyond normative expectations about the impact of a leave on one's career, this gendered difference in the available narratives speaks to differing moral pressures concerning motherhood and fatherhood, as well as the perceived affordances of paid work and care work, which I move on to now.

Greedy mothering expectations

In part, the differences in men and women's reactions to impacts on their career, at least in this group of non-sharers, emerge from their overall perspective on mothering and fathering roles. Many mothers articulated their role as a parent as more important than and separate from their paid work, as Pippa explained to Peter in their first interview:

> Pippa: I feel like it's my time to invest in being a mum and that I should be – you know, because I chose to have children, so um I don't feel like I should be trying to scrabble for a career, I guess, um when I'm going to be a mum. I think it's my duty [short laugh].
>
> Peter: Oh God, really?
>
> Pippa: To be a good mum, yeah.
>
> Peter: Duty? Well I didn't think that=
>
> Pippa: =Well as much as I can anyway. I want to be there for them [the twins].

It is interesting that Pippa situates career and motherhood as being in opposition to one another, and in fact suggests that a mother should not even attempt to pursue a career, which goes against the 'duty' of a 'good mum'. Peter is clearly quite shocked and in no way expresses similar sentiments about fatherhood and a career.

These mothers draw on familiar discourses about the importance of the first year in the child's development in accounting for the importance of their presence for their child and therefore of taking as much maternity leave as possible:

> I mean there's been a lot of research um about how a mother's full-time kind of care is really important [for] the structure of the baby's brain and how the baby kind of reacts later on in life, and I think we both want kind of a well-rounded baby as much as possible.
>
> Judy, Interview 1

> The first year is the most important for the development of the baby so obviously it would be nice to give as much as ah possible to her.
>
> Beth, Interview 1

These discourses are reflective of a wider pattern of increased moralising and guidance surrounding 'parenting' since the 1970s (Hardyment, 2007; Miller, 2023). Increasingly, parents (and particularly mothers) are called upon to follow this guidance to ensure optimal developmental 'outcomes' for their children (Faircloth, 2014; Gillies et al., 2017).

Although a *mother*'s presence was often foregrounded in these narratives, Cara and Beth articulated intensive parenting ideals in more gender-neutral terms. They told me about the importance of a parent's presence with a young child, as opposed to necessarily a mother, and both actively encouraged their partners to take SPL (unsuccessfully). Their main articulated concern was to support their child's well-being by delaying or minimising their child's attendance in nursery, even when by their own (later) accounts that their children enjoyed and benefited from nursery. Unlike in other contexts, such as in the Nordic countries (Eydal & Rostgaard, 2016), in the UK there is a strong discourse of the importance of family care for young children (Lee et al., 2023). This is coupled with very low government funding for formal childcare of children under school age, reinforcing the idea that young children ought to spend much of their time with their parents (though there are signs that this is changing: increased funding for the care of children aged under three was announced in the 2023 government budget) and making it more difficult for parents to combine paid work and care for their young children.

But even when the mother and father were posited as interchangeable in taking care of a young child, as in the case of Bart and Beth, somehow it always made more sense for the mother to take all the leave (because, for example, of the greater perceived risk to a career for a man taking leave, which was discussed above). Either way, non-sharing women emphasised to a greater degree than non-sharing men the importance of their parenting roles over and above their careers. Other studies too have observed that mothers in paid employment often continue to understand themselves primarily in relation to their maternal role and continue to be held morally responsible for children's upbringing (Duncan et al., 2003; Faircloth, 2021; Miller, 2005, 2017). As these studies so eloquently show, popular discourses about appropriate motherhood affect women's 'deepest yearnings and sense of self' (Gill, 2011:66, cited in Orgad, 2019: 3), influencing the ways in which they navigate family and work life.

In contrast, men in this group of fathers recounted a vision of combining father involvement with their careers. These findings echo those of Esther Dermott (2008): she observes a cultural shift towards an ideal of 'intimate fathering', in which the emotional connection between father and child is emphasised but can be disassociated from a time commitment. That is, the *quality* of the time a father spends with his child is prioritised over the quantity of time, which makes the amount of this time compatible with full-time or even extended hours of work. In terms of leave, this is shown in men's assertions that their lack of take-up of SPL will have little or no bearing on their relationship with their children. In this way Ian is able to claim that Ivy's 12 months of maternity leave will 'make us pretty involved parents', without any apparent reflection on how his two weeks' paternity leave may inhibit his own 'involvement'. This stands in strong contrast to sharers' accounts, in which SPL often figured as central to men's (future) close relationship with their children (see chapter 3).

Male-centred negotiations in relation to leave

As mentioned, some participants took a more degendered approach when considering the importance of parental care in the first year of their child's life. In fact, Beth, Cara and Debbie all attempted to convince their partners to take a share of the leave, but were unsuccessful. As I have discussed elsewhere (Twamley, 2021), even when these women were encouraging SPL, the ways in which SPL was discussed could actually reinforce gendered dynamics. This was apparent in the ways in which SPL was constructed as the father's choice, which maintained heterosexual scripts of the man as active decision-maker, and the woman as passively reacting to him. For example, in their first interview, Cara told me that she was keen for Chidi to take SPL, but they realised it wasn't affordable given that he earns more than she does. Chidi at this point mentioned that his employer offers three months' fully paid SPL. I record this rather lengthy (and confusing) interaction here so the reader can get a sense of the dynamics within their negotiations of leave:

Cara: I would love for him to have taken a month or two off [SPL] and then I would've had less um – like at the same time as me being off, especially because his mum is hoping to visit when the baby's born, so she would be around as well. Um but it just, well you felt it wasn't really practical with work / [inaudible]. [...] But it didn't, I mean financially it didn't make sense for you to be off.

Chidi: / Yeah, as well, yeah.

Cara: Like longer than / me.

Chidi: / Longer than you.

Cara: But um.

Chidi: So yeah I came to a decision of a, a lot of discussion and, yeah that it wouldn't work. So yeah. I've got one of my, one of my bosses at work just had a baby um and so he's, he's disappearing for something like two months, yeah?

Cara: Oh is he? I didn't know that.

Chidi: Yeah. But you know, for someone who's in that position, where he's, you know, he's at the top, you know, he can happily disappear and it doesn't impact him in any way really.

Katherine: So can I just check, so your company doesn't offer anything extra for SPL?

Chidi: Um it does, so ah I checked this, so they, they give you three months, and as far as I remember you get three months I think full pay or quite a lot of the pay um and then I think from that point on it goes to whatever the statutory amount is. Um so in that sense, you know, the, the package is actually quite generous. I don't know, I don't know compared to other places, but the package is quite generous, from what I saw, um and there's quite a lot of people in the company who are, have just recently have kid, are having kids. So, you know, people are taking sort of one month, a month and a half, and a lot of them tend to be the sort of more senior guys I think. Um so, so I guess from our perspective the issue would have been if I took sort of like six months.

Katherine: I see, yeah.

Chidi: Yeah, I think a month, two months would've been fine, I reckon, but more than that / I think then we would start to feel the strain really.

Katherine: Mmhmm. Mmm.

Chidi: Yeah. Do you agree or …

Cara: Yeah, I mean I don't know, I don't really understand what your work offers.

Chidi: No.

Cara: But I just know that, yeah.

Katherine: Because you're not getting any [extra pay], you're just getting the statutory?

Cara: Yeah.=

Katherine: =Yeah.

Cara: Um yeah.

Chidi: Mhmm.

Cara: I just know that I get paid [laughs] a lot less than you [Chidi laughs] all the time.

Cara and Chidi, Interview 1

This extended extract from their interview was at first listening difficult to decipher. Cara started off by telling me that she was hoping that Chidi could take a month or two of SPL with her at the time of the birth, but that she had understood that it would not be financially viable. Chidi agreed, but then went on to tell us that his SPL would actually be fully paid for up to three months and that several of his colleagues, including his boss, were taking this leave. Cara had apparently never heard of this, despite Chidi having said that they had discussed extensively whether SPL would be possible for them. This information puts into doubt the financial deterrent to his taking SPL unless, as he says, he took six months or longer. Since that was never suggested, it's hard to understand this line of reasoning, and it is clear that Cara does not quite understand either, as she says 'Yeah, I mean I don't know, I don't really understand what your work offers.'

There seemed a reluctance on Cara's part to probe Chidi's decision-making, though she repeated later her disappointment that he cannot take any SPL. There is perhaps an element of 'couple display' going on here, and maybe discussions continued beyond the interview, but the same interaction was actually repeated in their second interview. It is apparent in this, and in the interviews with the other two non-sharing couples who discussed SPL, that the take-up of SPL is not viewed as a couple decision, but as an individual choice that the husband may or may not take up. So, while on the one hand the transfer mechanism inherent in SPL may encourage so-called 'maternal gatekeeping', as discussed previously, in practice one can also see elements of what Tina Miller calls 'paternal gatekeeping'. In her studies exploring the gendered nature of motherhood and fatherhood, she observed that claims of incompetency from fathers could 'free them up' from undesired care or domestic activities (2017:155). Mothers could be complicit in this process as they sought to shore up their perceived competency as mothers. Chidi appears ambivalent at best about taking SPL and seemingly obfuscates his access to paid leave in a bid to deny its possibility. Both Cara and Chidi avoid any in-depth discussion of the possibilities of SPL, readily concluding that it is just not possible. This is not to deny that Chidi or other male participants had genuine concerns about the risks of taking SPL, but it highlights some of the difficulties which arise when women attempt to encourage their partners to share leave and some of their ambivalence about doing so. Their example shows the deeply relational nature of care negotiations, and how couples call upon and create particular 'leave narratives' about their decisions in a bid to uphold other narratives about themselves as a couple and family. Here we can see that 'maternal gatekeeping' is entangled with 'paternal gatekeeping' in a process of collaborative gatekeeping, so that each enables and co-constructs the other.

Similar findings about the gendered nature of leave negotiations were made in Austria by Schmidt et al. (2015). The authors argued that decisions for and against sharing leave were father-centred, and that framing the sharing of leave in this way reaffirmed hegemonic masculine ideals and therefore failed to transform gendered practices even when couples did share leave (which I will discuss further in later chapters). This reluctance to negotiate a more equal sharing of leave explicitly may partly be explained by participants' fears of the impact of such negotiations on their intimate relationship, which I discuss in the next section.

Fears of 'cold intimacy'

Participants in this study, sharers and non-sharers alike, spoke of equality within the couple as a taken-for-granted component of intimate relationships. They told me that 'obviously' they shared tasks and responsibilities, or that they held equal sway in decisions. Victor, for example, said, 'It's just everything should be shared equally between both parties, there shouldn't be a difference really', and Sarah said, 'Yeah, we sort of feel it's fair to share things out.' They told me proudly how they shared household work between them, or how they supported one another equally in their relationship, and sometimes compared themselves favourably with other couples (such as their parents), who they viewed as less equal. This facet of the couples' relationships emerged most forcefully in the first interview, when I asked each couple to fill in a Household Portrait, during which the participants discuss as a couple who does different household tasks most frequently (see chapter 1):

> Katherine: So um how do you feel about this chart, looking at it now?
>
> Pippa: Good, yeah, I feel it's fairly balanced.
>
> Peter: Yeah but it's a bit sort of gender-stereotypical isn't it, in a way? But um but the fact is it's how we operate / um and some things are more important to you and other things are more important to me, and those are the things that we each take responsibility for doing.
>
> Pippa: / Yeah. Yeah.
>
> Pippa and Peter, Interview 1

> Katherine: Okey doke. So um how do you feel about this? Do you think it's, are you happy with it? Is there anything you'd like to change, or …?
>
> Victor: Yeah, I'm quite happy with it really.
>
> Vicki: Yes, it's fair, isn't it? =
>
> Victor: = I enjoy doing the cooking so it doesn't really bother me.
>
> Vicki: And I, I like that he likes cooking and he does that and I am happy with what I do.
>
> Victor and Vicki, Interview 1

In both cases the couples expressed contentment with their Household Portraits, noting that they were 'fair' in their division of tasks. Any imbalances were accounted for by personal preferences or skills – such as Victor doing most of the cooking, but not much cleaning – or by differing contributions to the household in other ways: that is, one partner might do less housework or care work, but this was 'fair' overall because they did more paid work, or their paid work contributed more through either its current or future remuneration. This approach to gendered divisions of labour was typical amongst non-sharers, while sharers were more commonly aiming for symmetry in household tasks: that is, both members of a couple should do the same tasks for the same amount of time (as discussed in chapter 3; see also Twamley & Faircloth, 2023).

This narration of fairness resembles 'post-feminist' discourses, in the sense that gender was not considered relevant in shaping couples' divisions of paid and unpaid work. Rather, equality was reported as a general principle in life and a good way to treat others:

> If there's work to be done in the house it should be done by whoever's there.
>
> Sarah, Interview 1

> It naturally falls to what we do best ourselves or what we do, or we do what we hate the least, divide up the tasks that way.
>
> Peter, Interview 1

Sexism was downplayed as either non-existent within their peer group or only present in work scenarios, not in personal relationships. Unlike sharers, these participants were unlikely to consider themselves feminist; in fact, a few were actively anti-feminist:

> Victor: I believe in gender equality but I'm not a feminist.
>
> Katherine: Mmhmm. Can you tell me why or …?
>
> Victor: Well I j-, I just, from what, some of this, you get some very militant sort of feminists and things like that, and I think sometimes it might've gone over a bit too far. Don't get me wrong, I'm not about anything about sort of being negative or doing anything bad against women but I just think sometimes that some, I think the term is feminazis.
>
> Katherine: Mmhmm.
>
> Victor: And I think that's probably a bit too far over the edge sort of thing, if that makes sense=.
>
> Vicki: =Sometimes the feminists are really, really harsh on … women and men, I don't know. No, I don't like the stressiness of feminism, or like that, you know?
>
> Victor and Vicki, Interview 1

I don't kind of think [of] life [in] a feminist or non-feminist way. I think of life as in: these are the choices we make in life in our particular situation, with who we are, in terms of his job and his salary, and my job, and what's the sensible thing to do between the two of us in terms of the roles we take. I don't think of it as in I want to do this for my own self. I mean sometimes I think, oh, we could put his career to one side and focus on my career. [...] Which I kind of like the idea of for a bit and then I decide that I'm not sure I care about it enough to [short laugh], to really care about it enough, if you know what I mean, and actually I'm happy in the way that we are and our set-up as a family.

Olivia, Interview 3

I think the women I know who would claim to be feminists are very um strong-minded, strong women that I think people could find intimidating um and I don't necessarily think that that is the right way for it to be portrayed, I guess, so, and I don't want to be put in that box of someone who's a feminist and believes in all these things when actually I just believe in equality for human life.

Pippa, Interview 1

The discussions of feminism were in response to a survey question in which participants had been asked whether they considered themselves feminist, gender-egalitarian, or none of the above. In the qualitative interview, I returned to their responses to ask them about the reasons for their selection. In general, non-sharers rejected the term 'feminist'. Their reluctance to name or describe themselves as feminists appeared to be based on an understanding of feminists as aggressive (harsh and intimidating) or selfish (as Olivia says, 'I don't think of it as in I want to do this for my own self'), as these quotes show. Such characterisations of feminists are not uncommon (Ahmed, 2010; Tyler, 2007) and are thought to originate (in part) in a more general backlash against feminism that constrains women's ability to challenge a lack of equality in both private and public spheres (Oakley, 1998).

Along with the antipathy to feminism, or perhaps as a corollary to it, participants were keen to emphasise to me that household labour was not negotiated, but just happened 'naturally', as these quotes demonstrate:

So I think, you know, we're, we're each kind of pulling our, our weight in the, in the ways that we, we can um most effectively. So I think, you know, we don't, we don't discuss who does what, we just kind of get on and, and do stuff.

Ian, Interview 1

I really like that it's natural without any particular label. And we really, it's, it's natural, it's not ah, again it's nothing that we force each other to do or ah, it's, it's nice that we do stuff together and there is no particular men and women stuff that we, we don't put a label.

Vicki, Interview 1

So he, he's able to kind of predict already um what I would need in a way, and then he just does it and it just flows naturally for me. But I think it's just thanks to his sensitivity that he is like that, or empathy, I don't know.

Beth, Interview 1

This emphasis on things happening 'naturally' in a couple relationship reflects wider research on intimacy in which couples narrate love as something which is beyond rationalisation or control, something which 'just happens' (Carter, 2013) as people '*fall* in love' and are overcome by emotions and desire (Twamley, 2014). Stevi Jackson (1993) argued back in the 1990s that this understanding of love as beyond the rational realm is so potent that it has discouraged sociologists from researching love in any great depth. More recently, the construction of love and intimacy as irrational is positioned as antithetical to contemporary forms of feminism in which partners seek parity in paid and unpaid work (Hochschild, 2003; Illouz, 2007, 2012). Eva Illouz (2012), for example, argues that increased rationalisation and individualism in modern society leads to a greater range of choices for women, but also to a cooling of intimacy, since romantic decisions are now based on bargaining and reason. She critiques the 'contractual relations' of egalitarian couples as 'cold'. Similarly, Frank Furedi, in a response to a Norwegian study which found higher divorce rates amongst couples who shared housework than in those that did not, argued that the findings were not surprising, since those in egalitarian marriages are more likely to take a utilitarian and transactional approach to relationships:

> Intimacy, and the kind of emotions associated with love and trust, cannot withstand the corrosive consequence of the introduction of a contractual and transactional ethos. Pragmatism and calculation

are important for running a well organised office but they are likely to render formal what works best as an intimate and informal relationship. In effect they empty intimate relations of meaning. (Furedi, 2012)

His argument that a more egalitarian relationship is necessarily 'contractual' and 'transactional' is not based on any empirical evidence, other than the cited association between equality and divorce. In fact, other studies have suggested the opposite association: that is, that increased levels of egalitarianism between couples may increase relationship stability (e.g. Schober, 2013). It is important also to remember that internal and external estimations of equality may not be consistent (Twamley & Faircloth, 2023), and of course within-couple estimations have often been found to differ (Kiger & Riley, 1996; Van Hooff, 2011). Moreover, historically, and across cultures, marital and other intimate familial relations have been based on contractual and traditional systems of reciprocity or understandings of give and take, without a necessary absence of intimacy (Jamieson, 2011; Twamley, 2014). Nonetheless, these scholars' arguments reveal how underlying cultural constructions of love and intimacy may render negotiations of a more equal division of household labour (or division of leave) undesirable for some participants. Because of the influence of the idea of feminists as selfish and aggressive, there was little room for these participants to explicitly negotiate household labour, even when they clearly thought that equality was an important element of an intimate relationship. The result is an avoidance of explicit negotiations of parental leave, at least as it relates to equality or fairness, and ultimately a lack of any discourse around why SPL may be helpful or necessary in setting up more equal parenting (which was a motivation for many sharers, as discussed in chapter 3).

Conclusion

This chapter shows the ways in which participants relationally negotiate parental leave options, and the constraints they perceive to its take-up. The social context in the UK, where there is a historical norm of mothers' long maternity leave and very low numbers of fathers taking SPL, coupled with the policy construction of SPL as a transfer of maternity leave, shapes couples' decisions about taking SPL and their emotional rejection of it. Participants report a fear of the unknown consequences of SPL, particularly as regards men's careers. While women appear to have an emotional attachment to a long maternity leave as a kind of rite of passage of entry into motherhood, others around them reinforce these narratives of appropriate transition to parenthood. I also found that some mothers had long planned to take their full maternity leave and that these plans had triggered career choices which make mothers' leave more practical or more affordable than men's leave. Such planning amongst women has been shown by other research to continue to shape divisions of paid and unpaid labour as children get older and to 'justify' relationship inequalities as the most convenient or efficient 'choice' for couples (Daminger, 2020).

The maternity leave transfer mechanism solidifies an underlying belief that the mother–child relation is the most important one, and for some men forgoing SPL becomes a means of demonstrating their love for their partner by 'protecting' her leave and supporting her mothering role. Similar findings of men's reluctance to 'take away' women's leave have been observed elsewhere (McKay & Doucet, 2010) and go some way towards explaining why women are more likely to take gender-neutral parental leaves than men (Lammi-Taskula, 2008; Uzunalioglu et al., 2021).

Building on previous literature, I explore how ideals and understandings of appropriate paid work relations (in particular the ideal worker norm and a context of 'greedy work') mean that taking SPL is considered 'risky' for a father's career prospects, while women report less anxiety about how leave may impact on their careers, telling me that they had always anticipated their careers being delayed and interrupted by parenthood. That SPL is considered risky, even amongst a sample of participants who are relatively well off and in professional, often stable, careers, indicates that barriers for more precarious and lower-earning parents are likely to be higher still (even if they are eligible; see Twamley & Schober, 2019).

I also explored how participants' decisions are shaped by ideas about mothering and fathering roles, such as the 'intensive mothering' ideal which dictates that mothers should be present as much as possible, as opposed to a less time-intensive 'intimate father' ideal. Like Doucet and McKay (2020) in Canada, I find that the primary concern articulated by parents is that of maximising parental leave time (and household income) to sustain what they consider to be the best care for their children. 'Equality' is of lesser concern. This is, again, linked to understandings and practices of couple intimacy, including how intimacy intersects with understandings of gender equality, as some participants avoid 'cold' negotiations of gendered practices and parental leave that are perceived as antithetical to couple intimacy and harmony. Overall, the chapter highlights the emotional and relational nature of participants' negotiations of leave-taking, and how these come together with wider structural constraints to discourage participants' take-up of SPL.

3
Why and how some couples decide to share leave: 'sharers'

Edward, a sales executive for an antiques firm, was not initially keen to take SPL. He told me his wife Emily, a lawyer, convinced him to do it, but that before meeting her he would never have considered such a thing. In their first interview they told me the following about how their decision to share leave came about:

> Emily: So I, well we originally had a conversation, which I'm sure you won't remember [short laugh], um on our honeymoon about it.
>
> Edward: Whoa, no idea= [Katherine laughs].
>
> Emily: =And we were on a hike. I knew you wouldn't remember this [both short laugh]. […] I'd seen like so many of my friends where the mother is the only person who knows, you know, which nappy can be put on the baby or like, and then like, you know, which food they're able to eat or which one they're not. And if the father takes, you know, if they go out for the day as a sort of family then the mother's doing all the packing and everything because the father doesn't, you know, is, loves the child and is, you know, has, I'm sure has a wonderful relationship but it's the mother who all the burden of all the practical stuff falls on. Um and I think it must've been around then, and I just thought, wouldn't it be nice if like Edward had had a few months with, or some time with the baby to sort of actually know the routine and get to know the baby properly so that it's actually a genuinely shared enterprise that we're doing,

and it's not like something that I'd start getting annoyed with Edward because he doesn't know something or whatever.

Emily and Edward, Interview 1

Interesting here is that Emily recalled exactly when she first brought up the topic, several years before the interview. Mostly 'I' pronouns were used as she presented her perspective, including how she wanted to avoid being annoyed with Edward, and how she thought it would be 'nice' for him to spend time with the baby. The repeated 'you know' suggests she may think I understand her perspective, but also indicate some hesitancy. Interestingly, however, Edward very quickly refuted this portrayal, saying he took leave in order to bond with the baby and to ease Emily's transition back to work, not to create a 'shared enterprise'. She corrected herself then, saying that, yes, she had always known that he would pull his weight in childcare, and that it was about his bonding. Emily seemingly responded to and fed into Edward's preferred narrative of their leave division; she dropped equality as a motivation, even though in a survey taken immediately after this interview she wrote the following about their plans to take SPL:

> I think it will (and has) been good for our relationship to think about parenting, and leave, as such a joint enterprise. I think it will be good for my relationship with my child that Edward will have leave as we may be a more balanced family.

The references to 'joint enterprise' and 'balanced family' echo her original reasoning on shared parenting, later reiterated in an individual interview, but sidestepped in conversation with Edward. Emily also emphasised that SPL will be good for her relationship with their child and with Edward, demonstrating how SPL is figured within relational ideals of parent and partner.

As we moved on in the interview, Edward expanded on his reluctance to take SPL: he said it was an 'alien' concept to him, he 'just couldn't imagine' taking time off to look after a baby. He had never heard of anyone else taking SPL and he wasn't sure he wanted to be the first in his company or amongst his peers. Later, however, he started to meet other fathers taking SPL while he was attending antenatal classes:

> Edward: Yeah I am pretty traditional I'd say um but I think Emily's influence has mellowed that a little bit and, yeah, possibly living in somewhere like London and seeing like

our NCT group and the hypnobirthing group that it is really normal, you know? Maybe if we did this in like Richmond or like the Cotswolds then it would be like a, like I definitely would be the only guy doing that, but because we're doing it in London then it's less weird, and so, because I'm meeting loads of other guys and then 'Oh yeah, I'm doing that as well', it's like 'Okay cool'. So that has probably mellowed my kind of thoughts of it. Before I met Emily, like ten years ago, that would be a very alien thing for me to think of, and I'm pretty sure my parents are probably thinking this is probably a really nice thing that you're doing but=.

Emily: =Have you told them?

Edward: Yeah, I think so. Um but they would be like 'Well that was not something we did back in our day' kind of thing. So yeah it's something I have come around to. [Both short laugh]

Here we can see the relational and emotional matrices at play as Edward considered whether to take SPL or not. His initial reluctance to take SPL focused on what imagined others might think, and then shifted through dialogue with *real* others who are taking SPL (Burkitt, 2016) and who normalise the idea of taking leave for him. He repeatedly called SPL 'weird' or 'alien' in this interview, indicating a certain anxiety about this new practice. He mentioned his parents and how 'ten years ago' he would not have considered it, emphasising how leave was represented in his imagined (or real past) family life. He is clearly influenced by what Gillis (1997) calls 'the families we live by', but ultimately shifted his ideas through conversations with Emily and with other men. Their account shows how Edward's sense of what he wants is tied to others (Mason, 2004) as well as the ways in which even the introduction of SPL can create the spark for new ways of considering family life.

Emily demonstrated sympathy towards her husband's reluctance to take leave, and reminded Edward that he was never really on board with the idea of taking leave until he realised that the leave period would fall in the least busy period of his work. There are no remonstrations about this, indicating to me (and Edward) that this is a valid reason not to want to take leave. His work, while of less economic value to the family than hers (he earns considerably less than she does), is given equal (or even more) weight. The proposed leave period is unpaid whether taken by

Emily or Edward, so the potential wage loss is greater if Emily takes these two months. Yet they tell me that money was not a consideration in their decision. This is unlike most other couples, where the man was earning more or his perceived earning prospects were better; in those cases his job was explicitly focused upon in accounting for leave decisions. This is not to discount the different pressures that Edward may feel concerning paid work, but demonstrates the narratives available to couples in the UK as they consider SPL.

The exclusion or avoidance of her own motivations regarding the sharing of leave positions Edward as the ultimate decider of whether to take shared parental leave, and indeed the thrust of the whole of this interview is whether and how Edward decides to take leave, and then how much he should take. This complicates ideas about 'maternal gatekeeping' of leave, and shows that even when officially the leave belongs to women (in that SPL functions through a transfer mechanism) the decision-making power rests more with men than with women. Nonetheless, Emily has 'coaxed' (Phạm, 2013:37) Edward into taking leave, and while he may not agree with her motivations he did say 'I would never have taken it if it weren't for Emily.' Later, he expressed joy and pride in his experiences of leave, and suggested that he will take two months' leave again should they have a second child (see chapter 8).

As is clear, couples like Edward and Emily live in a similar context to non-sharers, a context which discourages, and makes it actively difficult to take, SPL. How is it then that sharing couples choose to take SPL? I have found that there isn't any one reason which precipitates sharing couples to choose SPL, but rather a combination of factors. In the case of Edward and Emily, Emily had a commitment and ideal around equality within the couple, which gave her a strong motivation to advocate for SPL; she did this in a subtle way, drawing on multiple 'relational resources' (Benjamin & Sullivan, 1999; Twamley, 2021) to do so. She earned a significantly higher salary than Edward, which meant that SPL made financial sense; and Edward's work schedule suited the period when the proposed leave fell. As with other couples in this study, for couples to actively choose and ultimately follow through with SPL a whole host of favourable elements must come together, which I go into in more depth now.

SPL sharers going against the grain

Just like non-sharers, sharers live in a context in which taking SPL is a minority practice. Few of the participants had personally known others who had taken SPL, and all the sharers in the study were the first amongst their colleagues to take SPL. Moreover, participants often reported that line managers and human resources (HR) colleagues had little or no experience of SPL and that HR were hastily training themselves or making up new policies in response to participants' questions about SPL, as indicated by these participants:

> I'm the first person in my company to do it. They had to write the policy for me, pretty much. So it's not even like the conversations are happening at work, so, I don't think anyone at work would've made me think of it because no one else has done it.
>
> Kate, Interview 1

> I'm the first, HR have told me I'm the prototype for shared parental leave. They've had to quickly brush up on the policy!
>
> Gerald, Interview 1

One of the participants, Nick, co-designed the SPL package in his company with colleagues in HR, which resulted in a comparatively generous package that shaped Nick and Natasha's final division of leave between them (with Nick planning to take seven and a half months of leave and Natasha four and a half).

Nick's employer was unusual, however, at least amongst the employers of this group of fathers. Other participants repeatedly noted a lack of employer support for SPL, either implicit (in terms of their failure to enhance pay for SPL while they did enhance maternity leave pay) or explicit (such as managers' or colleagues' discouragement of take-up of SPL). Their experiences with their employers were on the whole very similar to those reported by non-sharers. For example, in chapter 2 I recounted that David (physiotherapist) had initially planned to take six weeks of SPL with his wife Debbie (nurse) at the end of her maternity leave period. In interview 1 and later interview 2, however, he told me that he had doubts, related to a perceived lack of support from his employer and colleagues and to his sense that men are more likely than women to experience career penalties from taking leave. In the end, he did not take any SPL. Here we can see sharers express similar concerns and doubts about taking SPL in their first interview:

Tim: Well, that's the plan, that I take six weeks after Tara has gone back to work, but I am still not sure so we'll have to see em... It might not be possible.

Katherine: Oh?

Tim: I have a feeling that no one would say anything but it would be, I don't know, noted. [...] And [sighs], I don't know, I'm pushing to get promoted and sort of, it's – there's pressure on sales targets and things like that, so – which would be affected by taking all that time off and I don't know.

Tim, Interview 1

Katherine: How did you decide on one or two months of SPL?

Weston: I think in terms of, career-wise, it's a problem because it's, they're, women of a certain age are expected – well, not expected but it's an understanding: plenty of my colleagues are on maternity leave now. But if I was to say – turn around and say 'Oh I want to take', well even three months might be a bit, I would do it but I think maybe more than that I would start getting into, because I guess more, over, I don't know what it is, but over a certain period they would have to get a cover in.

Katherine: Mmhmm.

Weston: Whereas a month – that might be possible, just kind of, I'll do a good handover and then my boss will deal with it. Like they won't have to employ anyone else.

Katherine: Mmhmm. And what gives you an impression that the reaction would be different to you as a man?

Weston: I think it's [pause], I mean it's mainly, you know, there's a lot of old, it's not old-fashioned but it's not as modern of an industry, it's a big corporation. Ah so I would say part of the reason is not many men take it so it would be the unknown. Ah part of my job is, well, both of our jobs, but I guess my role in the company, it's quite demanding, so things happen in politics or whatever, in the business, and you're expected, you know, we rarely have quiet weeks really in what we do, so I think it would be the issue around the negative effects on the business of me not being there or someone being in that role.

Weston, Interview 1

Like non-sharing fathers, sharing fathers such as Tim and Weston felt that men are more likely than women to be penalised for taking parental leave, though they didn't have any concrete evidence of this other than that women more often take long leaves. Weston also, interestingly, narrated the nature of his job as a potential barrier to SPL, although he and his wife Winnie actually had the same role, though in different companies. This shows that *feelings* rather than facts or experiences can drive men's reluctance to take leave, and that work as a barrier to leave is a narrative more available to men than to women.

For her part, Winnie agreed with Weston that their employers were not supportive of SPL, noting the difference between how women and men's leaves were discussed:

> And so I think for women, at least at Weston's company, with women it's treated as um an expectation, whereas with men it's treated as a choice. Um and because of that the way that people speak about it internally is very different. Any support is about image management more than anything else.
>
> Winnie, Interview 1

Winnie argued that, since leave is understood as a 'choice' for men, men are perceived to make a choice *against* work in ways women are not (Mauerer & Schmidt, 2019). Such understandings of men's take-up of leave are most prevalent in contexts where men's access to parental leave is relatively new (K. Wall & O'Brien, 2017) and are also likely compounded by a system in which the leave belongs to women and not men. This shows the imperative of 'use it or lose it' parental leave policies to shift these patterns and to deviate from the idea of fathers 'opting out' of paid work when they choose to take parental leave.

Several sharers described to me, in addition to a perceived lack of employer support, the uncomfortable feeling of being 'different' or unusual in having chosen to take SPL. They told me that friends were often positive in theory about SPL, but few – or more often none – of their peers had decided to do it themselves:

> Keith: Yeah, I think that's been the overwhelming reaction, has been surprise and then kind of 'Go you' sort of [short laugh] / 'Glad you're fighting the cause'.
>
> Kate: / Yeah. 'I wouldn't have thought to do that.'

> Keith: [...] So you sort of feel like most of the people that we associate with at least are positive about men being more involved in parenting but are still very surprised about how that would actually work.
>
> Keith and Kate, Interview 1

> Helen: Like no one thought it was weird that Henry would want to, no one would, it's certainly a normal thing, it's a normal thing to want to pursue amongst our circle of friends.
>
> Henry: [...] Um yeah but, yeah people know the right answer but it's like, it's whether, yeah, when you actually, do you, do you go out and do it?
>
> Helen and Henry, Interview 1

> And I think a lot of friends actually, and family, are just also interested in how we'll get along. They want us, they want to see us flourish, sure, but they also, I think, want to see a little experiment also?
>
> Gerald, Interview 1

As both Henry and Keith mentioned, there appears to be a disconnect between general positive discourses about fathers' involvement on the one hand, and the actual take-up of SPL on the other. The positivity expressed by those around them was tainted with a feeling of being watched to see how this 'experiment' will work out, giving a sense of risk to their SPL practices, as well as the general feeling of being odd or unusual.

Other comments received were more explicitly negative or sceptical about SPL decisions, as seen here:

> They say things like 'Oh, I'm too selfish to give up my year off' and 'Are you sure you want to do that?' Things like that.
>
> Kate, Interview 1

> Adam: If anything maybe they're, they [friends] would be a little, not overtly, but a little bit kind of ah negative towards [pause] ... I think our choices are potentially a bit flaky, maybe. It's like [indicates a sceptical face] you know?
>
> Anna: Maybe they are [short laugh].

Adam: 'Well surely Adam you should go back to work', and I think there's a certain degree of, a lot of our friends are quite successful and I think there's a certain degree of um [pause], that that's just what successful people do, you know? You've got to focus on your work.

Adam and Anna, Interview 1

Most blokes were supportive and ah quite often the more ah surprised contrary reaction was from female colleagues ah or employers who were very much more of the sort of ah 'I'd be astonished if Natasha let you take any of her leave, I'd certainly never have let Jimmy take any of mine', and 'It's not just a baby holiday you know, it is actually really quite tough. You think it's all very easy, you've got no idea'.

Nick, Interview 1

Participants' parents were also frequently reported to feel 'concerned' about men's uptake of SPL.[1] Adam's parents, for example, sought assurances that his career in medicine would not be unduly affected by his planned three months of leave. And Filip told me his parents thought it was 'odd' that he was taking SPL and wondered whether he was being pressured unduly by his wife Faria, at which both Faria and Filip guffawed. Despite Filip and Faria's humour, the emotion work in managing the reactions of others is palpable across the SPL-taking participants.

The issue for friends and family appears to be the degree to which gendered norms of mothers as carers and fathers as earners were being challenged by sharer participants. This is an interesting contradiction, suggesting conflicts in moral discourses about families and parenthood: that fathers should be involved and women supported in their career development, but that fathers' priorities should remain in their paid work and women's in their caring role. Note that Adam's friends think he was 'flaky' for not prioritising work, which is 'just what successful people do'. Although he used a gender-neutral term in referring to 'successful people' women were not being encouraged to take less leave for career success. The social and cultural pressures on men and women are different. To successfully perform masculinity men must work for pay (Berdahl et al., 2018), while femininity is associated with putting family first (Collins, 2019). A survey experiment (with hypothetical scenarios) in the US found something similar: fathers who take parental leave are viewed as good parents and likeable when they take short leave periods, but there is a reverse association if they are perceived to take leave that is 'too long' (Petts, Mize & Kaufman, 2024; Petts, Kaufman & Mize, 2023). Amongst the participants in this study, men's taking 'long leave' (anything more than a month) was also reported as contentious, as Faria and Filip found:

> Faria: And I would say certainly the negative reaction we've had from your work or anybody else we've spoken to has never been 'Don't do this at all', but 'Is six months really necessary? Could you do it'=.
>
> Filip: =Yeah, 'That's a long time / you'll get bored'.
>
> Faria: / 'That's a long time', yeah, exactly=.
>
> Filip: =You'll want to come back, yeah, yeah, all that stuff.
>
> Faria and Filip, Interview 1

Then, just as described in chapter 2, for many couples, to take SPL is to transgress sometimes deeply held beliefs about what the transition to parenthood should look like. Some participants, such as Edward, found the experience of being different particularly uncomfortable. Others were more readily able to laugh off what they saw as old-fashioned concerns, such as Filip, who appeared to revel in being the first in his company to take SPL, telling me that he had organised a parents' group in his company and was encouraging other colleagues to consider SPL themselves. But it was clear nonetheless that most men (including Filip) were influenced by this situation, many limiting their SPL weeks in response to such an adverse environment. Now that we have established the similar circumstances in which sharers and non-sharers make their decisions, I consider how sharers differ from non-sharers.

Involved fathers and breadwinning mothers?

In chapter 2 I discussed how ideals of intensive mothering shaped non-sharers' decisions about SPL. Might the opposite be happening amongst sharers, that is, that sharing fathers prioritise their parenting role and mothers their careers? It is not so clear-cut, though there are elements of this, certainly. Consider the following extracts, in which Mark and Filip described their reactions to unsupportive senior colleagues in their workplaces:

> Mary: Do you want to say about what your colleague said to you, off the record? [laughs]

Mark: Oh, when I first brought this up he did say something bizarre to me about how it can be career-limiting, but then he's never mentioned it ever again and I think he probably regrets saying it now [short laugh]. It was a bit silly=.

Mary: =Realised he shouldn't have said it.

Mark: It was a bit silly. Because I'm quite junior, he is quite senior, it was realistically not going to affect my, I'm quite new in my organisation as well, so it's not like I'm going to apply for a job in the next year or eighteen months anyway, so um, but I think he was quite sort of ignorant of the, the policy, and actually he's not been any problem since then, eh, in signing any of this off.

Mary and Mark, Interview 1

Filip: He [the team leader] reacted … positively … but he also was, he didn't, yeah he, to start with he didn't get it and I saw the moment in the conversation where his brain went 'uh-oh' [short laugh]. Like because he, he started off with 'Yeah, that sounds fine if that's what you want to do. Have you thought about six months? Six months is quite a long time. Is that, um well before, well before you go you should um before you go you should talk to people and make sure you kind of know what you're doing while you're out so that you can kind of not lose touch and sort of get back in.' Very sensible advice but I cheekily, slightly, said 'Oh well I mean I presume there'll be a sort of process for women when they go on maternity leave, so I'll just go through the same process, because that's what I'm doing really', and I could see his brain just go 'Oh shit' [Faria short laugh] because we're not, they're not supposed, one of the big things that HR say is, you know, you can't ask a mother-to-be how long she's planning on taking off.

Faria: Mhmm.

Filip: You could see his brain go 'Oh, I've just talked about how long he's taking off and tried to discourage him from it' [Faria laughs]. Like I could just see his brain wasn't treating me as a parent going on leave in the same way

> he would a mother going on leave until that moment, and then it/ then it, then it changed.
>
> Faria: / That's very true ... Yes, that's right=.
>
> Filip: =And then he [inaudible] got it.
>
> Faria and Filip, Interview 1

Mark and Filip seemingly managed to brush off the reactions from their senior colleagues; in fact Filip portrays himself as enjoying the provocation of his team leader by bringing up norms about maternity leave. This nonchalance is buoyed by a combination of strong job security and high motivation to be an involved father. Filip, Mark and also Gerald told me that they had long expected to share leave (even before their partners got pregnant), and thought that they might become stay-at-home fathers at some point in the future:

> Gerald: I think I was just always of the mindset that when the baby, when a baby would come along I would, I would probably have just taken the time off anyway [if SPL wasn't available].
>
> Gina: Yeah, you just, that you would've just eaten through all your savings to do so, if it was necessary.
>
> Gerald and Gina, Interview 1

> My chunk as the, I suppose, I don't know what the term is, the primary carer I suppose, at the end when you [partner] go back to work, it's just such an opportunity for the male partner to have I think, which is unusual. And I, yeah I just think it's just, it's just a really good, it's a good idea. I mean we should, would never normally be able to take that amount of time off to just be the carer, and everything you read about it says it benefits the, not just the child but the parents and their relationship as well, with the child and your partner, and it's um yeah it's just something I'm sort of looking forward to doing, have looked forward to.
>
> Mark, Interview 1

While all the men in the study expressed a desire to be in one way or another an 'involved father', only these men positioned fatherhood above or on a par with their career aspirations. Their reported 'long-held' desire to take leave is similar to mothers' reported aspiration to take all their maternity leave. Those mothers reported taking steps in their careers, even before meeting their partners, which would ensure that such leave and the later practical issues of motherhood could be accommodated in their career. These men did not report making specific choices about careers or work patterns, which suggests that they anticipated being able to combine paid and unpaid work in the future. They will not have been exposed to the same kinds of narratives as women about the difficulties of combining paid and unpaid work, or they will not have seen them as relevant to themselves.

On the other hand, a lack of interest or drive in a particular workplace, rather than a desire to be a more involved father per se, gave other participants the confidence to negotiate SPL with their employers. For example, Nick was keen to change careers and saw SPL as a chance to think through his next steps while allowing his (higher-earning) wife to progress in her chosen career. And Henry appeared not to attach a great deal of significance to career progression with his current employer, who he claimed he hated. These may be called 'circumstantial sharers', like many of the primary care fathers identified in Brooks and Hodkinson's study (2020), which demonstrates that changes in gendered parenting practices are sometimes a result of pragmatics rather than of attitudinal shifts (see also Jones et al., 2021). Whether such an entry into SPL has lasting implications for care practices will be discussed in Part III.

Women sharers tended to earn either similar amounts to or more than their partners (Anna (theatre set designer) was the only exception, earning less than her husband Adam (medical doctor)). Such patterns are noted more broadly in quantitative studies (Wood et al., 2023). Women with higher salaries are usually viewed as having more bargaining power, and so as being able to negotiate less care and housework, as if the preferred option of all parents were to spend less time on caring for their child. The data in this study demonstrate a more complex picture, with higher- or similar-earning wives giving some men the opportunity to take a greater role in fatherhood. The relative earnings within the couple could rather be interpreted as giving men leeway to negotiate for access to more parental leave.[2] These men reported long-held dreams of being 'involved', or even stay-at-home, fathers, which suggests they may have been attracted to their partners partly because they could facilitate such desires. Indeed, in their narratives of getting together as a couple, these participants often reported having discussed ideals of future life and perspectives that included being involved or primary care fathers or being attracted to women who were 'career-oriented'. Meanwhile, amongst women sharers, the importance of their career was articulated alongside their desire to be present mothers, and motivations for SPL were more about improved work–life balance than purely career progression.

The case of Faria and Filip is instructive here. Faria (lawyer) earns upwards of £400,000 a year, significantly more than her husband Filip (business consultant), but since she is a partner in a firm she does not receive any maternity leave package (she is essentially categorised as self-employed). Self-employed mothers receive a statutory maternity allowance from the UK government to facilitate leave from their work. She forwent the opportunity to take this, which would have paid her around £140 a week (a very small amount of money for her). This meant that Filip could take the leave as SPL instead. He works in a company which enhances SPL statutory pay to 100 per cent salary compensation for six months. Since Faria did not return to work for a year after the birth, they were both off work for the first six months. They told me that, given the very favourable circumstances they found themselves in, it would be 'crazy' for Filip not to take this leave, but they feared a potential detrimental impact on his career from taking six months of SPL. When I asked Faria whether she worried about the impact of leave on her career, however, she paused, and then said:

> Well no, now that you mention it, I didn't. I guess I have known women who essentially took off four years in order to have several children at once, and I think that would have a negative impact, so I wouldn't consider that.

Thus, only a hypothetical case of an extended career break is viewed as potentially problematic.

Like women non-sharers, women sharers expected to take extended maternity leave in some form or other. They did not articulate their desire to share leave in terms of aspirations for their career or to reduce the impact on their career progression. Rather, the focus in their narrations was on the importance of *shared parenting* more generally, and their belief that SPL would facilitate this:

> I hope the fact that Keith is having a month off when the baby is born will mean we have time to get into habits together and establish how we want to do things jointly. The fact that Keith is intending to take 12 weeks of parental leave after my 40 weeks of maternity leave has meant that he is already more involved in decisions and is more interested in what we do when the baby is a newborn and the decisions we make then, than some other fathers I know.
>
> Kate, Survey after interview 1

> I hope that by sharing our parental leave it will help our child to develop a strong relationship with both parents and that going forward Weston and I will continue to jointly care for our child.
>
> Winnie, Survey after interview 1

Faria: Well I think it can have a, I mean I think it has a positive impact on the family in the kind of, the long term because I know far too many people where the fathers are just unable to cope with taking care of children for a long period of time, and I don't think that's because they're not competent, because all these people are / perfectly able to handle other things in life.

Filip: / Yeah.

Faria: So babies, okay they can be difficult but only because they're unfamiliar, not [short laugh] because it's rocket science and you can't actually manage a baby. But I think traditionally as a society, whether it's here or back home in Singapore, we're very geared towards that role being fulfilled by a woman. Um and I think this sort of policy, if people actively take it up, I think it will for us, I mean just means that in whatever life situation you might be so if you need to share the care, you can do it, and it's not such an unfamiliar thing, because if your father thinks, 'well I was there for the first six months', or for the first year or whatever period of time, 'and I did manage to take care of my child um without, you know, too much diffi-. Yes my wife may have been around, my wife may not have been around, but I was, I could do it.' I think that's very positive.

Faria and Filip, Interview 1

So rather than an articulated commitment to their careers comparable to that of non-sharing fathers, sharing mothers emphasised their hope to share the role of parent with their partner while continuing in paid work. Their motivations for shared parenting may have been to facilitate engagement with their paid work (and one can see that more shared parenting would be important for that), but women rarely explicitly discussed this. In fact, more often it was their partners who articulated a desire to support women's careers, as seen here:

[SPL is] partly so I could spend some time with the baby and partly so Emily could sort of ease herself back into work. So the first few months she's working I'm not also working so there's no like, a nanny or a nursery looking after the child that she has to worry about um for those first few months. I will be looking after the baby full-time so she can get home whenever she wants, she doesn't have to be worrying about it, like another parent is looking after our child, so those first two months she can sort of ease herself back into it. And if she is like slammed at work it actually doesn't matter so much because I'll be looking after the baby.

Edward, Interview 1

Katherine: So, what would you say is your motivation to take SPL?

Winnie: I ah feel that it's important for Weston to have a better relationship or a sort of more steady relationship / than my father had with me growing up.

Weston: / Yeah. But I think on the other hand we're both very keen um to continue our careers, you know? =

Winnie: =Yeah.

Weston: Our careers are important to us.

Katherine: Mmhmm, okay. And it seems from the way you were talking that the main motivation for you to take up shared parental leave Winnie is so that, that you'll both be able to be involved with the baby. Is that correct?

Weston: I would say, well let me answer and see if you agree [laughs].

Winnie: Yeah.

Weston: I would say yes, but also secondly is um Winnie wants to go back to work and, you know, I wouldn't ever try and stop her doing that or even want her to do that. I think she should, she should go back to work, she enjoys what she does. So I guess yeah [pause] mostly we want me to be around to help with the baby, or to have time with the baby on my own, but also, yeah, because I don't think, we never considered you not going back to work so it kind of just made sense that way.

Winnie and Weston, Interview 1

In both of these cases the women emphasised the importance of their partner learning to take on half of the care of their future child, while the men emphasised supporting their partners' careers. Weston also said that he would never stop Winnie going back to work, a curious addition which to me suggests that women leaving the workplace is a norm he is claiming to fight against by taking SPL. This is also a potential 'intimacy display' at work. These and other comments make it clear that amongst sharing men there is a moral imperative to show themselves as committed to work and amongst sharing women the moral imperative is to demonstrate their commitment to their roles as parents. Amongst the sharers (and the non-sharers), then, there are no examples of women who portray themselves as primarily career-focused, such as those uncovered in Hochschild's study *The Second Shift* (Hochschild & Machung, 2012). Perhaps this is because the moral imperative for mothers to want to spend time with their child has grown stronger since that study (Lee et al., 2023; Miller, 2023).

Equality good for intimacy

Like non-sharing parents, sharers expressed a desire for gender equality in their couple relationships. The difference is how they understand that equality and the role of SPL within it. While in chapter 2 I noted that non-sharing couples tended towards a definition of equality which prioritised 'fairness', sharers more commonly expressed equality in terms of 'symmetry': that is, a desire that each partner should do an equal share of each work task, with sharing leave often seen as a core aspect of this symmetry (see also Twamley & Faircloth, 2023). In the first interview, sharing couples often outlined their plans to ensure such equality in parenting and household work more broadly. For example, Adam and Anna told me that Anna intended to express milk so that she and Adam could share the feeding of their child fifty–fifty. Helen and Henry, meanwhile, kept a spreadsheet to keep on top of leisure time, ensuring that both enjoyed equal amounts of 'me time' after the baby was born.

Sharers also spoke more favourably than non-sharers about feminism and were more likely to articulate the necessity of interventions to support women in the workplace, as these extracts show:[3]

> I think I said [in the survey] I was feminist, I was pro- and, and a feminist, I think. As to reasons why, I guess it's, I ought to be able to articulate this by now but, in that [clears throat] [pause] I think there's a definite gender imbalance in society and that's not fair. Um

it shouldn't be that I continue to have a benefit just by being born that way um it works to my advantage if Gina has equality through every aspect, through work if she gets the pay she should have um it, you know, I believe in equality in general I'd say.

Gerald, Interview 1

And I think challenging society that [pause], that it isn't a gender-equal society, so that you have to do things and act in a way that promotes women um promotes girls and gives them more of a chance and opportunities, because I think, yeah I think the information we receive and the society is, in general, geared towards men as decision-makers, as having the power kind of within society and that we have to challenge that.

Mary, Interview 1

> Nick: Um [pause] I don't know really. I, I, I have [pause] started, I started reading a column in *The Guardian* by Laura Bates about feminism and there's a whole, a whole load, a whole load of it that um I, I recognised in myself and other men of this, an unconscious degree of um bias or prejudice. So I think having read that on a fairly regular basis and ah Helen Lewis, *New Statesman*, and things like that I've become a bit, [inaudible] being all shouty about it. I think I read more feminist writing than you do, or, you know, expressly feminist / writing.
>
> Natasha: / Mmhmm.
>
> Nick: So perhaps I am more finely, not finely attuned, but more conscious of it on a day-to-day reading basis [inaudible] experience of gender discrimination but um [pause] yeah.

Nick and Natasha, Interview 1

With this in mind, it is perhaps not surprising that fears about 'cold intimacy' as articulated by non-sharers were not apparent amongst sharers. On the contrary, couple equality, in particular as regards parenting, was posited as important to *ensure* intimate connections within the couple, as demonstrated by these multiple quotes:

> Adam: I think we just, you know, the, the limited reading we've done on the subject, you hear about how, you

> know, um fathers feel resentful against mothers because the mother gets to stay at home all day with the child and they have to go off to work. Then you feel, you hear about mothers who feel resentful about the father because he gets to go to work and see his friends while she's stuck at home with the child. […]. And I just think that we've, throughout our relationship we've always had, been at our strongest and had most fun when we're doing things together and we're a team together, and so I think if we can try and apply that moving forward it'll just make parenting more fun and enjoyable and easier maybe.
>
> Adam, Interview 1

Katherine: And um you mentioned that it um that you being the primary carer, or the father being the primary carer, for a while would have potential implications for your relationship with Mary. So what are those implications?

Mark: I suppose I've just seen some people's relationships where the male is a bit sort of, you have to sort of, the mother seems to just be the main parent and the, kind of the man sort of wafts in in the evening and does, I don't know, either as much as he can or as little. I don't know, it depends um [Mary short laugh] on the person you're talking to. It just, it just, I think it's just um it'll give me an appreciation of what you've been through in the previous six months I think, it's just, I think just in terms of equality in the relationship. But it's, I mean it's obviously, you're doing the childbirth and the carrying it at the moment, so obviously my share of responsibility is still small there. But it just gives you an idea of what, of the responsibilities you've had in the previous few months I think.

Mark, Interview 1

Tara: I feel like if we're both learning at the same time early on then that's sort of good because it means that one / of us doesn't sort of take ownership

Tim: / Yeah.

Tara: and kind of become the expert parent and then the other one is like shunted off to the side, which I think=.

Tim: = We have seen some friends who are a bit like that and it doesn't work out well for them I think, yeah=.

Tara: =Yeah, it can be, yeah it can be really easy I guess to fall into that like um kind of pattern.

Tara and Tim, Interview 1

Helen: The plan is that neither of us will feel, you know, more responsible than the other or that the other person is doing it somehow wrong or inadequately / because I think that would be really awful for you as well, like I think to feel that I didn't trust you or, or whatever must be, you know, bad, and a lot of the couples I know I think they have a little bit of that, and.

Henry: / Mhmm. It sounds like it's also kind of a factor in your first round of friends' divorces.

Helen: Mhmm, yeah.

Helen and Henry, Interview 1

We're going to make the mistakes together and learn the best, hopefully, the best way of the baby and just go, 'Okay so this is the way we do it', but actually if you want to try one, a different way, I won't go 'Oh no, no, you mustn't do it like that because x, y, z', but there might be occasions when you say, say 'It's because this way brings him out in a rash', but I'd know that already ... So I don't want to miss out on that bit of knowledge. Certainly we will learn together, we'll learn, we'll get to know the baby together, and there won't be the gaps in the knowledge, or at least we'll be able to communicate really quickly to fill in the gaps.

Gerald, Interview 1

[SPL will] help in solidifying and improving the relationship. Time to communicate and focus on each other without other distractions. Shared challenges will make them easier and ensure that we have strong foundation for growth.

Adam, survey after interview 1

These participants' desire for SPL was articulated as a means to establish symmetry and, relatedly, it was anticipated that SPL would benefit the couple relationship. They told me that if the woman takes all the maternity leave, she may end up bossing her partner around, or their lives would diverge in ways that they had not been used to. They emphasised the importance of a shared understanding of one another's experience as mother or father, leading to more empathy and understanding, as well as a sense of them as 'in this together' as parents of their new child.

An emphasis on 'shared responsibility' for the future child was repeated in several of the above quotes, as it related to care and domestic work. As discussed in chapter 1, while time-use scholars have tracked differences between mothers and fathers in time spent on paid and unpaid work tasks, less attention has been paid to gendered responsibilities or to the 'mental load' or 'cognitive labour' involved in organising care and housework (Daminger, 2019; Dean et al., 2022). In the accounts in this study, mothers were very alert to potential inequalities in cognitive labour and were keen to avoid taking on the bulk of care responsibilities after the baby was born. They discussed how detrimental a single 'family manager' could be to intimate relationships. As Helen said, overseeing the participation of a partner is 'the death of romance, 100 per cent'. An important part of avoiding the primary–secondary parent dynamic for these couples was that one parent (the mother) is not overseeing the work of the father or asking him to do particular tasks, rather 'he just knows' when the baby should sleep, eat, etc., and how to facilitate it.

Underlying this desire is an understanding of intimacy as something 'natural' or spontaneous, as observed (but in a different way) amongst non-sharers in chapter 2. This desire for a natural dynamic in the couple relationship comes out most forcefully in the stories that participants tell me about their relationships, as well as in their views on what makes them feel good about their relationship. They told me that their partner 'knows things without necessarily being told them', 'understands what I need', is 'sensitive' and that they just 'naturally connect'. Having to tell one's partner to, for example, prepare a snack for the baby or remember to pack nappies for a day out was positioned as damaging to couple intimacy. Thus sharers (mostly) are trying to set up shared knowledge and responsibility for their baby so as to avoid the mother taking up a position of nagging or instructing her partner. SPL was seen as a key means to establish this.

'We'd be crazy not to ...' (enabling structures for SPL)

While some non-sharers struggled to see the logic of SPL, sharers tended to have multiple factors which encouraged them to consider it, cost being an important one. A clear observable difference between non-sharers and sharers was couple earnings. None of the non-sharers have a mother who earned more than the father, but four of the couples amongst the sharers did (Edward and Emily, Faria and Filip, Nick and Natasha, Gina and Gerald). In fact, in only one couple did the man earn more than the woman: that was the case of Adam (medical doctor) and Anna (theatre set designer), where he was prompted to take leave in part by the high remuneration offered by his employer (fully paid SPL for six months). Amongst non-sharers, mostly men earned more than their partners (in seven out of eleven cases). Moreover, in all cases except two (Sam and Chidi), non-sharing fathers were only offered statutory SPL pay, while amongst sharers half of the fathers' employers topped up their SPL pay. Given this combination of high-earning female partners and subsidised SPL, the financial case for fathers' uptake of SPL was often clear and decisive. Filip, for example, told me it was a 'no-brainer' and Adam that 'we had to take this fantastic opportunity'.

For other couples, finances were not explicitly discussed as a motivation to share leave, even when the financial case was clear. This was the case with Edward and Emily, as outlined at the beginning of this chapter. Emily's significantly higher salary is portrayed as of no importance at all in their decision: they told me she would have lost all her salary in the 'normal' run of things, meaning they were prepared for the financial cut anyway. In contrast, they considered a man's higher salary to be decisive in SPL decisions; they discussed this in relation to friends who are not taking SPL:

> Emily: I think in those cases the men are earning more, so it doesn't make any sense for the man to sacrifice salary [by taking SPL].
>
> Edward: Yeah, the woman might as well just take all twelve months.
>
> Emily and Edward, Interview 1

What these discussions (or non-discussions) of finances make clear is that fathers' leave is often positioned as a bonus by participants – something to avail themselves of when appropriate conditions align.

Such a framing of leave discourages many men from taking SPL, as we saw in chapter 2. It can also influence *how long* men take SPL for. For example, Adam had initially suggested to his wife Anna that he should take more leave than her, since his pay during leave is higher than hers, which is only at the statutory level:

> Adam: So I kind of was just thinking, you know, so I was never really serious, but kind of did discuss with Anna that actually financially the best thing for us to do would be for Anna to have her six /weeks'
>
> Anna: /Yeah.
>
> Adam: statutory and then go back to work, and then I raise the child, I take my eighteen weeks and, you know?
>
> Anna: […] And I was like 'No way [laughs], I've been waiting for this non-working year for like my whole working life'.
>
> Adam and Anna, Interview 1

We see echoes here of the 'maternal gatekeeping' discussed in chapter 2, indicating the limits of finances as a factor in determining the share of leave. This is accentuated by the maternity leave transfer mechanism, which obliges women to give up part of their maternity leave in order for their partner to take SPL.

Conclusion

In this chapter I have outlined various factors which shaped couples' decisions to share leave. Since SPL is so unusual, with various factors working against take-up, parents must go against the grain if they are to choose to share leave (or swim against the tide, as Schmidt, Zartler and Vogl (2019) put it in relation to non-normative parenting practices in Austria). Thus, *several* factors must come together to support a decision to take SPL; there is not just one.

First, less distinction was made between mothers' and fathers' roles amongst sharers than amongst non-sharers, though distinctions still lingered. Sharers expressed less emotional attachment to the idea of mothers' long and uninterrupted maternity leave and some fathers had a long-held desire to be equal or primary care fathers. Fathers were open to interrupting their careers, either because they had a low attachment to career progression (like Mark) or because they disliked their jobs and were keen to use the leave to consider other options (like Keith). This was important, since participants observed that men's take-up of SPL was understood as a 'choice' *against* work in ways women's take-up of leave is not, and taking SPL was therefore experienced as a risky choice by male participants. Similar findings have been reported concerning men's reluctance to take up opportunities in flexible working (Chung, 2020). This reluctance is compounded by the maternity leave transfer system through which the SPL functions. On the other hand, mothers' similar or higher earning dissipated the 'risk' of men's taking leave and even facilitated men's negotiation to take some leave.

Second, for some participants, having a social network that supported and encouraged a non-normative sharing of leave was very important. Edward, for example, was eventually persuaded to take leave after meeting another expectant father in his antenatal class who was intending to take leave.

Third, sharing parents all had a financial incentive to take SPL. Either the mother earned more than the father, which meant it made financial sense for her to take leave, or the father received enhanced pay during his SPL. This shows the importance of high remuneration for fathers on leave, as seen in multiple contexts (O'Brien, Brandth & Kvande, 2007; Valentova, 2011).

Finally, sharers drew on understandings of couple equality which favoured symmetry in men's and women's paid and unpaid work, and expressed strong support for the idea that inequality would disrupt couple intimacy. This shaped not only their visions of future parenting practices, but also their interactions and negotiations concerning leave. Still, parents modified their plans for leave in response to the unsupportive conditions and opinions of those around them, in particular by fathers' reducing their leave time, as has been observed elsewhere (Atkinson, 2023; Mauerer & Schmidt, 2019).

Notes

1   Less so about women's shortened maternity leave, which participants understood as related to the fact that their mothers had generally had much shorter maternity leave themselves or were full-time mothers and had less of a preconceived idea of how much maternity leave women 'should' take.
2   I am grateful to Eva-Maria Schmidt for this insight.
3   These conversations arose in response to a question about whether and why participants defined themselves as 'feminist' or 'egalitarian' in the survey through which the couples were recruited.

Part II
Experiences of the leave period

As discussed in chapter 1, most studies on parental leave are retrospective and cross-sectional in design, focusing on barriers to and facilitators of sharing leave, or 'outcomes' of different leave patterns. There is very little investigation of what parents actually do on leave on a day-to-day basis and how these experiences shape the kinds of fathers and mothers men and women become. Building on participants' accounts in Part I (in which they reported their perspectives, preferences and expectations in relation to leave), I apply a 'sociology of everyday life' frame (Back, 2015; Neal & Murji, 2015) to interpret their diary entries and their descriptions of leave in later interviews. This means paying close attention to their reported practices and the meanings that are attached to such practices, as expressed in their narrations. In particular I pay close attention to everyday forms of relating between parents, and between parents and their children, in order to understand the relationship work (Gabb & Fink, 2015) at play and what this says about the perceived (and potentially shifting) responsibilities in these relationships at different time points.

4
Non-sharers' experiences and practices during the first year after their child is born

Chidi is back at work today. I am trying to plan to see someone everyday [sic] as I felt so lonely in the period between Christmas and New Year when he was working. ... I dread not seeing someone else all day. I spent some time with my sister but baby C was a bit unsettled and I wanted to hand him over to her to give my back a break but then he slept on me for three hours after feeding and was still sleeping when I got home. I probably could have put him down but it was so special to be cuddling him in the recliner and to enjoy some time relaxing and watching tv!

Cara, Diary 1 (baby 4 weeks old)

Went to local gardens with a friend and then baby C was grumpy and overwrought when we got home so I put him to bed at 6.20. Then he woke up and was just all croaky, poor boy. So maybe he is coming down with something. ... I hope he sleeps okay – might have to crack out the Calpol [paracetamol]!

Cara, Diary 2 (baby 6 months old)

First day at work was fine. Checked on Cara to make sure she was okay. Working late so didn't spend much time with baby C. Very strange having a baby in the house!

Chidi, Diary 1 (baby 4 weeks old)

Work has been very busy so Cara has been doing most of the caring, even when I am at home as I have to bring work home. Feel guilty about that.

Chidi, Diary 2 (baby 6 months old)

As is clear from these diary extracts, Cara and Chidi had very different experiences of the transition to parenthood. Cara's diaries are full of the preoccupations and everyday activities of care and housework, while Chidi's diaries are dominated by paid work hours and his struggles to spend time with baby C. Cara's original vision of shared parental responsibility and engagement with their baby, as articulated in chapter 2, has not been fulfilled during this period. In fact, both of them characterised Chidi as 'helping' her in taking care of the house and baby, rather than taking any kind of shared responsibility. Cara celebrated moments of intimacy with baby C, while 'dreading' being alone with him. Her love for her baby was punctuated by the anxiety she felt about the care he needed and her capacity to meet his needs by herself. Her diaries are almost entirely about baby C and her interactions with him. Chidi's life, on the other hand, proceeded more or less as before the birth of their child. He continued to go to his office for work, but 'checked in' on Cara and the baby on the phone. At times he expressed sadness at missing out on time with his son, but mostly he focused on how much he enjoyed the (limited) time he spent with their child.

Cara described feeling lonely and anxious, despite various kinds of support from family and friends who lived nearby. As she, and later other mothers, told me, such support is 'not the same' as having one's partner or husband present. Cara felt unable to share the responsibility of the care of her baby with anyone else, even if they might give her some practical support and company. But Cara struggled to share with Chidi, since he was working so many hours, a situation compounded by the master's degree he had recently started, which involved weekends away and studying late at night. He clearly feels highly motivated to excel in work and mentioned more than once in his interviews that he was relatively junior in his company. These differences continued over the course of the maternity leave period and ultimately shaped Cara and Chidi's relationship with one another and with their son. As I detail in this chapter, Cara and Chidi's experiences of leave were quite typical of non-sharing participants and illustrate how the usual maternity–paternity leave split sets up normative gendered parenting practices.

The paternity leave period: too short

Upon its introduction in 2003, the two weeks of paternity leave was heralded as a potentially transformative policy which would alter parents' experiences for the better. Arguably, however, its very short duration of just two weeks has not kept pace with changing ideas about fathers' involvement in family life (Brannen, Faircloth et al., 2023). Indeed, the chief reflection from participants about paternity leave was that it was too short to provide any meaningful level of care and support for the mother and child. Few parents had clear memories of this leave by the time I interviewed them at six months. The predominant narration of this period revolved around the anxiety that mothers felt as the leave came to an end, experienced as particularly daunting by mothers who had had a C-section or experienced difficulties with breastfeeding:

> Sarah: After those initial two weeks, I was crying one day, I had mastitis, I was alone, I didn't know people ... I guess I basically had the baby blues. I hope, I have never felt this crappy, this lonely. I said to Sam 'I hope this isn't postnatal depression' and he said to speak to the health visitor. It was just the reality of transition was awful, hard, a big change. I felt worried and exhausted all the time.
>
> Sam: Yes, it was tough. I felt vulnerable, and on edge, just so tired all the time. I felt psychologically weak, I was just so tired.
>
> Sarah and Sam, Interview 2

> Going back to work, obviously I didn't want to, I can't believe that two weeks' paternity leave as a statutory is relatively new, because the thought of going back after a few days ... I mean, Pippa was not physically able to get out of bed after her Caesarean section. It's nuts!
>
> Peter, Interview 2

As we can see from Sam's reflection, returning just two weeks after the birth of the child was also not easy on fathers. Spending the whole day in paid work meant it was difficult for fathers to support their partners, since they themselves were often suffering from sleep disturbance. These accounts also highlight how the physiological experience of birthing and feeding can shape leave experiences, as do children's health or sleep issues.

Despite an overwhelming sense that two weeks is very little and is felt by many participants to be insufficient, four fathers did not take their full paternity leave allowance, or worked through their leave. Chidi reduced his paternity leave to one week with the idea of taking annual and national closure days off over the Christmas period, which later did not quite work out. Bart and Olly worked through their leaves, though Olly changed jobs shortly after, which meant he was able to take some time off after this official paternity leave ended. Beth and Olivia did not seem to be overly perturbed by this situation, probably because of the alternative support they received – Beth from her mother and Olivia from a maternity nurse. They both also seemed to understand and empathise with their husband's need to work at that time, which was later offset through Bart's flexible working pattern and Olly's time off as he transitioned between jobs. However, Cara and Rita reported feeling 'cheated' about this reduced paternity leave, even reflecting back on this period in their final interview over a year later, as seen here from Rita:

> Katherine: Just to start off, if you could tell me in your own words how you think the last year and a half has gone since we first met? Thinking about maybe what were the high points and what have been the more difficult low points.
>
> Rita: Mhmm okay. I think it was quite an up-and-down eighteen months [blows raspberry]. High points, low points? Well I think um [4 seconds], well it was quite an experience [short laugh]. Um I think we are now at a point where it's quite good, so, I don't know. I think the first year was quite okay um, the birth was quite tricky, eh, and I guess the first two months were quite hard [both short laugh]. It's quite emotional. [Crying] Em […] I guess it was also hard because we don't have family here, and also friends. I mean they couldn't really help. So the first weeks were hard, and also because Riley went to, back to work, I guess, after one week. That was tricky. Also because I had um a Caesarean, so I couldn't move.
>
> Rita, Interview 3

> That was one of the times I found really hard because he, he was like 'Oh, I won't take it off but I'll be working from home', and then he wasn't, he was in the office, so, and everyone else was busy in that period, so I just sort of had a really like hard few days on my own [laughs] with a really tiny new baby, you know, [who] I was really struggling to keep fed and asleep and happy.
>
> Cara, Interview 3

The lack of family and other networks of support means this short leave is experienced as even more difficult. But, as Cara explained, having family around did little to relieve the heightened sense of responsibility brought about by motherhood:

> My sister lives nearby, even then, and even after friends at church on leave, but [with] Chidi away from 8[a.m.] till 7[p.m.], it's a long time to be alone. … He works in the city. I was trying to meet people, but only one person in the day. […] My mum came, and brother and a friend, but it's not the same.
>
> Cara, Interview 2

Since all of these fathers were eligible for full pay during their paternity leave (topped up by their employers) they did not reduce their leave because of the financial cost of taking it. Rather, these cases demonstrate the pressures fathers feel if even two weeks off work is considered difficult to manage. These pressures continue to shape parents' later experiences of maternity leave too.

Divergent experiences at the transition to parenthood: after paternity leave ends

Women's diaries and later interviews chart the everyday care practices, such as those involved in feeding their babies and getting them to sleep, that demonstrate the all-encompassing nature of caring for a newborn during the maternity leave period:

> — Baby B did not have [a] very good day today. She cried and it seemed something bothered her. Not sure what it was. Maybe she was just tired as she does not sleep well during day.
>
> — I ordered a playmat for her on Amazon so we can do some tummy time.
>
> — in the afternoon we went for a walk with my friend and her baby. It was nice but I had to feed baby B outside and I am still not comfortable with it so I think she did not get enough and that is why she cried on the way home. It was nice to have a chat with another mum though.
>
> — our landlord has finally sent a guy to look at TV cable. He will come to fix it tomorrow.

— I am happy that it is Friday and tomorrow it will be all 3 of us at home.

> Beth, Diary 1 (baby 4 weeks old)

Really bad night['s] sleep, waking 4 times and is more alert overnight so spent much of the night in the spare room, David ended up getting up to her the last time so he is tired for work. Finding it easier to just get up with her than try to get her back to sleep beyond 6am as she's not having it. Also finding getting out useful – tends to wake me up so I don't feel so sluggish. Went to baby sensory, baby D really enjoyed it, she seems very social/interested in the other babies.

> Debbie, Diary 1 (baby 4 weeks old)

I'm still constantly questioning if she's had enough food and reading books to try and understand feeding and its relationship with sleeping. We mess around with expressed breast milk and a little formula and I get terrified I'll fall behind in supply, her catch-up and end up giving up breastfeeding which I love to do as I feel closer to baby O. Hopefully it becomes more intuitive. [...] With baby O all daily interactions from feeding, soothing to nappy changing make me feel close to her as she is so dependent upon me for everything.

> Olivia, Diary 1 (baby 4 weeks old)

As is apparent from these diary extracts, women often recorded their uncertainty about appropriate care and described how they went about learning and adapting to their babies' needs. They discussed experimenting with different techniques for improving the sleep of their babies and were often preoccupied with their child's weight gain and establishing breastfeeding in the first months. They described challenges in care, but also their growing love for their babies as they spent more time with them. As Lynch and Walsh (2009: 38) write, 'Maintaining love and care relations involves work that is often pleasurable but also burdensome', a sentiment that is apparent in the women's accounts. Olivia, for example, made the link between her baby's dependency on her 'for everything' and her growing feelings of closeness towards her. Mothers' diary extracts show how they monitor and attend to their babies' needs. This love labour has emotional, moral, physical and cognitive aspects. We can see the sharp learning curve that women on maternity leave experience and how completely they are immersed in the care needs of their children.

Men's (and women's) diaries also record fathers' daily interactions with their children, which are necessarily more limited than women's given their paid work responsibilities and hours:

> We're very much in a routine now – as I go to work and baby J sleeps through the night. I do all I need before 6.50am then start waking her up at 7 (new clothes, clean nappy, skin oil) before Judy gets down for her first feed of the day. In the evenings, it's pretty much the opposite as I get home from work but it's good to at least be of childcare use!!
>
> John, Diary 2 (baby 6 months old)

> Did all baby D's care until David got home, he played with her for a short time and then bathed her, I settled her to bed – this is our usual routine. It's lovely to see how excited they are to see one another when he gets home. D is slightly more cuddly now which is lovely.
>
> Debbie, Diary 2 (baby 6 months old)

> Working today, home at 18.30. Bathed baby S. Cried getting out of bath – hard work! Then Sarah fed and put him to sleep. Good night (I think! I was sleeping in spare room).
>
> Sam, Diary 2 (baby 6 months old)

These quotes are indicative of men's diaries more generally during this period. They often reported spending some time playing with babies in the evening and bathing them before bedtime. There was less focus on learning to care in these diaries, perhaps because their care was rarely conducted alone, and was therefore less intense, meaning their learning was at a slower pace than women's. Nonetheless, engagement in bathing and putting children to bed was clearly important for the fathers and evoked feelings of intimacy with and closeness to their children.

At the weekends there was more scope for men's participation in care, and mothers reported vastly preferring weekends to midweek days (as hinted at in Beth's diary extract above). Men often referred to care for the baby then as also care for the mother, offering mothers some respite from the relentless nature of full-time maternity leave:

> [Taking the baby from Beth in the evenings] gives me the chance to play a bit of music to baby B and calm her down. I enjoy it a lot. And hopefully this gives a break to Beth too.
>
> Bart, Diary 1 (baby 4 weeks old)

NON-SHARERS' EXPERIENCES AND PRACTICES

> Looked after baby S in the a.m. to let Sarah rest.
>
> Sam, Diary 1 (baby 4 weeks old)

> With baby J being so little, the 'care' I can give is balanced more towards ensuring Judy can get enough sleep and correctly eats. Wanting to make sure Judy keeps time for herself, I offer to take over the reins for a while.
>
> John, Diary 1 (baby 4 weeks old)

> Weekends I take her [baby D] for walks to give Debbie a break. Now she is older, she sleeps for part of it, but now it's 2–3 hours I can take her out and Debbie can sleep.
>
> David, Interview 2

Here men's love and concern for their partners is expressed through care for the baby. This 'relationship work' (Gabb & Fink, 2015), involving both practical and emotional support, is central to supporting the intimate couple relationship. Men could express frustration at times at their inability to be more involved in the care of babies, especially when witnessing the difficulties their partners were experiencing. Olly, for example, described his (and Olivia's) annoyance at his inability to do more care, particularly during the night, which mothers reported as most difficult to cope with:

> On the whole nighttime feeding thing – we are in the position where baby O is reliant on being breastfed to sleep and she won't take the bottle. This has left me in a rather impotent position where I want to do more at night but there isn't anything I can do other than run errands. I still don't get that much sleep but Olivia isn't best pleased and wants me to do all the early mornings. Which I do do intermittently but I struggle with given I am often burning the candles at both ends as well as being woken up at night. We will need to resolve this soon as it is a real struggle for both of us but mostly Olivia and it is creating a bit of inevitable tension. It is making us question my job and other things.
>
> Olly, Diary 3 (baby 9 months old)

Olly's long work hours (he gets up very early and often works late at night) restrict his ability to be more active in baby O's care. He perceived that this provoked tension between himself and Olivia, which other couples also noted. This shows how paid work, particularly when it involves long hours as in Olly's case, impacts on the intimate relationship between partners during this period.

Olly's ability to share night-time care was also hampered by a physical inability to feed the baby, since Olivia was exclusively breastfeeding. Most of the non-sharing mothers exclusively breastfed their children in the initial months. This goes against national statistics on breastfeeding, which show that only 12 per cent of mothers are exclusively breastfeeding their babies at 4 months (McAndrew et al., 2012: 25). However, exclusive breastfeeding is more common amongst university-educated women (McAndrew et al., 2012). Feeding dominates the care needs of a baby in the early months and therefore breastfeeding is an important factor in shaping the division of care at this time.[1] Some parents had hoped to share feeding, with the mother expressing breast milk and the father later giving a bottle, but this was found to be too time-intensive for the mother and often babies preferred being fed directly from the breast. I discuss breastfeeding in more detail in chapter 5, where it is also seen to shape sharers' leave together and their division of care labour.

These accounts demonstrate that hands-on care for the baby is not a shared endeavour during the maternity leave period, but rather the responsibility of the mother, which the father intermittently helped her with. Moreover, as the following accounts demonstrate, women were understood as basically responsible for babies' care during this period, and men's care activities described as more of a bonus:

> Spent the morning in [city in England], had another lie-in as David and his mum took baby D for a walk. Feel grateful that David feels so confident to take her for a couple of hours.
> Debbie, Diary 2 (baby 6 months old)

> He [Olly] did a babysitting evening recently, which was hilarious. I came back and found him holding her on the bed …. [laughs] She was asleep, but he didn't want to put her down in case she woke up. I feel like it was a great experience.
> Olivia, Interview 2

These two quotes have different timbres, but both highlight that men's care for babies can be seen as supplementary to women's. Debbie expressed gratitude for David's confidence in looking after their baby alone, which afforded her a lie-in, while Olivia characterised Olly's night-time care of their child as 'babysitting'. For these mothers and fathers, care for the baby can be said to be part of a 'gift economy' of couples.

Drawing on her research with parent couples in the USA, Hochschild (2003) explains that in a two-working household, a man may feel that any contribution to taking care of the house or children is more than either what the average man does, or what his father did before him. He therefore sees this work as 'extra' and as a 'gift' to his wife. Agreement in the understanding of 'gifting' is important to maintaining a relationship since, as Hochschild says, 'the sense of a genuine giving and receiving is a part of love' (2003:105). Non-sharing couples did appear to understand fathers' care during the maternity leave period as a gift. Moreover, women reported feeling particularly close to their partner as they observed him taking care of their baby, as illustrated here:

> Felt very close to David when watching him so carefully change her or change her clothes and talking to her.
>
> Debbie, Diary 1 (baby 4 weeks old)

This sense of fathers' involvement in childcare being akin to a gift may not be permanent, however, and it is likely to be influenced by the fact that mothers were on maternity leave, and therefore considered care their realm, while men were working full-time hours, as demonstrated in the following discussions:

> Peter: I still feel twinges of guilt with how stereotypic the division of work between us is, I wish ...
>
> Pippa: But you go to work every day, this is my work.
>
> Peter: [...] I wish it was more even because, you know, I am under no impression that I have the harder day, ha ha, we have had enough days together to know that looking after the boys and looking after the house is way way harder than it is for me to go to work, way more tiring ... so I am very grateful to you Pippa for doing it all so well. [Pippa laughs]
>
> Peter: What are your thoughts?
>
> Pippa: It's quite fun, this activity! I am quite pleased with myself! It just shows that we, that we are quite a good team, you appreciate the work I do and I appreciate what you do. We know how hard we both work to make this work, otherwise it would be a disaster.
>
> Peter and Pippa, Interview 2

I feel like we are [a] team in the end of the day and he is out there to earn the money and pay for stuff and I try to do project management stuff at home. And it would be really inefficient and, he would be exhausted, if he had to do work stuff and home stuff and I guess if I was back at work, would things be different? That is what is interesting? How the allocation of chores goes then?

Olivia, Interview 2

As reported in chapter 2, Pippa embraced the idea of herself as the primary carer, while Olivia expressed more ambivalence. Both articulated a sense that the division of care and paid work was 'fair' during this time, but for Olivia this was justified by their temporarily differing paid working patterns.

As is clear, women and men were conscious of the difference in their experiences of the transition to parenthood. In their interviews and diaries, they reflected on how such different experiences shaped their relationships with one another and their baby. Here Sarah and Sam, for example, discussed their experiences of the first month after paternity leave when Sam returned to his work as a surgeon:

> Sarah: I just knew that this was a difficult month that we had to go through, well that I had to go through I suppose. I do remember saying to him 'I am envious that you can go to work and mix with adults, and sleep during the night'. While I was looking after the baby which doesn't give much at that stage. [...] I was envious of Sam, and even now I say that to Sam that he has it easier – he can sit and have a breather, make a cup of tea, he just can.
>
> Sam: I can't.
>
> Sarah: Well, not in the middle of an operation, but the rest of the day, even walking to work I am quite jealous of, you can listen to a podcast. I can't even go to the loo! And I have said to Sam a few times that I am envious and 'Would you swap places with me?' and he said 'No, I wouldn't' ... which slightly goes towards the crux of your research!
>
> Sam: I think I get the best of both worlds, it's nice looking after him and I don't have to have the horrible sleep deprivation that Sarah has ... And I don't have to do it all the time. I think I am really lucky. I looked after him this morning, if I am not busy then I will look after him for

an hour or so so Sarah can sleep a bit more. […] But an hour is a very different matter to 24 hours. Lots of time to get to know him, but also get time away from him.

Sarah and Sam, Interview 2

Sam and Sarah largely agree that Sam has an easier time of it, but other couples reported less agreement. David, for example, reflected in his second interview with Debbie that 'There is an unsaid thing about "Oh, work is more difficult" or "Being at home with a child is more difficult" and it's how you negotiate that'. This created some tension within couples, heightened by stress in paid work and sleepless nights, and indicating some shifting understandings around the 'gifting' of men's involvement in care over the period of the study.

'The challenge is being responsible but learning at the same time'

As we have seen, mothers were the main caregivers during the maternity leave period, and expressed some ambivalence about this role. The title of this section is a quote from Sarah (interview 2) which encapsulates the main concern in navigating the initial months of their maternity leave that women described. That is, Sarah and other mothers expressed their anxiety about feeling largely or solely *responsible* for the care of their newborn and for overall care decisions, with little or no prior knowledge of caring for a baby. In response, women reported seeking information about care from multiple sources: books, health visitors, friends and their own mothers.[2] They detailed many and varied instances of learning to care, some of which were experienced quite lightly, such as when Beth reflected on some reasons why her baby might be crying. But other instances, usually concerning feeding, could provoke high levels of anxiety. Rita described her concerns about her daughter's drop below her birthweight in the first weeks after her birth (in fact she had visited her local accident and emergency department a few days before, so great were her worries about her baby's slow weight gain):

> Today I went again to the Nurse centre to weigh baby R. She gained another 130g in only two days. Only 50g missing till birth weight. I am so happy and text everyone. I guess that when my parents came last week to basically cook all day and take the baby so I could eat quietly helped. We really haven't organized this very well. Now

> I would ask my mum to come for several weeks to help. I totally underestimated this or maybe it's just our baby which needs a lot [of] attention. But she cries almost all the time and never really sleeps. She only falls asleep on the breast during her very long breastfeeding. When I try to put her down she wakes up and cries again. She also doesn't take the dummy. I wonder if we should go to the osteopath as my friends suggest. It's not normal, or? I don't know what to do. I talk to Riley, he thinks all is fine and I just worry too much. Well, what does he know. He does not have more experience than me, or? He just never worries about anything.
>
> Rita, Diary 1 (baby 4 weeks old)

Unfortunately, Rita found her partner Riley's reassurances unconvincing; in fact, the more time she spent at home with her baby the more she saw herself as the greater authority on her (I will discuss this further later).

These feelings of being alone could be alleviated by a sense of shared endeavour with the father, as shown in the following account in which Sarah reflected with Sam about her decision to stop breastfeeding after experiencing recurring mastitis:

> Sam said something lovely, that I suppose was true ... Sam said 'Look, if you stop breastfeeding, it's not that you have failed, it's that we together haven't been able to work this, not just you. I haven't been able to sufficiently support you to allow or enable you to do this.' I still felt a bit guilty, but Sam was supportive, emotionally supportive, we discussed it every day. It was a big issue, but finally we got over it.
>
> Sarah, Interview 2

We can see how grateful Sarah is for Sam's assurance that they *share* the responsibility for the care of their baby, even when in this example it is Sarah that was breastfeeding and mostly taking care of baby S.

In other instances, women participants explicitly asked their partners to be involved in decision-making. David and Debbie had a discussion in interview 2 about the sharing of household and domestic tasks, prompted by their reflection that Debbie was doing a disproportionately large amount of the care and housework:

> Debbie: Maybe we need to find a concrete way to organise the thinking tasks?

David: Is there anything you think you are not happy with?

Debbie: Em well, sometimes like grocery shopping isn't very interesting, I don't mind cooking. I don't mind stuff at the moment. Taking photos is irritating.

David: So I should do more groceries. Should I be more involved in the washing and stuff?

Debbie: No. The other thing I get on [at] you about is like reading about having a baby and weaning etc. If you don't do that, I feel like I am=

David: =choosing the path.

Debbie: Yeah, in charge of it all. Yeah, I'd like to decide with you about that. And you were so into having a baby so you should read a chapter and you are hands-on with her, but not so interested in the like …

David: And you likened it to when I want to visit a city, I like research it, I get books out of the library and make notes and I know where I am going. But maybe for me, it's a pride thing, maybe it's being arrogant, I kind of vaguely know and we will wing it and get through it.

Debbie: I think you know what you are doing but you don't find it as a subject to read about interesting.

David: Yes, it's mundane.

Debbie and David, Interview 2

As discussed in chapters 2 and 3, women reported being most concerned about the burden of 'thinking tasks' or cognitive labour when discussing household work. Now that the baby has been born, the *weight* of these thinking tasks has increased. Debbie told David she would like to decide *with* him about the care of baby D. Interestingly, David reflected that perhaps he feels he doesn't need to read or seek advice about baby care, but Debbie pushed him to consider that he just wasn't as interested, with which he agreed. Why isn't David more interested, given that he was so keen to have a baby and has a history of reading about other subjects, for example travel books? The reasons are twofold.

First, the diaries and interviews show that men did not *feel* the same kinds of pressures to care for children that women did. As discussed in chapter 2, in general it is mothers who are held to be morally responsible for children's upbringing (Hays, 1996; Lee et al., 2023). Optimising child development and minimising children's exposure to risk are thought to be two of the defining features of contemporary parenting culture, with a particular focus on the care of young babies as formative in later health and well-being (Hays, 1996; Faircloth, Hoffman and Layne, 2013). The focus on the mother as the key determinant of babies' future lives puts huge pressure on women (Rizzo et al., 2013) and, as is shown by this study, reduces the possibility for sharing care, either with the partner or with other kin or formal childcare services.

Other research has found that men are less likely than women to express anxieties about appropriate parenting or to seek advice (for instance Shirani & Henwood, 2011). Here we see how the experience of leave alone for mothers is *formative* in creating these gendered differences, as they are often quite literally left alone to make such decisions. As reported in chapter 2, some mothers, such as Pippa and Vicki, appeared to adhere to intensive mothering ideals before the birth of their child, and so their continued feelings in this regard are not particularly surprising. Other women, such as Sarah, had not expressed such opinions, but seeing and understanding the baby as particularly vulnerable and 'at risk' shaped Sarah's relationship with her son. She came to see the baby as inextricably linked to her as a mother, and struggled to have even short periods away from the baby, although her partner actively encouraged it:

> Sarah: maybe I should have made more effort for 'me time' … I have a general feeling all the time that I don't have enough me time, I feel like that all the time.
>
> Sam: I am constantly saying to you, go do something while I am here. I took baby for a walk yesterday so you could have time.
>
> Sarah: It's hard, just an hour – it's having the mental space too, to enjoy being on your own … I worry about her. I don't know.
>
> Sarah and Sam, Interview 2

Few women reported being able to spend regular time away from their children, but almost all non-sharing men continued to engage in sports and leisure activities weekly and sometimes more often. Women occasionally complained about this, but more often appeared to facilitate their partner's leisure activities as important for health and well-being. The differences demonstrate the *felt responsibility* of mothers to be always there for their children, a feeling that notably increased as time went by and their knowledge of how to look after the baby became greater than their partner's.

Second, and perhaps more importantly for this study, when fathers were not on leave they did not experience the consequences of the nitty-gritty of care to the same extent as women who were on maternity leave. They did not appreciate to the same extent as women, who were at home all day, mostly alone, with a baby, that, for example, small shifts in nap schedules may result in an overtired cranky child:

> I certainly aren't as, aren't as intense around as many things as Judy is, which I think annoys her, but again it's not my character, and if I was massively intense about everything like ah, it has to be done like this, has to be done like this, has to be done like this, has to be done like this, it's yeah, it just feels a bit … feels a bit much, when you're already, you know, quite, you know, like tired […] but I don't think there's a right or wrong with a baby.
>
> John, Interview 3

> The week started quite busy because of work. I had a meeting till late and I was at home only at 7.30 pm. I spent only an hour with baby B but at least we had dinner together. B seems to enjoy the new food. We tried carrots. It's so sweet and funny seeing her coping with the bowl, the spoon, the dirty hands. The late time rushed us a bit with the usual routine. I am not too strict with that. Beth is a bit more careful. I understand her point. Especially because she arrives to the evening very tired as she takes care of B all day. […] I worked till 00.30 and I am now super tired. Work is a bit stressful at the moment.
>
> Bart, Diary 2 (baby 6 months old)

> Settling in [baby D into nursery] day two which means I had to drop baby D off and leave her. She was really crying as I left and in my mind I worried that she would remain upset. I sat in a local cafe and felt a bit guilty that in a way I was enjoying being out on my own while I knew she was upset. When I went back I was told that she'd been pretty upset most of the time. Seems like settling in might take a few weeks, I am worried about getting her properly settled before I get back to work. We met David for lunch as he works nearby which was nice – he is more sensible about the settling in, 'more mind over matter'.
>
> Debbie, Diary 4 (baby 13 months old)

The general tenor of fathers' diaries was more upbeat than that of mothers'. They celebrated small triumphs in care and more often expressed positivity about their and their partners' experiences as parents. But, as illustrated by Bart's diary entry, paid work was often portrayed as pulling them away from time with their children, a point I return to below.

These accounts show that parents recognise the unevenness of anxiety, as well as its potential source: see where Bart acknowledged that Beth is more tired by the end of the day, and therefore more anxious to ensure a smooth transition to bed for their baby. They also observed (and perhaps previously felt) that women knew more about their babies because of having spent more time with them; therefore they left decisions to women as better placed or suited to understanding babies' care needs. This is a bit of a chicken-and-egg scenario, as the very experience of providing everyday care supports the position of the mother as the knowledgeable one; so does men's neglecting to find or develop expertise through interacting with others or reading books. As Sarah noted in interview 2, 'I make the decisions [about baby S's care] because I have read the books and I have spent more time with him. I know what the noises mean, so I direct Sam, and sometimes Sam asks me.'

Engendering responsibilities for household work during maternity leave

Diaries and interviews show that in most cases it was the woman who took on the responsibility for household work, such as cleaning and laundry, during the maternity leave period:

> I use the evening for 'me time' – to read or watch tv, if I'm not doing chores that is. Chidi is trying to help me out more and he is doing but I always notice what needs doing first!
>
> Cara, Diary 3 (baby 9 months old)

> Lowlight[3] – Olivia got annoyed with me for not putting on a wash on request – I didn't follow what she was saying properly so got into trouble :-(but we made up quickly.
>
> Olly, Diary 4 (baby 13 months old)

> Katherine: Ah, did you find any periods particularly difficult over the past year?

Linda: Mmm yeah, even now I feel like difficult. I try to ask, like I ask for his help and he is like ah, he says like 'I'm doing my best' but I want him to come from automatic from within, not like me pushing, like 'do this and that'. I feel like I'm giving him like more of duties than he [is] doing by himself, you know? [short laugh]

Katherine: Mmhmm. Like what kind of things?

Linda: Ah like um when I'm, like if I'm cooking or doing the laundry like he needs to look after baby, like just have her, or like he do the laundry! Like he does help, but he's like these days on the Playstation 4 and playing, and like sometimes he gets annoyed and even I'm ... like I'm getting annoyed and we start arguing.

Linda, Interview 3

As we can see, non-sharing women appear to hold the responsibility for housework as well as care work. While men and women reported men participating in care when they can and, on the whole, women appreciating this participation, tensions arose when women felt responsible for housework and, as Linda says, having to 'push' the partner to participate in it. Just one woman, Rita, reported that she willingly took up the responsibility for housework during the maternity leave period. She said she liked to get as much done as possible during the week so that the weekends could be devoted to family time. She particularly missed Riley, who was working very long days, and so completing the housework was a bid to facilitate intimate family time at the weekends. As we shall see in chapter 6, later Rita reflected that, having taken on all the housework and care work during the maternity leave, she was unable to shift it back to a more shared allocation after the leave period ended.

Two non-sharing fathers, Bart and John, explicitly discussed doing housework. Beth described the 'good feeling' she got from sharing this work with Bart:

Our plan today was to tidy up the flat which was in terrible condition. I went out with baby B to make her sleep so Bart can start tidying. Eventually she fell asleep, so I came back home. We parked her in the garden and she gave us 1½ hours to continue working in the house. We managed almost everything except one room. Such a good feeling.

Beth, Diary 4 (baby 13 months old)

These accounts from women suggest that while men's care work might be received as a 'gift' during the maternity leave period, women's feelings about housework are not so clear-cut. They were more likely to express frustration at having to take sole responsibility for housework, and unevenness here was likely to provoke conflict. Housework and care work are often conflated in studies of division of labour (Doucet, 2023), but the meanings attached to them can differ substantially. Research which does unpack the differences between care work and housework shows that, increasingly, men (and women) aspire to more involvement of fathers in *care* work, without necessarily holding a concomitant desire for or practice of gender equality in *housework*, which is valued less highly (Doucet, 2006; Eerola, Närvi, Terävä & Repo, 2021; Twamley, 2019). My reading of the participants' accounts is that the maternity leave is particularly formative in shaping divisions of housework and care work. Since fathers have limited time in which they can connect with their newborn children and support their partners during the maternity leave period, they prioritise care practices with children, which they experience as more emotionally gratifying.

Importantly, however, it wasn't just the *doing* of housework which women complained about, but the fact of the assumed *responsibility* for this work. Their Household Portraits, undertaken in interview 1, indicated that women often took on the 'mental load' for housework even before becoming mothers. At that time, less tension was reported. Once women held responsibility for the care of their babies, which as we have seen they experience as meaningful but also anxiety-provoking, inequalities in the mental load were less tolerated.

Greedy work influencing maternity leave

As recounted in chapters 2 and 3, the 'greedy work' scenarios of male participants shaped their decisions about leave, by encouraging them to avoid SPL or to minimise the amount of SPL taken. Greedy work and men's attitudes to their work also shaped their ultimate take-up and experiences of paternity leave. But we can also see how men's long work hours impacted on the rest of the maternity leave period. Specifically, participants continued to report that very long hours were worked by men, which left women alone for long days at home with a small baby:

> Riley comes home at 11pm, too much work. I hate this! A birth does only happen once and it's only 3 weeks [since the baby was born]. I really need him to help me.
>
> Rita, Diary 1 (baby 3 weeks old)

> Days are going faster and faster. I feel already a bit drowning at work. I have a deadline this Saturday and I am struggling more than usual. Day at work was short. Afternoon was spent at the tongue tie clinic. We decided not to go ahead with the intervention. It was a nice day but unfortunately no time nor equipment to go for a walk on the south bank. Hope I will be able to organize myself a bit better and enjoy the girls more.
>
> Two nice moments today. I changed baby B by myself in a public toilet. Good fun. And I tried to work a bit tonight with baby B sleeping next to me in the living room. Nice feeling having this sweet human being next to me.
>
> Bad moment (sort of): when baby B and Beth went out for a long walk this afternoon I stayed at home trying to work. At some point I was missing them a lot.
>
> Bart, Diary 1 (baby 4 weeks old)

Even if fathers managed to get home on time to see their child before bedtime, they often reported sitting down to work again, sometimes until late at night. The pressures of work were clearly impacting on their enjoyment of this period and their ability to support their partners and care for their children. The flexibility afforded by employers, as in Bart's case, meant he could join his partner when she went to the tongue-tie clinic with their baby, but he still needed to 'catch up' on work later. As reported in other studies, employees with flexible work schedules may end up working longer hours than those with less flexibility, as boundaries between home and work become blurred (Chung, 2022; Kvande, 2007). This creates tensions for fathers who struggle to reconcile the demands of a high workload with their wish to spend time with their partner and child. Here we see how such flexible work schedules can affect the experience of leave.

Two mothers also reported working during their maternity leave, namely Beth (marketing executive) and Helen (publishing editor). Both had been particularly 'grateful' to their employers for topping up the statutory maternity pay and as part of this arrangement had agreed to work some hours during the maternity leave period. Perhaps because of this gratitude, they did not appear to grudge this time at work. Nonetheless, this example illustrates how the poor statutory remuneration of maternity leave, as well as work norms, shapes parents' experiences of leave. Rita and Riley, for example, were clearly worried about the financial implications of Rita's maternity leave and often discussed their anxieties about meeting nursery care costs after the leave period was over. Rita explained the impact of such worries on her experience of maternity leave:

> I always feel I have to do something because I don't earn any money, except the 640 pounds [monthly statutory maternity leave pay] which especially in London is nothing. It's quite stupid cause this makes it a bit difficult to actually enjoy time with your baby as you are a bit stressed most of the time. Somehow, I imagined maternity time [as] more enjoyable. I guess it's just my thinking and I should just stop as I cannot really change it. I should relax more and worry less.
>
> Rita, Diary 2 (baby 6 months old)

These financial worries put extra stress on Riley as the primary earner. As discussed in chapter 2, at the time of recruitment to the study Rita and Riley were earning the same amount and even working in the same firm. They decided that Rita would take all the maternity leave so that the impact of a break from work would be entirely experienced by her, thus making Riley the primary earner. Soon after the maternity leave started, he changed jobs to improve his earnings, which led to longer work hours as he established himself in the new company. Similarly, John (IT manager) changed jobs at the beginning of the maternity leave period to improve their family finances, as Judy (administrator) anticipated taking a career break after her maternity leave period ended. While women felt weighed down by the responsibility of taking care of a newborn, men were more likely to report feeling weighed down by their responsibility to earn sufficient money to support the family (Shirani & Henwood, 2011). This had implications for the women, meaning longer hours alone with their baby. These accounts emphasise the importance of job security and well-paid leave for supporting parents' transitions to parenthood, whatever the pattern of leave take-up. We also begin to see how role specialisation during maternity leave sets up a pattern which, I show later, continues after the leave period ends.

The final months of maternity leave

In mothers' accounts, the final months of maternity leave, from around 6 months onwards, came across as much less stressful and more relaxing. At this point, mothers felt they had acquired a routine with their children, most of whom were now sleeping at least some relatively long stretches in the night and the day. The babies were also taking solids, meaning there were fewer feeds overall.

> Today is Thursday, on Thursdays I take a shower in the morning for a few weeks now, it makes me very happy. Before I was only taking showers on weekends or evenings when Riley was home to take baby R during that time. But now baby R is happy to sit in her chair and watches me taking a shower. And I explain what I am doing. So nice to take a shower it's one of the things you normally do every day but you stop when having a baby. It gives me the feeling that I manage the new situation.
>
> Rita, Diary 2 (baby 6 months old)

> I am really really well organised now. I have to be. Then I can enjoy my time with them, then I know everything is in its place and on hand etc. And I need to make sure I have done everything in a day, so I can relax in the evening.
>
> Pippa, Interview 2

> Things have have just gotten much easier, each week it gets easier, and I think I know what we are doing. And I get to see my NCT [antenatal group] friends, I see them 2–4 times a week, and/or have a class.[4] I had yoga today. Breastfeeding is fine now too. Sometimes he doesn't sleep well, but hopefully I can get a nap during the day or Sam isn't always working so he can help out then too.
>
> Sarah, Interview 2

> She's her own little person, she's more, I think as babies get older they're just a bit more independent, a bit less fretful. Um so it, it seems like she can give you a lot more back, which has been like lovely, to see her grow up. So I would say the first half of the year was harder in terms of lows. I think finding that rhythm with her, because I started, when she was about four months old I started kind of trying to go to a class or just going to something every day, and that was great I think, getting out of the house. It's really important.

> Like before that I was probably just too tired to think about what we were [short laugh] going to do every day. But um yeah, being able to go out with her really helped.
>
> Debbie, Interview 3

Mothers expressed feeling more confident in the care of their babies. This isn't to say that everything was suddenly straightforward: they were still tired and sometimes felt overwhelmed, but they compared this period favourably with the first six months. They had also set up networks of support with other women on leave and had clear timetables for their days. They expressed more enjoyment in spending time with more 'interactive' babies, noting that newborns do not express the same kinds of joy and recognition as older babies. As might be expected, while fathers noted that mothers were more relaxed, they narrated less change over time in their own experiences of the first year, as they had been less affected by changes in the babies' behaviour than women. These accounts highlight again the differences between non-sharing women's and men's experiences in the first year of their baby's life. They also hint at the differing experiences of mothers taking leave in the first half of the year and sharing fathers taking leave in the second half (the more usual pattern), which I will discuss in the following chapter.

Conclusion

The innovative use of diaries during the leave period exposes the difficult experiences of mothers on leave alone, particularly during the first six months, accentuated by fathers' short paternity leave and long work hours after the paternity leave period ends. A sense of job precarity or financial insecurity pushed fathers to work long hours; some didn't even take their full two weeks of paternity leave. This demonstrates the importance of secure employment and well-paid leave in supporting shared care responsibilities at the transition to parenthood. This includes well-paid maternity leave, since some men worked longer hours to make up for the low maternity leave pay received by their partners. It also affirms the argument of Joan Williams that, for transformational change in family practices, a reconstruction of workplace norms is required (2012).

Women's accounts of maternity leave are a vivid reminder of the challenges of caring alone for a newborn child (Arendell, 2000). Ann Oakley (1980) found that a segregated division of labour was a factor in women's low feelings after birth and in their being labelled as suffering from postnatal depression. Through these diaries we begin to see why this may be the case. In particular, the women reported the challenge of being (or feeling) solely responsible for their children's health and development, while at the same time learning to care for their newborn. Arguably there is a heightened risk of mothers suffering in this way, given that, as several scholars note, consciousness of risk to young children and the responsibilisation of mothers for the negotiation of these risks has increased over the last 30 years, reinforced by a multi-million-pound industry of parental advice and support services (Furedi, 2001; Lee et al., 2023). Women's accounts certainly reflect high levels of anxiety. The more time they spent with their babies, the more confident they grew in their ability to meet their children's needs. But this increasing expertise affirmed sociocultural narratives about the importance of mothers for their children and their assumed superior skills in parenting as compared to fathers (Gaunt, 2013; Petts, 2022).

The difference in the time spent on leave by men and women that don't share leave is stark, and has a large impact on parents' relationships with their children. Women's extended maternity leave alone leads to a building of expertise in taking care of their children (see also Miller, 2005). Non-sharing fathers' time with their babies is necessarily much more limited and their expertise correspondingly lower. As shown by other research, even when fathers become the primary carer when the children are older, the expertise developed during maternity leave can continue to shape the division of parental responsibility (Brooks & Hodkinson, 2020).

The little time that men did have available during maternity leave was spent with the baby, rather than on housework. This was in a bid to both 'give the mother a break' from relentless and stressful care responsibilities, and build a relationship with their child. This was encouraged by women, as a kind of mutual relationship work and an effort at family intimacy building. As we shall see in later chapters, this had knock-on consequences for men's involvement in housework, which women increasingly took over during the leave (see similar findings in Canada: Fox, 2009). Since non-sharing fathers tended towards an ideal of intimate fatherhood (Dermott, 2008) rather than necessarily towards equal participation in care and housework, they were unlikely to push for changes in the parenting responsibilities established during this period. For this reason, caring for partner and child entailed sharing some childcare, but housework not so much.

Notes

1. Breastfeeding was also reported as a key deterrent to SPL take-up in the survey (Twamley & Schober, 2019).
2. A health visitor in the UK is a nurse or midwife who specialises in supporting families with a child from birth to age five.
3. Participants were asked to report 'highlights' and 'lowlights' of their days in their diaries.
4. The National Childbirth Trust (NCT) organises paid-for parenting and birth classes for parents in the UK.

5
Leave sharers' experiences and practices during the first year after their child is born

Most sharing couples had the mother on leave alone for the bulk of the year, with men taking varying lengths of leave, usually towards the end of the maternity leave period. Thus, like non-sharing mothers, sharing mothers were often on leave alone from two weeks after the birth of their child. The two weeks of paternity leave that most sharing fathers took was (again as among non-sharers) recalled primarily for its brevity. Helen, for example, told me in interview 2 that 'It's harrowing when the father goes back to work. I was like hysterical from lack of sleep and not being able to breastfeed'. Few parents recalled these two weeks in any detail, except to say that it was good to be with their partners but the leave ended too soon.

Then the following initial months continue to follow the pattern of the non-sharing mothers, as these diary extracts illustrate:

> Baby was up a lot last night. She had the end of a cold, and so was waking herself up sniffing and coughing. Poor little thing can't breathe properly. It's so hard to listen to! It also means she slept extremely loudly. I didn't get much sleep after about 3am. Baby woke up about 1, 3, and was then awake(ish) from about 5. […] Did a load of washing. Baby woke up so did a change and had a really nice time singing with her, giving her a good clean, her vitamins, cleaning her gunky eye etc. She then got quite grumpy and so tried to cheer her up. Did a feed. Tried for ages to put Baby down for a nap. She wasn't interested. Maybe 30 mins or so. She rested for a bit eventually, but then cried again. […]

Evening – Edward got home at 7. E had bath and massage etc, which she really enjoyed. Then she went crazy – got incredibly upset for about 20 minutes, crying frantically. Had no idea what was wrong and tried everything; eventually some wind came out and she calmed down and went to sleep.

          Emily, Diary 1 (baby 4 weeks old)

V tired after broken night (as per usual). Baby T has accepted no night feeds but woke several times for the dummy. Rang [sleep trainer] who suggested trying a couple more nights with the dummy to see if she settles, and if not to go COLD TURKEY. Terrifying prospect.

Joined the NCT people for lunch. [...] I have to refrain from asking the others how their babies are sleeping as I can't bear to hear the answer if positive. Didn't confess to them about sleep training.

High point was when I got T to nap in her sling at the pub – I thought she had lost that ability. Low point was when T was playing with her arch [baby gym], being v v cute, but I was just too tired to play with her properly and lay on floor beside her.

          Tara, Diary 2 (baby 6 months old)

Henry struggled last night – he did have him until 11pm trying to get him to sleep but I do 11–6am when my mum takes him for a few hours if it's awful, which is most nights with baby H's reflux. I got 7 hours broken over 5 lots. Henry got over that in one lot after the horrible getting to sleep. Tonight he's at football so he's out [of] the house from 9 – no pre leave childcare – and home 12 hours later. I feel resentful though that's not fair because I said he could go ... I can't pee without rushing. I'm so tired and it's all on me.

          Helen, Diary 2 (baby 6 months old)

As we can see, these mothers were very tired, focused on trying to encourage longer and more regular sleep habits and variously worrying about and dealing with the health of their children. The diaries from when the baby was 4 weeks old and 6 months old show that these mothers were usually alone with their children. Fathers were present in the early mornings and evenings, but the women were clearly tired and sometimes overwhelmed. They reported, like non-sharing mothers, that they found taking the primary responsibility for their newborn child exhausting. Perhaps because of their expectations of shared parenting, many of these mothers also described the emotion work (Hochschild, 2003) of dealing with uneven care responsibilities, as when Helen described grappling with her feelings of resentment about Henry's absences.

Not surprisingly, men's diaries of their time during maternity leave were strikingly similar to those of non-sharing men's diaries, with work hours structuring their interactions with their families:

> Overslept this morning! Emily had got baby E at 5:30am and fed her. She went straight back to sleep and all 3 of us slept through until 7:45am. Hurriedly got changed and left for work.
>
> Got home at 6:15pm and did bath-time with baby E (my favourite time of the day!). Emily fed her and she went to sleep at around 7:15pm. We had dinner together and a quiet evening in.
>
> Edward, Diary 2 (baby 6 months old)

> Very rough night with Baby. He's teething and refluxy and hates the heat, and it's boiling out. Three hours effort to get him down for about the same. Helen then picked him up again in the small hours. This is on the back of two previous nights of the same. We are both pretty run down and snappy with each other, necessitating hasty no-fault apologies. Nappy changes, feeds etc. Off to work in the morning. Back home via football for an hour, which was a mistake – too exhausted to play properly. Had a phone interview for a job which I think went well but took last reserves of emotional energy. High point – none, frankly, I think I even left for work in the morning without seeing Baby. Low point – arguing with Helen. She thinks I'm not doing enough, and she's not wrong, but it's difficult to see where in my day I can do more if I also have to earn a living. I've wanted to drop out of football on a number occasions and have offered to do so to spend more time at home but she has insisted that I carry on for health/exercise reasons.
>
> Henry, Diary 2 (baby 6 months old)

> Slept all day. Feels a bit off to be so self-centred but was working all night and am back to work tonight so have to just get some sleep. I find it particularly stressful much more than I used to and really struggle to get to sleep. When I wake up Anna and baby are not around. Depressing to be in a flat alone but get ready and off to work. Aside from the state of the flat, you would almost not know

I have a son. This must be what it is like for fathers with jobs with long hours. I'm lucky this is not the norm for me.

Adam, Diary 2 (baby 6 months old)

As with non-sharers, men's care during this period was concentrated in early-morning wake-ups and night-time bath/bed routines. Fathers expressed sadness at missing out on seeing their child and a sense of guilt about the lack of support they could give their partners when they worked late. This sense of guilt was heightened for Henry, who recognised how much his wife Helen was suffering in caring for a baby with reflux. Here we see the impact of the individual baby on the leave experience. Others had babies who were 'natural sleepers' (Filip, interview 2) or at least did not have health issues which impeded sleep. In these cases women were able to shelter their partners from, for example, night-time wake-ups during the maternity leave period, as Edward explained:

> So yeah it's been great, it's been absolutely great. Um I feel like I've been sheltered from the worst of childrearing a six month old by Emily quite well. It hasn't really affected me. Like the bad parts of childrearing I haven't seen that much of actually, like sleepless nights and that sort of thing. Um Emily's been really, really good. Like if E gets up then pretty much always she will get up and do whatever needs to be done so I can just continue sleeping and go to work the next morning.
>
> Edward, Interview 2

This is not to say that Emily's leave was 'easy'; she also struggled with the months of maternity leave alone, but the load was more manageable with a baby that was healthy. This impacted on the couple relationship: with easier circumstances it was easier to care for one's partner, a key aspect of the relationship work (Gabb & Fink, 2015) necessary to maintain intimacy (as reported also in Bonnie Fox's study in Canada, 2009).

Like the non-sharing mothers, sharing mothers discussed the impact of men's long working hours on their maternity leave experiences. This was particularly the case for Helen and Tara, both of whom considered their partner to be the primary earner. Helen and Henry's situation was made more difficult by several factors: baby H had severe reflux; Henry was not eligible for SPL, which meant he used unpaid parental leave and saved up four weeks of annual leave to take two months off alone at the end of Helen's maternity leave (which meant more time alone for Helen in the run-up to this leave); and he changed jobs during her leave. Helen told me:

I mean like Henry had so much schmoozing towards the end and trying to get this new job, you know, he it ... It was just a nightmare for me, like I'd be looking after baby H and ... The way that the sleep worked, like I remember [laughs] I don't even want to remember this but the way that the sleep worked was I would get my most sleep if Henry could be home and I could give him the baby by seven, and then I could sleep from seven until one. Now it would still take me a while to wind down, but then even then if I then fell asleep between eight and one it meant that if I didn't sleep at all after that, even if I only had an hour or so I still had that little bit in the tank. It was horrible, and so if he had to go out and say have a drink with someone because it made total sense, but da da da, getting this new job and all the rest of it, I would maybe not get that sleep. And it was like sometimes you know it would work out that I could fall asleep or whatever, but often, my sleep was just so broken that I would get up.

Helen, Interview 3

Henry and Tim, as the primary earners in this group of couples, are the most similar to non-sharing men in their paid work situations: they both reported increasing their time at work during their partners' maternity leave. The other sharing fathers felt less pressure to work long hours or to seek promotion or a new job. Thus, these accounts suggest that it is not just work contexts more generally that enforce or encourage long hours, but men's position as the primary earner in the household, that encourages them to focus on paid work at the transition to parenthood. This can be a matter of circumstance, i.e. in relation to relative earnings, or design – as seen with Rita and Riley in chapter 4, who earned similar amounts but decided to foreground Riley's career. The pressure to earn more was heightened when their partners intended to move to part-time work or take a break from paid work, like Helen and Tara respectively.

Whatever the situation, though, parents noted that mothers became the 'primary parent' during their maternity leave alone because of their extended hours with the baby. This was not necessarily welcomed by sharing parents, as we can see in these accounts:

Anna kept trying to interfere while I was putting him [baby A] to sleep. Sometimes she seems like she checks up on me. She's definitely the boss when it comes to knowing what to do but I'll ask if I need advice.

Adam, Diary 2 (baby 6 months old)

> Um so I began to look forward to that [SPL alone], but was also nervous as it's sort of the responsibility I suppose, because, um, I suppose I felt like very much a sort of secondary parent because Mary was at home with him all the time and he was being breastfed, um, so I didn't do anything. All I sort of did was I suppose just, yeah sort of nappy changing and baths.
>
> Mark, Interview 3

> Sometimes I think Edward thinks I'm pretty precious about exactly when she [the baby] sleeps, but he doesn't understand what changes in her schedule mean!
>
> Emily, Diary 2 (baby 6 months old)

> High point – I got a lot of house work done bc [because] I had Henry to help with baby.
>
> Low point – I got a lot of house work done bc I had Henry to help with baby. He still struggles to do literally anything when he looks after the baby. He struggles to empty the dishwasher or hang out washing.
>
> Helen, Diary 2 (baby 6 months old)

Their position as the primary carers could also slip into responsibility for housework, which, as we can see in Helen's account, was particularly negatively experienced by women.

However, unlike the non-sharers, sharing couples explicitly stated their expectations that the primary–secondary parent dynamic would shift once fathers started SPL alone, as expressed by Mark above, for example. Moreover, some mothers told me that they felt their partners were more involved in decisions about the baby's care because they were anticipating their own leave alone:

> The fact that we decided we would do shared parental [leave] made him more involved from the beginning because he knew that he was going to be solely responsible for like three months, so he kind of couldn't just like let things slide and be like 'Oh, I don't really know like what baby K wears or where the food is', like heaps of people are. You'd think they wouldn't be these days but it still happens.
>
> Kate, Interview 3

In the following section, I explore in more depth what happens when fathers are on leave alone, and whether parents' predictions are realised.

Fathers on leave alone

Fathers who took leave alone did so when the babies were around 9 months old and the mother had returned to paid work. As indicated in the quote from Mark in the previous section, expressing his anxiety about becoming a 'primary parent', fathers approached their leave alone with some trepidation, as well as enthusiasm. They told me that while they looked forward to spending more time with their children, they also felt worried about shifting from full-time paid work to full-time care of their child. Some of these worries were about their jobs – what kind of workload they might return to – but most were centred on whether and how they would cope with being at home alone with a small child.

Mothers too expressed some anxieties around this shift. Since they have been the primary carers, they worried about 'letting go' and how their partner and baby would cope:

> I found it hard to kind of let go of her, I suppose. So even though, you know, I knew that she would be happy with Tim, for example at, from, from early on in his leave, but I was kind of anxious to sort of um, build up the time so that, so that she wouldn't get completely, like have a bad experience with him or kind of have too much time at the beginning. So maybe I should've been a bit more confident with that um, although it worked out okay.
>
> Tara, Interview 3

> Henry complains of being tired even when he gets so much more sleep than me. I worry what him doing the childcare will look like.
>
> Helen, Diary 2 (baby 6 months old)

These extracts demonstrate that maternity leave builds mothers' expertise, which may then shift into a distrust in a partner's ability to care. Sharing mothers arranged to take some leave together at the beginning of their partners' leave alone to support them; several told me they took a week off together to 'ease the transition' (Winnie) for the baby as well as for the father.

Mothers reported other measures to help fathers have a better experience while on leave. Similar findings were made amongst non-sharers, in that those mothers encouraged their partners to take on care responsibilities at the weekends and in the evenings. That was necessarily more limited and, as I argued in chapter 4, did nothing to destabilise gendered divisions of parenting and sometimes meant that women took on more housework while their partners were spending time with the babies. Here, the mothers were supporting their partners' roles as fathers as they transitioned to SPL alone. They arranged baby classes for them to attend (many of which the women had already been attending), introduced them to people (mostly mothers) they had met while they were on leave, and explained the babies' routines. This shows their concern about and attention to fathers' anxieties, but also their personal investment in fathers having a good experience of leave.

Given when the leave occurred, that is after the baby had been weaned, most of the babies were settled into a good routine of sleeping and eating by the time men took leave alone. They also had experience of caring for their children, even if this was confined to evenings and weekends, and they reported that they had learned how to approach the leave from their partners' experiences. For example, Henry told me that he was planning to see people every day of his SPL, as Helen had told him that having adult company was key to 'feeling sane', and Edward said he 'reaped the rewards' of Emily's maternity leave, since 'Baby does what she's supposed to, in terms of like sleeping and eating, pretty much when we want her to, and that has been very much Emily's influence over the first like six months I would say.'

Although it is possible to take SPL in chunks of time, I did not come across any couple in the survey who planned their leave in this way. The preference for the woman to take the first part of the leave was to ensure that she had sufficient time to recover from the birth and was able to breastfeed. The timing of men's leave alone clearly shapes men's experiences and their accounts of their leave, which were largely positive:

> Katherine: And ah what was your shared parental leave like?
>
> Edward: It was great. Um, two months, just over, it, I'd say for the first like week and a half, first two weeks, it felt pretty full on. I was like looking after an entire other human being and it was up to me. Um just like remembering feeding times, sleeping times, eating times, all that sort of stuff. Ah but other than that it was brilliant. […] Yeah it was really nice just like hanging out with baby, you know, going to the park, doing like um like Gymboree type things, you know? There was like one thing a day that we used to go and do um I had a really fun time.
>
> Edward, Interview 3

> Within a few days just sort of ah it was all, it was all sort of fine really and he was, and we really enjoyed the ten weeks off together um to the extent where I really didn't want to go back to work … So I tried to sort of replicate some of the classes Mary did and visit my mum a fair bit and my sisters whenever they were off, and we would just sort of go around and go to art galleries and things, and I actually quite enjoyed it.
>
> Mark, Interview 3

> This recent ah time off um […] kind of ah has, well it, ah it went really fast. I was kind of a bit um nervous going into it because baby T was going through quite a clingy period where if she was the other side of the room from her mum she would be starting to, to, to grinch and get upset. So just the thought of sort of taking her for full days where she was going to be like that um felt, ah yeah I was a bit nervous anticipating that. But I think it, it worked out well. She, she was good and we had, and we did all the, we went to Tiny Time and Monkey Music and Zipzap and, and she started enjoying going on the swings, so we spent a lot of time in the park on swings and feeding the ducks, and it was really nice.
>
> Tim, Interview 3

The negatives that were reported were the boredom of leave, the repetitive nature of taking care of a baby, and the lack of other men on leave, as is visible in these accounts:

> I was feeding him, he was just getting into food but not really eating it, and so I would sort of spend an hour feeding him in the morning and then I'd be trying to put him down for about forty-five minutes and he'd sleep for forty-five minutes, and then you start lunch [short laugh], and then you're doing that for an hour, and then um you've got a little bit of playtime before then you're trying to put him down and he fights you for an hour, and then, you know, you get the, you know, then you put him down and then um and you sort of, you look at it and half the day just is, is gone with bits that aren't very enjoyable, and where he was unhappy or fighting you or whatever. And so there were some great bits in there and um but more than I expected that, that was, it was not hard, but nor was it particularly enjoyable. Um and, and so I think I found, I thought I would, I would find it harder than I found it. Um and I found it easier but not as satisfying in some ways as I thought I would. And I'm glad I did it,

on the whole, um but day to day I was fairly ambivalent about it I think. The, I mean, I am glad I've done it and really enjoyed some of the moments of it but I prefer being at work.

Keith, Interview 3

Definitely felt like I was entering a woman's world very often, especially like these like Gymboree like playdate type things. I would be the, you know, the only guy, maybe one other guy, but it'd be me and mmm like fifteen women and sixteen babies. It did feel kind of weird. It felt a bit lonely every now and again actually. Like they would all go off and like chat, because they'd obviously been like NCT friends or something and on their, on maternity at the same time, and I was just like sort of parachuted into this group.

Edward, Interview 3

Keith recounted more challenges with his child's sleep than other fathers (by the time Henry took leave, baby H's reflux was largely under control), but he still told me that the leave wasn't 'particularly challenging'. Part of the lack of challenge, other than the timing of the leave, is that the moral responsibility of fatherhood is not comparable to that of motherhood. Men do not hold, and nor are they held to, expectations of perfect parenting in the same way as women (see also Shirani et al., 2012b). This was clear in the diaries and interviews, but also expressed explicitly by some participants. Tim, for example, told me that he did not experience his leave as 'intensely' as Tara experienced hers. This shapes the emotional experience of men's leave, which is less anxious or lonely than women's narrations of leave.

The lack of other men on leave was recorded by SPL-takers as of little consequence in the general experience of leave. This is in contrast to some other research findings, in which men report a lack of male company as a key issue they struggle with while caring for children alone (Brooks & Hodkinson, 2020; Doucet, 2006). Perhaps part of the difference here is that the fathers are not on leave for a particularly long time – none of the fathers reported on in this chapter took more than three months' leave alone, and all intended to return to paid work – and none are (yet) primary care fathers, as the fathers in those other studies were.

Although men's leave is perhaps less challenging overall than women's leave, men's accounts do demonstrate that they experienced leave as quite a radical shift in their day-to-day life, and that children came to be the focal point of their days in ways comparable to women's narrations of leave. For example, here Weston discusses how he came to experience a child-centred temporality while on leave:

> There was no pressure to get anywhere, well apart from a class, but obviously um you knew what time that was. So yeah it was nice to just not be constrained by any like, oh we have to be there by a certain time, or we're meeting these people, blah blah blah. It was just, what does he need? Well he needs to be fed, he needs to have a nap, let's have some fun and play um and that's it. And then you got home in time for, for dinner and bath and bed, you know? And it was kind of that. So yeah I mean it was very tiring, but ah it was nice to do all of the things obviously Winnie had been doing. And yeah, as I say, just not being pressured by having to be anywhere. Just, I don't know, it sounds cheesy but living in the moment [inaudible], just being with him and seeing how, especially during that time he was starting to learn to stand, kind of try and walk a little bit.
>
> Weston, Interview 3

Like fathers who experienced leave alone in Norway, Weston experiences what Brandth and Kvande (2002) call a 'slow time', in which time is organised in relation to the needs of their child. They argue that such time alone between father and child is necessary for fathers to become competent in reading and responding to their child, and ultimately to take independent responsibility for care. So even though, as Helen says in interview 3, men's time on leave was 'a lot more fun and ours [women's] was a lot more get through the day', there was still a sense that this leave gave men an insight into 'how exhausting it can be looking after a baby all day' (Mary, interview 3). Thus, from the perspective of sharing parents, men's leave alone increased empathy and understanding between mothers and fathers (a key motivation to share leave, as reported in chapter 3).

In terms of shifting gendered parenting practices, until now I have reported two main ways in which mothers had the primary role during maternity leave: first, she took on most of the everyday care activities, and second, she took on most of the decisions about care, such as whether or not to try a particular 'approach' in encouraging sleep, whether to call the doctor when the baby has symptoms and so on. It is a limitation that I do not have diary accounts from fathers and mothers during this time to show the kinds of everyday tasks and responsibilities of parents during men's leave alone. From their interview accounts, though, it's clear that fathers were the main 'hands-on carers' during their time off, and indeed this is not surprising given that they were at home full-time while women were in paid work. In terms of decision-making, fathers clearly took up routines established by mothers and were often 'coached' in taking care of the babies in anticipation of the leave. Some mothers also reported that fathers called them at their workplaces about various issues at the start of the leave. However, the mothers were in general keen to shift responsibilities to the father during this time, given that this was a motivation for SPL in the first place, and mothers also reported that men started to care for babies 'in their own way', indicating that they took responsibility for at least some aspects of care during leave:

> He [Mark] was able to do some of the things in, and look after baby M in his way, which was maybe different to how I did, and that was also good for me, to, to learn that that's, you know, [...] that there's lots of different ways of doing things.
>
> Mary, Interview 3

> The thing I found with Weston especially is that I think his confidence grew a lot during that time where he was solely responsible for baby W. I think at the beginning he would very, very often defer to me and ask me 'What does baby W need? Do I need to do this? What should I do? Shall I, you know, what do I do if this happens?' et cetera. And I think throughout that time period I saw, you know, obviously Weston became a lot more comfortable looking after W without having me around or me to ask questions. [...] He came on a lot as a father in his ability to care for W during that time period.
>
> Winnie, Interview 3

Thus, just as women's maternity leave was a time to learn to care, men also reported learning to care, first from their partners, and then, the longer they were on leave, through their own trial and error as their babies developed (as seen in Keith's account of feeding his baby). Such findings are duplicated in other research on fathers' leave alone (e.g. O'Brien & Wall, 2017), demonstrating that leave alone can result in fathers becoming 'confident and competent caregivers' (Doucet, 2017:17). What this study adds is the detail of everyday care and how it contributes to such increased competence specifically during the leave. In chapter 6, I discuss whether and how this lasted beyond the leave period.

Taking SPL together

Five fathers took some SPL with the mother at the time of the birth: Keith, Mark, Tim, Filip and Gerald. The reports from these parents indicate that the extended time off together from birth was crucial in avoiding the 'harrowing' experience (Helen, interview 2) reported by other mothers when the two weeks of paternity leave came to an end. The diary extracts from this extended time off together give a taste of how their experiences differed from those of mothers on leave alone at four weeks (as reported in chapter 4 and in the opening section of this chapter).

> Had a fairly good night's sleep as baby K went down easily after each feed. Highlights today were sitting in our garden with ice cream (it was really nice weather), going out for coffee and bath time this evening. Baby K loves the bath and gets a really cute look on his face! Baby K has been having what we think is colic and been quite unsettled (we're trying infacol; hope it works!). This photo [pasted in diary] was when Keith managed to settle him and it was so nice how he is sort of holding on to Keith. This is when I felt closest to them today, along with bath time. We both like bathing baby K together. Lowlight was probably this evening. Was feeling quite low in spirits after a nap, but Keith made me go for a 20 min walk on my own which really helped.
>
> Kate, Diary 1 (baby 4 weeks old)

> Baby fed 2–3am and then awake for an hour or so. Went into baby room. Not really settling in Moses basket. Feed in bed and then sleep w baby. Partner awake at 7.30am and I have sleep after feeding.
>
> Main achievement was breastfeeding all day. Partner made all food/drinks. Put on one load of washing! Not sure what else I achieved.
>
> Managed to feed in 'laid-back' way on a Poäng chair [an armchair model made by IKEA], while watching Wimbledon. Much more comfortable and less back ache.
>
> Weather hot so feeding a lot. Try to keep us cool, by closing blinds and putting up curtain. Fan on. Play w baby gym and peekaboo.
>
> Partner did tummy time and baby 20 mins naked in the morning (two poo!).
>
> Walk in evening once weather cooled. Baby in pram. Too hot for carrier. Relax and feed in park, goes well on left breast using normal hold.
>
> Feed while watching Catastrophe (tv prog about a couple who have baby!) and eating my dinner. Baby falls asleep on nursing pillow.
>
> Mary, Diary 1 (baby 4 weeks old)

While baby was cluster feeding in the evening, hubby made me dinner – he made one of my mum's traditional Indian recipes. It was delicious!!

Faria, Diary 1 (baby 4 weeks old)

A good day on the whole although we were worried in the morning when she had that very snuffly nose again and trouble breathing – it kept her awake after her 6 am feed which was a pain, though I did go back to sleep while Tim got up with her. Feeds went smoothly on the whole and she slept between them (again, mostly). Tim and I went for lunch with her and I went for a half hour massage afterwards (at Tim's suggestion). Made less attempt to wean myself off the nipple shields. She had a mild version of her witching hour in the evening – Tim took her out for a walk at 8.30 pm which didn't help a whole lot.

Tim made dinner and brought me snacks all day while I was feeding her.

Highlight: cuddling baby T in the morning after a feed and feeling her snuggly little body on my shoulder, completely peaceful.

Low point: she had her 'witching hour' from around 8pm. Tim stayed up with her while I went to sleep.

Tara, Diary 1 (baby 4 weeks old)

Like non-sharing mothers, we see sharing mothers trying to figure out how best to feed their children and to help them to sleep. They described various issues, such as colic and a blocked nose, and their worries about how best to treat their baby. The differences are that mothers here reported sharing their worries with their partners ('we were worried', for example, said Tara), as well as making decisions together on potential solutions. Sharing mothers also recounted the practical support which non-sharing mothers so craved: Kate put a photo in her diary of Keith holding the baby after he managed to get her to sleep and Mary reported having all her meals cooked for her by her partner while she focused on feeding. These diary extracts show how different the early weeks can be when fathers are at home with their partners: no mother talked about being lonely.

This is not to say that everything was perfect, but the diaries and later reflections are much more positive in general than those of the non-sharing mothers. All parents who had extended time off together in the first four weeks after the birth made a point of expressing how helpful they found SPL at the time of the birth, as exemplified in the following interview extracts:

Katherine: Can you tell me about your, your two different periods of leave? So you had one around the time of the birth and then one after about nine months, I think it was meant to /be, yeah?

Keith: /Mmhmm. Yeah. So ah first month great. I think that is, I think that's an excellent thing to do. I think everybody should do that if they're able to do that, and think it, you know, your life's been turned upside down and it's a whirlwind, that first sort of um first couple of weeks, first few weeks. And so [...] it, I think it would've been really difficult going back after two weeks as a lot of people do, because you, you're only just finding which way is up after a couple of weeks, and I think that it was really good having that extra couple of weeks to just try and understand what was going on together um before going back to work and leaving Kate to it. I think it would've been pretty difficult otherwise. Um so very, I think that was absolutely great, and easy as well, in the sense that I di-, you know, it doesn't feel at the time, but um easy in the sense that there's two of you, you're doing it together, it's all fine, you just plan, you just work around what you're doing.

Keith, Interview 3

I think having my partner there at the beginning was a really important step and really, I think just having, if he'd only had those two weeks of paternity leave it would've made things even more difficult.

Mary, Interview 3

I certainly wouldn't have breastfed if Tim hadn't been off those six weeks, it was just too labour-intensive. Breastfeeding is a full-time job, it takes up all the day, then who feeds you and ensures the house is running? I guess people have their mums coming to stay? My parents aren't in that position to help in that way.

Tara, Interview 2

These accounts suggest that an increased length of statutory paternity leave (taken at the time of birth with the mother) could be very beneficial for mothers and fathers, particularly those who have had a C-section or other health issues.

However, these benefits do not necessarily entail changes to gendered divisions of parenting. Tara and Tim, for example, told me that the initial weeks of shared leave together, though experienced as beneficial during those weeks, are to a certain extent 'undone' later, as she, like mothers on leave alone more generally, became the primary carer. As they explained in their second interview, their first six weeks off together were 'very much a shared project', but as she spent more time with baby T she became more necessary to her, since she only seemed to go asleep in the evenings if it was Tara putting her down:

> That was a vicious circle so then I 'do maternal gatekeeping' as it works and that has been tricky. I am trying to be less controlling, but it's natural if she doesn't see you during the day and then suddenly you are putting her to bed that she doesn't, that she isn't okay with that.
>
> Tara, Interview 2

It's also clear in interview 2 that Tara has more knowledge about their baby now that Tim is back at work. For example, Tim recalled that he wasn't able to put the baby down for a nap the day before when Tara had gone out to the shops; Tara responded, 'I wouldn't even have attempted to put her down for that nap as she had slept too long during the first nap, so I knew that she wouldn't sleep then and had I been here I would have told you not to.' Both attributed this shift to Tim's reduced time with the baby since returning to work. Thus, shared leave at the time of the birth eases the transition to parenthood, but my study shows that it does not challenge gendered norms around parenting roles, at least in the short term.

What happened if men took a period of leave together with the mother at a later time point? Adam and Weston took around two months off at the end of the mothers' maternity leave, while Gerald took nine months of leave with Gina (they only took SPL together) and Filip took six months together with Faria (who went on to have another six months of maternity leave on her own). Since Adam and his wife Anna did not complete their final interview or diaries, after a death in the family, I have no record of their experience of Adam's SPL, but their two months' leave together was intended to be taken while they were travelling together in East Asia. Similarly, Weston took two months' SPL at Christmas, most of which was taken with Winnie and by their own account was similarly conceived to facilitate visits to family living in different locations. As Weston described, this leave together was experienced as more akin to extended holiday time than to parental leave:

> It was, it was nice to have it [the leave] over Christmas, but obviously that meant from, in terms of one-to-one time like it was less for me, because obviously we were going to families and, which is nice obviously [short laugh], for them and for me and baby W, but I didn't have, I probably had, I can't remember exactly, but say three weeks, three and a half weeks ah where it was like a daily me and baby, what are we doing today, from, you know, wake up to, to dinner, which was nice because, you know, as I say I wanted to do it, but also it gave us time just together rather than, and doing like normal things rather than, because we went on holiday, we went to stay at my mum's for a couple of nights. So yeah I would've done probably a bit more alone if I could have.
>
> Weston, Interview 3

Although he enjoyed the leave, both he and Winnie later described Weston's leave alone as more influential in shaping his relationship with their baby and his confidence as a father.

The other two couples, however, were able to take much longer leaves together. Again here we see the impact of time off around the birth. Gerald, Gina, Faria and Filip described these initial weeks together as hugely beneficial:

> I think the first four to six weeks were, it was really important for me to be there, and, and Faria would have coped on her own but her C-section kind of recovery would have been impeded for sure, she would have had to do so much more lifting and movement which isn't ideal when you've just had major surgery. And there would have just been one of her to cover kind of everything, including when I was home, not letting me do too much so that I could function at work.
>
> Filip, Interview 3

> In terms of SPL, I have to say I don't know how people do it without SPL!? I am so tired – after each night where we have broken sleep, which is every night, I get up at 7 am and bring him in to Gerald, and Gerald you take him, and he will walk with him for a few hours so

that I could sleep. Especially the first few months, I wasn't actually that tired, because Gerald was taking the baby in the morning.

Gina, Interview 2

Moreover, the shared *decision-making* established in those initial weeks continues *right through* to the end of their shared leave. For example, see the following extracts, when the baby was around 6 months old, in which the participants use 'we' terms in describing their attempts to encourage their children to sleep for longer periods:

> Baby G woke at 7.12am, fed for 30 mins then I handed him over to Gerald, who walked him around the park so he had an additional 35 mins nap. He had hardly slept the night before, so I was very tired. When they returned, I fed him for 30 mins and eventually topped up with a bottle. […] The low point of the day was the lack of sleep at night. He also woke several times after I put him to bed at 7.15pm. He woke 3 times before 1am. He was awake for nearly 2hrs and I ended up leaving him to cry it out for 50 minutes. I was sobbing outside the door whilst he sobbed in his cot. It was awful but he eventually fell asleep and stayed down for 4hrs. He hasn't slept that long since before his 4-month regression. After a night of CIO ['cry it out'] Gerald and I resolved to get longer naps in during the day.

Gina, Diary 2 (baby 6 months old)

> We couldn't figure out why baby was crying – it's because he wasn't feeding properly and it didn't improve until we upped the formula.

Gerald, Interview 2

> We managed to get her to fall asleep herself, which was great. That would have been really hard if I was on my own, if Filip had been sleeping in bed or not here during the day, and I was trying to get her [to] nap … it would have been really really hard, to get her to sleep without rocking her, or getting her to sleep on me, would have been really hard. He was the one initiating it, he started doing the morning nap, trying to put her down awake … really if I was on my own, I don't know whether I would have had the patience for that. I was tearing my hair out, and now we are reaping the rewards because we spend no time making her sleep, we just put her down and walk out.

Faria, Interview 2

Additionally, unlike parents who did not share leave, these couples reported a consensus on the care routines of their babies since they experienced together how variations in naps and feeding could impact on their children. Filip, for example, told me in the second interview, 'Some people find our routine too strict, sometimes people rock up but we have our routine and it works so we don't break it.' This also demonstrates a sense of shared endeavour in caring, without a 'lead parent' who takes on the primary burden of the 'mental load'.

The evidence, then, is that parents on leave together share the cognitive labour (Daminger, 2019) or 'thinking tasks' of parenting. This might lead us to assume that these would be the most egalitarian couples in the sample and that leave *together* is the most fruitful for transforming gendered parenting practices. In fact, despite sharing many aspects of care, including the cognitive labour, all four parents on extended leave together positioned the mother as the primary carer during these months. This is interesting, since cognitive labour is often thought to be constitutive of parental responsibility (Daminger, 2019). This situation largely came down to feeding, which was led by the mothers. Both fathers therefore reported doing more housework and cooking in order to support the hands-on care their partners were doing, as demonstrated in these diary entries from Filip:

> Breakfast was made with baby F in a sling, to allow wife to shower. Lunch was then prepped before I went to church. After church I cooked lunch and we ate. Then some clothes washing. I finished baby F's passport application before the three of us headed out to the shops.
>
> Filip, Diary 1 (baby 4 weeks old)

> Cooked wife's regional food for dinner as a treat, her mum's recipe. She liked it so I am feeling great!
>
> Filip, Diary 2 (baby 6 months old)

Filip's care for his wife is palpable in his diaries. He celebrated her skills as a mother and clearly enjoyed supporting her throughout the leave period. Here he shows love and care for his wife by bolstering and supporting her mothering role. While this is 'indirect care' for the baby, it is arguably direct care for the wife and a key aspect of relationship work (Gabb & Fink, 2015) between Faria and Filip. As Nancy Folbre notes, 'even seemingly impersonal tasks can have personal valence' (2021:7).

The fathers' supportive role is not interpreted as 'equal' to the mothers' parenting role within these couples. Once Faria and Gina had recovered from the birth (from around four to six weeks after their babies were born), both Filip and Gerald reported feeling 'redundant'. Filip, for example, expressed guilt at taking so much time out from work when he was clearly no longer 'completely necessary', further showing that he saw himself as a support for Faria rather than as an equal carer for their baby. In their second interview they discussed the gendered nature of these feelings about leave:

> Filip: The doctor signed you off, the baby was in a routine. I am helpful now, but not necessary. I felt a bit guilty.
>
> Faria: Yeah, I felt guilty too [about Filip being on leave], it makes you wonder why. I mean, I could be back at work too. I think frankly she would be fine with a childminder or nanny at this stage
>
> Filip: or a father!
>
> Faria: yeah! But I don't feel guilty about it, so you shouldn't either
>
> Faria and Filip, Interview 2

Gerald was less content with such an ancillary role. He discussed this with Gina in their second interview after I asked them whether, in retrospect, there is anything they would have done differently in the first few months of their leave:

> Gerald: I think, I think I would do things differently in terms of the time off ...
>
> Gina: Would it be fair to say that for the first few months you were looking after me?
>
> Gerald: Yeah, I felt a bit redundant not being able to feed with a bottle, and knowing that you were always the backstop.
>
> Gerald and Gina, Interview 1

Here, Gerald directly reports that supporting Gina, which (as with Filip) involved cooking meals, doing housework and taking the baby for walks to encourage him to nap, did not live up to his aspirations for leave, so much so that in interview 2 (and again in interview 3) he reassesses their division of leave, telling me that in retrospect he would rather have arranged to take leave alone for a period of time.

The use of the word 'redundant' (which Faria and Gina never used to describe themselves) positions the fathers as 'extra' to the mothers. It seems that these men considered themselves as unnecessary for the care of the baby. This is particularly puzzling in the case of Gerald: Gina repeatedly says in her interviews that it was crucial to have Gerald present, as she would not have been able to care for the baby without him. Unlike baby F, who according to his parents has a 'natural tendency to sleep' (Filip, interview 2) and started sleeping through the night at four months, baby G struggled to feed and sleep well, with broken nights still reported after a year. As Gina recorded in her diary (quoted above), they ended up trying the 'cry it out method', which involves letting the baby cry himself to sleep for some nights until he learns to 'self-soothe'. These sessions were apparently very upsetting and had little impact on G's sleep. Gina attended to all the night-time wake-ups over the project period, so she was extremely tired during the day: she told us that she relied on Gerald's help to catch up on sleep and to make sure the house kept running. This decision was perhaps more explicit on Gina's part than on Gerald's, as we see in her diaries. The following extract, for example, comes at the beginning of the leave:

> At 7am Gerald took baby G out for a 2hr sling walk which allowed me even more sleep. I've often used the time to have a shower and do some tidying. The house was a bit messy from yesterday and I could have tidied and taken out the take away trash but I decided against doing that in favour of sleep. I felt I deserved some rest after the nightly feeds and I should learn to a) let go of my need to control the household and b) let Gerald do the housework. It turned out to be the right decision because when Gerald came back and I fed the baby he tidied the house. I resolve to step back more now and not take so much responsibility for the house.
>
> Gina, Diary 1 (baby 4 weeks old)

How, then, does Gerald consider himself 'redundant', when he is clearly valued for the support he gives to Gina? Here we see that the higher value accorded to (direct) care work than to housework shapes evaluations of leave. For Gerald, the mother is taking on the 'real' or more valued hands-on care work, as opposed to other work relating to the baby that might also be considered necessary, such as the tidying of the house and laundering of clothes.

In Gina and Gerald's case, the ideal of equality is in tension with the gendered and physiological expectations of parenting (Faircloth, 2021; Hamilton, 2020). A key aspect of this is the central and highly moralised place that breastfeeding holds within understandings of good motherhood (Faircloth, 2013). Both Faria and Gina were committed to breastfeeding, but while Faria managed to breastfeed fairly easily and breastfed exclusively for the recommended six months, Gina struggled. In fact, baby G fell perilously below his original birthweight before she finally agreed to start mixed feeding, as they detailed in their second interview:

> Gina: Everyone knows breastfeeding is best! I put it into my identity of how good a mother I was, and to see him not thriving then made me feel that it was my fault and it kind of was because I was so ideologically driven that it put him in danger.
>
> Gerald: It caused a lot of rows.
>
> Gina: Yeah.
>
> Gerald: 'Cause I was wanting to stop it, but not knowing how to bring it up.
>
> Gina: 'Cause I was quite insistent, yeah. So that was horrible. I still feel like a failure, even if I can rationalise it. And I hate formula, I hate the smell of it and dealing with it.
>
> Gerald and Gina, Interview 2

While the move to mixed feeding might have given Gerald an opportunity to participate in feeding, ironically the reverse happened. Gina's perception of herself as having failed her son meant that to make up for this 'failure' she took on ever-increasing amounts of hands-on care work, while Gerald was 'relegated' to a supportive role for the mother.

Their accounts demonstrate the ways a sociocultural narrative of breastfeeding as intrinsic to good mothering shapes parents' experiences of the transition to parenthood, even when mothers do not exclusively breastfeed. By their own account, the moral pressure to breastfeed was so strong that it even put the health of baby G at risk. What is also interesting here is that Gina and Gerald were amongst the couples most committed to egalitarian parenting in the entire study. In their first interview, Gina told me that she wouldn't even have considered being a mother unless she had been sure that her partner would take on an equal share of the parenting and the parental leave. Her apparent ideological shift in understandings of motherhood after the birth of their child explains Gerald's frustration with his perceived lesser role in the care of the child, but also stands testament to the powerful discourses about the primacy of motherhood and its links to breastfeeding. Here we see how initial (egalitarian) plans begin to unravel and how partners diverge.

Gerald and Filip did similar tasks during their leave, but attached different meanings to them. Filip saw his work in supporting Faria as part of the relationship and family work of a father. Given that Filip and Faria have discussed the likelihood that Filip will become a full-time stay-at-home dad in the future, it's clear that this more traditional gendered division of labour was a temporary situation for them. Gerald also told me of his hope to one day be a stay-at-home father, which Gina explicitly said in couple interviews that she was not keen should happen. This probably contributed to the friction over Gerald and Gina's divisions of labour during the leave period. Either way, in both couples their prolonged leave together was not seen as disrupting the position of the mother as primary carer. In Part III, I consider the implications of SPL together (and apart) for practices once the leave period was over.

Conclusion

As in the previous chapter, on non-sharers' experiences of leave, I have drawn on diaries and interviews with sharing couples to explore the everyday practices and experiences of men and women during leave. Mothers' experiences of leave all occurred in the immediate aftermath of the birth and were focused on establishing sleep and feeding babies. Just like non-sharing women, sharing women described their maternity leave alone as very difficult, as they got to grips with caring for their newborn. Likewise, the standard two weeks of paternity leave was considered too short to provide sufficient support for new mothers; Helen, for example, described the end of the paternity leave period as 'traumatic'. In contrast, couples in which fathers took four or more weeks of leave at the time of the birth (using paternity leave and SPL) gave very different accounts of this time. The presence of the father helped mothers to establish their preferred method of feeding and gave them a sense of parenting as a 'shared endeavour', which was a priority for sharing parents. But leave together, even when extended, was not seen to destabilise gendered parenting norms. The emphasis was on supporting women as primary carers. Thus, couples who only or mostly took leave at the same time continued to position the mother as the primary parent carrying the bulk of caring responsibilities. Similar findings are reported by K. Wall and O'Brien (2017), who note that paternity leave is often understood by fathers as a time to support mothers, but that a shift to more gender-equal parenting responsibilities is more likely when fathers take leave alone.

Although fathers took leave alone after the baby had been weaned (at around 9 months), and when sleep routines were generally established, they still reported a sense of learning to care while on leave. Mothers and fathers told me that fathers developed confidence in their ability to parent during this period, learning to parent 'in their own way'. Fathers also described building a sense of intimacy with and knowledge of their children while on leave which had not been present before. In such a way, fathers on leave alone were able to foster a sense of themselves as primary carers, even if only for a short time, thus counteracting popular discourses about the primacy of the mother for young babies, and destabilising gendered parenting norms.

Part III
After the leave is over

The final diary entries were made and the (individual) interviews took place once the maternity/SPL leave period was over, between 13 and 18 months after the birth of participants' children. These data give an early insight into how parents organised family and work life once they returned to employment (if they did return to employment). They demonstrate how their leave trajectories influenced their division of labour after the end of the leave, and the other factors which came into play.

This part of the book differs from the previous two in that it is not organised by participation in SPL, although I continue to examine how parents' experiences of leave shape their reported practices. Instead, the chapters are divided according to how participants described their divisions of paid and unpaid work. But this is not a 'time-use' study in which the participants account for every minute of their day. My grouping of the parents in these chapters relies on their narratives of their days and the ways in which they speak about the various responsibilities of family life, with a particular focus on financial provisioning, childcare and housework. Using these accounts, I have identified three principal patterns according to which parents divide care, and each of the three chapters in this part considers what led couples to take up these different arrangements and how they felt about them.

In these chapters I also discuss participants' hopes and expectations for their lives when their children will have turned 10, and a further round of data collection is planned (in 2027/8). Drawing on the narratives of the couples about what this future family life will look like, I apply a 'sociology of the future' framework (Cantó-Milà & Seebach, 2015) to analyse their visions. In this way, I consider how these visions of the future are grounded in the experiences they have narrated of the first year of their child's life. I outline their articulated future imagined barriers and constraints to the kinds of lives they hope to lead, which demonstrate their awareness of structural impediments and the differing ways in which they link a sense of agency to their partners and children.

6
Breadwinning fathers and primary care mothers

Katherine: Okay so the other thing that I wanted to talk about was you remember in the first, and the second, interview we did that table and you put stickers about who did what? I didn't bring the table today but um what, how do you think the division of /labour is like in the household and care activities /just like now?

Rita: /Yeah. /Um that is quite, actually quite interesting, because before baby R we were both doing [pause] I guess quite equally. I was doing some bits, Riley was doing other bits, but it was somehow equal. Yeah. But everyone did what they liked more. So then ah with me staying home with baby R I was doing most of it, just because I had the time and I was happy to do that. But then when I went back to work it, it didn't change much. So Riley somehow was still used to me doing everything, but then I didn't actually, I mean it was just becoming all so crazy because there was no time, yeah, because I was back to work. And also […], in addition to, not just the household, it was also the child, which somehow he always assumed that I take care of her. It's, it's always, the normal line is 'Rita takes care of her', you know? He goes ah smoking, has his coffee in the morning, has a cigarette with it, and yeah 'You, you have to take care of her'. But I can almost never do this, you know? I never have time off, which is very annoying […] because I'm, yeah, there is nothing like 'Oh I want my cigarette and

> a coffee' [short laugh] or 'I want to play a game on the computer'. It just doesn't exist.
>
> Rita, Interview 3

When the maternity/SPL period was over, the seven couples discussed in this chapter followed the pattern Rita described, with the father taking primary responsibility for earning and the mother for caring. In all these cases, the women either reduced their paid work hours to part-time or left employment entirely, while their partners continued to work full-time. Rita was clearly unhappy with this situation and narrated their division of leave as formative in the current division of labour. Other participants were more content with this split. In this chapter, I explore the extent to which experiences of parental leave shaped these final practices and their assessments of their work and care divisions as well as their imagined future practices.

Parent practices a year after the baby is born

When I visited these participants for their final interview, they described how the mother was the primary caregiver with overall responsibility for the child and usually for household work as well. The fathers were responsible principally for earning. This pattern was typical amongst couples who had not shared leave; only one sharing couple, Tara and Tim, divided responsibilities in this way (see table 0.1). Diaries and interview extracts show how these parents' everyday lives have become separated into different spheres, in which mothers organise their time around their children, and men theirs around their paid work:

> Got up and dropped baby C at nursery and then when I picked him up later he was really irritable. I was working from home today. It's my last day before Christmas so a lot to get done, a bit stressed! I am guessing he [baby] had a bad day too, although they said he had been fine for them! So I put him to bed early but we did have a lovely moment just before when we sat and cuddle[d] on the armchair – he chewed on his cracker and then hugged me, then chewed again and then another hug. He makes me so happy even when he is being grumpy!
>
> Cara, Diary 4 (baby 13 months old)

So, yeah, usually, you know, get up at around seven. Um, baby C would probably be waking up at around the same time so I'd go and have a shower and usually what Cara does is she picks him up and she brings him like to the shower door, so like we've got these see-through ones and I like greet him from there, and she takes him to have breakfast, so I probably like have a shower, get dressed and everything, and then I'd come in and spend like maybe two or three minutes with him, just sort of playing around rather than anything, just you know, making noise or … tickling him or something. And I then leave, um, then, go to work and I'd come back home at around, I'd probably be in the house at around maybe six-thirty roughly on average, and baby C would usually be awake for like about half an hour, until he goes to bed, and we'd usually put him to bed together, read him a story, and … Yeah, put him to bed. But often I have to work late too though, so then I wouldn't see him sometimes in the evening at all.

Chidi, Interview 3

Um I, I wake up at six thirty or six forty-five, um I have my morning rituals, you know, the coffees, the showers, the, the teeth, dressing, ironing, if I don't have a shirt ready. Then at about eight to eight fifteen I leave the house, I come to work on my motorbike, I end up in meetings doing a bit of office work and, you know, meetings, depends on the day. Now I, at the previous firm, so I ended that engagement in March, um I would, I would do a nine to five-thirty strictly. In part that was because of, of baby R, but also because I had lost the will to progress in that firm and I just didn't care about the overtime anymore, you know? And now the office hours here are different. The office hours here are from nine to six, so I lose half an hour, and because it's a new environment, and because you want to make, you know, a good impression, and there's a lot to learn as well, and there's a lot to, to get through, so it naturally takes you a little bit longer, I tend to be working until, you know, seven, eight, and then another forty-five minutes to get home. So I get home sort of for eight to nine o'clock, by which time baby R is either just about ready for bed or already in bed. […] And then after baby R goes to, obviously Rita goes to bed with baby R, so that's somewhere between eight thirty and nine, she either stays in bed with baby R and falls asleep and I end up doing, you know, relaxed stuff in the, in the living room, either, or, you know, catching up on, on emails, sometimes doing a bit of work or doing, you know, a video game or watching a film or whatever.

Riley, Interview 3

Katherine: Okay. And can you describe a typical day for me, if you have one?

Vicki: These days have been okay. Baby V is awake at like seven, six thirty, six sometimes. It's six to seven. And we [short laugh] come down to have lunch, ah breakfast, I make his breakfast and he starts playing with the toys. I try, he starts playing with the toys, he makes a mess, all the, all the toys on the floor, and I start doing the, if I had the time to, to go to have a shower while he's playing with the mess. I leave him playing with the mess. And I just change, change my clothes and everything, and I start to do some, something for lunch, and when I am planning to go to a, a baby group in the morning, just nine, nine thirty, just we leave something done for food and we go away, we go out for the baby group. And we come back for lunch and after that we just, I sit here having lunch with baby V and I start cleaning something. Baby V has a nap during that ah after lunch [...] when he's having the nap sometimes I, I feel tired and I sleep with him [short laugh], or sometimes I, I just go down and clear or something, check the, collect the toys or something like that, and the time flies, and now it's dark, four thirty-five, and we start to do something for dinner. Baby V is awake like four, and we start doing something for dinner. We go to, to Tesco sometimes just to go away, to go out in the evening, and we come back like six, and he starts eating his dinner. And at seven when um start the, at six thirty I put the CBeebies to start *The Night Garden* and at seven he knows he's going to sleep, and we go into his room to put him to sleep, and at seven-thirty he's gone to sleep and I come back and start taking the toys and put [on] the washing machine, I put the, the, for these, the dishwasher, and checking what I am going to do for next day. If I have to buy something for food or what-. [...] And I, I, I start, the moment that is for me. I may have a herbal tea and I sit here and I start checking my phone [both short laugh], I start checking my mails at that time, when I don't feel so tired I check my emails. I call my mum sometimes at that time. It's the moment that I have to, to have a look for something that I need on the internet, or something like that. I don't have time now to check in my Facebook, and I feel tired ten thirty, I go to sleep. And that's it.

Vicki, Interview 3

These diary and interview extracts demonstrate how such divisions operated on a day-to-day basis. As we can see, the mothers were mostly with the children. Cara, for example, barely mentioned her husband in her diaries between Monday and Friday, while Chidi's everyday life was clearly dominated by paid work. Likewise, Riley's life seems to have scarcely changed since before he was a father. Riley was perhaps the most 'extreme' amongst the men in that he devoted himself entirely to paid work from Monday to Friday. As recounted in chapter 2, Riley argued before the baby was born that one of them would have to focus on their career and that, since Rita would take a career hit from maternity leave anyway, it should be him.

All the fathers in this group except Tim had either been promoted or had sought a better employment after the birth of their child. This change of work prompted longer working hours than before the birth of their child, as they attempted to establish themselves in their new workplaces and sometimes juggled with longer commutes, as detailed by Riley. The men presented themselves as solely or mainly responsible for earning. There is a notable shift between the first set of interviews and the final set. Although in the first interviews many of these fathers accounted for their not taking SPL by reference to their higher salary or the feared impact on their careers if they did take it, the decision was expressed in terms of what made practical sense within the couple. In these final interviews they articulated a *moral responsibility* for providing for the family and an increased awareness of their role as providers for their children and sometimes for their partners. For example, Peter told me how fatherhood had affected his attitude to work:

I've um I think I'm finding I'm, I'm getting more of an appetite to to try and accelerate my career, but it's, you know, it's not a personal ambition, it's um, it's you know, it's a, it's an ambition that I have for, for us as a family to be able to, you know, be able to support the children if they have hobbies that [short laugh], you know, require, you know, money and, and, and stuff like that, you know? You know, I want them to ha-, be able to have experiences and opportunities and, you know, we're kind of very hand-to-mouth at the moment.

Peter, Interview 3

Peter here positioned his earning as being for the family and the children. He is somewhat hesitant here, reflecting perhaps his previously expressed ambivalence about the 'traditional' division of labour between himself and Pippa. Nonetheless, like other fathers in this pattern, he clearly saw himself as the *breadwinner* of the family. As Schmidt (2018) has recognised, the attention given to what 'breadwinning' means for parents has been limited. Drawing on research with fathers and mothers in Austria, she argues that parents' earning does not necessarily equate to 'breadwinning', which entails a particular responsibility for family provisioning usually associated with fathers. She found that men consistently reported themselves as responsible for family finances, while few women shared this responsibility with their partners (and no women felt themselves to be primarily responsible in the way men did). Schmidt argues that while breadwinning is often distinguished from care work, it may be conceptualised as 'care' if it is undertaken with a 'caring disposition' (p. 456). Peter's approach to earning, which suggests that he regards his job primarily as a means to support his family, may be conceived in this sense. On the other hand, earning may be used in leveraging power in the relationship or as a means to avoid other forms of unpaid labour. This seemed to be the case with Riley and Chidi, who enjoyed significant gains in their work lives over the period of the study but, on the flip side, whose partners were left feeling unsupported in their own paid work and care labour at home (discussed further below). The breadwinning–caring split may, then, be experienced differently by different couples: some, such as Peter and Pippa, narrated the two as equal contributions to the household.

None of the women discussed in this chapter expressed a moral responsibility for breadwinning, and all reduced their paid work hours after the leave period: Pippa, Cara and Rita were working part-time, and Judy, Tara and Vicki left paid work entirely. Such reductions in women's paid work increased the pressures on men's earnings, a responsibility some fathers assumed reluctantly (see also Schmidt, 2018). John in particular expressed the stresses he experienced from becoming the sole earner in the family:

John: Obviously you know, there's the, I'm, I'm always, I'm a little concerned about, I am concerned a little bit about money. It's just me [laughs] it's just like=

Katherine: =How do you mean, how do you mean it's just you?

John: Well she's, Judy's not working, I don't think there's much of a plan for her to go back to work really. Erm … So yeah, it's, it's all landed on me but I'm lucky that I'm in a fairly well paid job, but again still, you still feel a bit poor every now and again, which seems ridiculous [laughs] when it's all like you, you know, you earn, what, probably earning three times what my mum and dad ever did, and you know, you still feel like 'Oh, better, you know, better not buy that just in case', and [laughs]. It's like oh, 'Need a new car'. [scared voice] 'Okay, I don't know where that's going to come from really?' [laughs] where it's like yes, we can afford it but then we probably won't be able to afford anything else for a while …

John, Interview 3

While the feelings associated with care work, in particular the mental load (Dean et al., 2022), are often discussed in the literature, less attention is paid to how parents experience the responsibility for financial provisioning emotionally. In this group of fathers, John experienced money pressures particularly acutely, despite earning what he calls a 'good salary'. He also said, 'I don't think there's much of a plan for her [Judy] to go back to work', suggesting a certain ambivalence towards and perhaps a lack of agency in their arrangement. For a mother to leave paid work entirely is increasingly unusual in two-parent households in the UK (Connolly et al., 2016), as few families are able to sustain themselves financially on only one income. That some mothers give up paid work despite the ensuing financial penalty speaks to the powerful discourses of the importance of a stay-at-home mother in the UK, especially when children are young, as well as to the perceived attractions of such a role relative to being a mother in paid work (Orgad, 2019).

When men are positioned as responsible for earning, women are positioned as responsible for children, not just in that they take on the everyday care tasks, but in that they make the chief decisions for the children and organise their lives. Women reported organising social activities, finding and choosing the nursery or other childcare, reading books on childcare, and leading decisions about the care of the children.

Women and men also explicitly designated women as the 'primary carers'. For instance, Peter discussed how he followed Pippa's lead around decisions on childcare:

> So, you know, I, I, you know, Pippa has kind of driven a lot of that um and, and I've, you know [13 seconds], and I've um ah, you know, s-, gone a-, gone along with it um because, you know, there's, there's no reason to, to do otherwise. So we haven't argued over, you know, 'Should we be doing this with the boys or that with the boys?' which again is, you know, just a, you know, another way that I think we've avoided kind of unnecessary stress. So so yeah so I think it's, it's been a fantastic time, I can't imagine life without having them. And, you know, they're, we just have so much fun together. Um so it's been, it's been brilliant.
>
> Peter, Interview 3

And in the following extract Cara talks about her feelings of accomplishment in having reached the first birthday of her son:

> I felt, on his actual birthday I felt like it was a big achievement for me to have got to that year mark. Like he's not going to remember it but I said to Chidi, I was like 'I want to make it, a big deal of it for my sake' [laughs] because it's been, it is like a big achievement to get to the year mark and still be in one piece I think.
>
> Cara, Interview 3

Note the first-person singular pronouns that Cara used as she emphasised that it was her achievement to have made it 'in one piece' to one year after the birth. Moreover, she and Chidi situated his participation in childcare, and especially in housework, as 'help'. Chidi said, for example, 'And like I said I try to help where I can, but I could probably do more, and maybe I should do more, but yeah, that's the balance at the moment.' Despite the vague assertion that he should 'probably' do more, he did not. Cara's diaries indicated that she was at times unhappy with the division of labour between them, particularly when it came to housework, but there seemed little suggestion that things might change anytime soon.

How did this situation arise amongst these couples, and with what implications? One very strong and compelling factor was the sociocultural narratives about childcare, and another was the high formal childcare costs in the UK. As was discussed in chapter 2, discourses about appropriate parenting in the UK, arguably particularly amongst middle-class parents (Lee et al., 2023; Orgad, 2019), stipulate that parents (especially mothers) are the best care providers for their own children, with other relatives second best and formal childcare last. Vicki and Judy clearly held these beliefs, telling me in their first interview that it was important for children's well-being to have a stay-at-home mother, while Pippa expressed ideals of intensive mothering, such as that mothers should devote as much time and energy to their children as possible, maximising their own presence in their children's lives. These views continued throughout and after the leave period. Vicki, for example, had always intended to reduce her hours of paid work after her leave, with her mother-in-law taking care of their baby during the hours she was at her job. When her mother-in-law passed away during the leave period, Vicki decided to leave her job as a sports coach entirely:

> Katherine: And what happened about you, so you were working as a sports coach um when you were /pregnant?
>
> Vicki: /Mmm.
>
> Katherine: Did you go back to that or …?
>
> Vicki: They, when I finished the maternity leave they offered me just like a few hours, like eight hours per week or something like that, and, and was not really, we discussed between me and Victor and it was not really worth it to go there just for a few hours and leave baby V with someone else that I don't know, you know? Really I prefer to stay with him at this age you know? He needs me.
>
> Vicki, Interview 3

Vicki went on to tell me that even when baby V starts school she will only work the hours he is at school, as she feels it is important that he has a full-time mother available.

Other parents were less consistent over the course of the study. Tara, for example, increasingly came to see herself as the primary carer during the maternity leave and as necessary to her daughter's well-being. She told me that at one year of age baby T is 'too young' for nursery and 'maybe' in a year's time they will send her for a few hours a week to a childminder. Tara therefore stopped doing paid work after her partner Tim's SPL, and was intending to return part-time after her daughter started school. Similarly, at the time of the first interview Cara was working full-time. She decided to drop down to three days' paid work a week so that baby C could have 'more days at home with family than days at nursery' (interview 3). She combined nursery care with care given by her sister, who is a stay-at-home mother, so that baby C is only at nursery for two days a week.

Their decisions must also be understood within the context of their relationships. Mothers were expected to be the ones who would reduce or give up paid work, either because they earned less (for example Judy) or because there was an underlying assumption that it would or should be the mother. For example, here Riley discusses why they decided to have his mother move in with them to help with childcare:

> Now we would like my mother to look after her full-time, because we read babies need a sole attachment for the first two years ... So even though we were in nurseries [when we were small], once we have read that and combined with the economics – the cost of nurseries! £2,000 a month, the cheapest is £1,600! It's too expensive. It's mad, we couldn't believe it. Do governments really want women in work? It's nonsense! The support is terrible, and now we have the option of someone who is the best person in the world after us. It's a no-brainer.
>
> Riley, Interview 2

Notice that the lack of government support for nurseries was interpreted as a lack of support for 'women in work'. Rita and Riley never apparently considered Riley working fewer hours even though at the time of the first interview they were earning the same amount and even worked for the same firm in the same job. They had decided that Riley's career would be the focus in their couple relationship. But also at that time, they had both committed to the idea that Rita would not become the primary parent, even if she took all the maternity leave:

> Riley: There shouldn't just be one person doing everything. I think the burden should be shared, absolutely.
>
> Rita: I just hope that it's going to be equal, I mean, yeah, that I'm not going to end up as a housewife and [pause], and that Riley also takes care / of the child.
>
> Riley: Yeah, I / I completely agree with that.

In the final interview, however, it is clear that the pattern they had hoped for has not emerged, as Rita explained in the opening quote to this chapter. Rita's situation was difficult since she was working four days a week in a demanding career, while also taking full responsibility for childcare and housework. She told me that it would not be possible for Riley to work part-time, echoing the reasons for his inability to take SPL, and saying, 'I guess for a man it's even harder, well because for a woman, okay the woman, they have to take care of the child'. She thus both challenged and reinforced essentialised gendered ideas around work and care. She told me that she wondered whether it would be better for her to give up paid work entirely, given the difficulties of juggling everything and the high costs of nursery (in the end her mother-in-law could not regularly care for their daughter).

Thus, Rita and Cara expressed frustration about their situations, and both reported some tensions in their relationships related to housework and childcare. Their leave patterns, both having taken all of the maternity leave, have shaped the current divisions of responsibilities between them and their partners. Likewise, Linda had hoped to return to paid work after the birth of her child but was effectively fired during her maternity leave period. She struggled with taking the responsibility for all the housework and care work and became very upset in her final interview (which her husband Larry did not participate in). However, her salary as a care assistant would not cover childcare costs, and Larry was earning more than she could. Their financial situation is strained, and they live in a cramped and shared apartment. She told me in her final interview, 'I feel like I'm giving him like more duties than he is doing by himself, you know?' What Linda, Rita and Cara have in common is that they had not anticipated having to take on the primary care role, or that their partners would be largely absent from care and domestic work and have little appreciation of what it involves (see above, where Chidi admitted that he probably should do more, but ... didn't). This has already created some grievances with potential knock-on effects on the intimate couple relationship.

John and Judy present a different case. As was clear in the first interview, they had always planned that Judy would give up paid work at the end of her maternity leave, expressing a strong conviction that a stay-at-home mother was necessary to a child's well-being. Moreover, John had historically taken most of the responsibility for housework, as Judy has a mobility issue which makes some household tasks more difficult for her. His diaries indicate that he continued to take the responsibility for various household tasks in a bid to ensure that Judy had more time to care for the baby and for herself. This relationship work (Gabb & Fink, 2015) is practical in nature and bolsters Judy's mothering role. But despite the planned nature of their role specialisation and John's participation in housework, they expressed tensions over the year in their diaries (see chapter 4) and final interviews:

> To me, that's what, babies do the things that they're doing, you know, and ours is massively better than any other, and, you know, I'm working as hard as I can so you [Judy] have that opportunity not to have to work, and can enjoy, and I think, you know, I think in the long term, you know, it's, it's a good thing to do, 'cause you get a much stronger bond, you get, you know, all this opportunity to, you know, really just enjoy her in the fun years. I don't get that. Erm, would I like to? You know, I'd like it to be the other way around, I'd happily give up work. But unfortunately practically can't.
>
> John, Interview 3

> So I kind of took that loneliness out on John because it seemed to me like he was going out and having all the fun and I was stuck at home with a baby who didn't really communicate. Um but saying that, you know, he was working all hours of the day, you know, providing for us and he should be allowed kind of out at night as well as I should be allowed out at night.
>
> Judy, Interview 3

As is clear from these extracts, both John and Judy presented themselves as having had the more difficult position in the family. There is a sense of resentment, perhaps compounded by both feeling that they have sacrificed for the other, without mutual appreciation. In order to improve his earnings, John took a new job which involved a longer commute. This change of job, a long commute, and his ongoing involvement in domestic work in their home, he recounts, severely limited his ability to socialise with others or participate in leisure. His final interview demonstrates the high levels of stress he was experiencing, as in this (shortened) extract of a long stream-of-consciousness narration:

> The only time I've really had for anything like healthy is like five o'clock in the morning but that's like counterproductive 'cause then you get less sleep, which is also a thing you need to be healthy, so it's like oh, what can, what can I do, I can't go any later 'cause then I won't get into work, which is weird, feels strange, and then won't be able to help out with her in the morning routine. I can't go, I can't, you know, I can't go after work 'cause then I miss the night-time routine, and it's like okay, so what do you do, it's like well, you know, I'll I'll put myself under the hammer and … okay, right, what can I chop? Mm, dunno, lunch, that'll be, I'll chop lunch [laughs], yeah, then you get a bit, you lose the energy 'cause you haven't had enough food or something,

and then when you haven't had enough food you just crash when you get home, and crashing when you get home isn't great, so that's not, not what you're meant to do or not what I want to do, let's say ... But then yeah, just totally got to get that stuff done and then it's like ah, nice. You know, just, just feels like, um, spinning a lot of plates, and they're all kind of, you know, wobbly. They're up, but they're a bit wobbly. But you know, when that's done, that's spinning, I can forget about it. When we've done, yeah, when we've fixed the work thing, which is ... fixable up to a point ...But it's very much a rollercoaster, work's always a rollercoaster, right? When that's balanced, um, that's fixable and that's gone. [...] But then it's like everything in between just feels a bit funny because, yeah, people, Judy's struggling and you're like oh, want to help out but, I can't when I'm at work or only so much, I'm at work.

John, Interview 3

The mode of speaking, including the multiple asides and quips, is telling of the stress that John was experiencing. His worries about his health were compounded by the fact that both his parents died young (before they reached retirement age). He describes the multiple spinning plates in his life as 'wobbly' and says that he was neither earning sufficiently for their family nor sufficiently supporting Judy. He speaks to an 'imagined other' (Burkitt, 2012) in this piece, of what he is 'meant to do' as a father and partner but clearly feels unable to do. The example of John demonstrates that shifting ideals of fatherhood clash with more traditional models of family in a context of 'greedy work' (Gatrell & Cooper, 2016; Ranson, 2012). He must be ever-present in his job, but also present for his wife and son. The difficulties experienced are compounded by Judy's switch to a full-time carer role and the increasing division between their daily lives. Such divided lives can drive couples apart and affect their relationship satisfaction (Fox, 2009).

In contrast, Vicki, Pippa and Tara expressed satisfaction and overall contentedness with their situation, as did their partners. In part this satisfaction reflects the expectations that had been in place since before the birth of their children: unlike Cara, Linda and Rita, these women had actively chosen to take on the bulk of the caring responsibilities. But it also reflects a concordance in the 'economy of gratitude' (Hochschild, 2003) in their relationships, in contrast to that of Judy and John. A mismatch in understandings of gratitude within couples can lead to relationship strains, as a mutual sense of giving and receiving is integral to love (Hochschild, 2003:105). This concept of gifting is shaped both by the couple's relationship and by broader societal influences, including comparisons with other couples and with their own parents. John and Judy expressed clashing understandings of gifts, arguably provoked by broader shifts in fatherhood ideals. Judy wanted to mother their daughter intensively full-time, but struggled with the demands this entailed, and envisioned 'involved fathering' from John, who felt under pressure to provide financially. In contrast, Vicki, Pippa and Tara told of a shared sense of gratitude with their partners, each feeling they were contributing equally to the family, albeit in different ways, as demonstrated in an extract from Peter's final interview:

> I think during, certainly more latterly I think I've, you know, changed job and, and I'm just a bit busier and, and stuff, and Pippa's kind of, I think, been more on the front foot in terms of getting out of bed first to try and let me sleep, which I've hugely appreciated, ah particularly on, you know, on the days that, that she hasn't worked. And I'm fully aware that having, you know, done my fair share of, or done some days of, you know, solo childcare, that, you know, the idea that me going to work is, you know, tougher than staying at home just isn't true at all.
>
> Peter, Interview 3

When I pushed him about the possibility of his taking a greater role with the twins, he admitted that it was not his priority. It suited him and Pippa well to have this role specialisation:

> I definitely, you know, would like to be more involved and, you know, to be fair there are choices that I could make or sacrifices that we could make as a couple in order to facilitate that, but I guess it's, what that means is it's not my number one priority I guess, you know, being perfectly honest. So, so it would be like nice to have but I'm not losing sleep over it because it's not the most important thing to me right now.
>
> Peter, Interview 3

Pippa and Peter recognised that in some respects their division of care responsibilities (Pippa for all the house- and childcare and Peter for financial providing) might be considered 'old-fashioned' (Peter, interview 2), but in interview 3 they both expressed satisfaction with how it worked. Peter's recognition of and gratitude for Pippa's role in parenting is key here, and, in turn, Pippa repeatedly in interviews expressed her gratitude for Peter's role in providing for the family financially. These couples had expressed a preference for equality as 'fairness' (see chapter 2) and their described practices fit into this pattern.

Tim and Tara are the only couple within this pattern who shared leave. Key again to the mutual satisfaction with this arrangement is their joint commitment to parenthood and their gratitude for one another's participation in different facets of caring for the family and household. In her final interview, for example, Tara reflected on how she and Tim divided household and care work:

> I think they're probably divided about as equally as they can be when one person is, like I'm working at home with baby T all day and Tim is working in the office all day. We're both working, but um I suppose I care more about certain things. Like I want, I wanted to hoover this carpet before you arrived actually. Tim would never have noticed it, like ever. So I suppose I care more about certain things like that and he is probably better at like keeping up with family birthdays and whatnot. Um, how has it changed? I'm not sure that it has really changed. I mean I'm still doing most of the cooking, but I don't mind that. But he's doing, like he cleans up the kitchen every morning before he goes. Um yeah it's probably, I'm probably doing more but it's kind of broadly fairly equal.
>
> Tara, Interview 3

Tara went on to say that she felt their shared engagement with their child had brought them closer as a couple:

> But, you know, we've also, eh, become closer because we're, you know, we have this shared bond now of, of loving baby T and being her parents and, you know? He's, he's, he's the only other person who's going to really want to look at five hundred photos of her with me and like discuss how exciting it is when she can like [short laugh] crawl along the coffee table. So, you know, that's a big bond, and hopefully the other stuff will kind of come back into play when we're, you know, a bit less like tired.

Tim's experience of SPL also seems to have been key in shaping his attitude to parenthood and paid work. Thus, while he was the only earner in their family, they both reported that he engaged in housework and parenting as much as possible given the differences in their available time:

> Katherine: Mmhmm. Has your, have your work hours shifted since you've become a parent?
>
> Tim: I try and make as ah, try and leave as close to, to, to five or, or even before if I can and, and try and make staying late the exception, whereas I think there was, it was easier to, 'Oh well I'll just stay and get this done because it will make my life tomorrow easier' before. […] We've also moved to a new office where it's, it's very hot-desking and you kind of don't really know where, where people are at any time of the day, so it's, it's easy to just ah, to slip out if there's nothing sort of super-compelling keeping you there.
>
> Tim, Interview 3

In interview 2, when baby T was 6 months old, Tim was still working long hours, well past 5 pm. Therefore, it seems that the office move to hot-desking which allowed him more personal flexibility (and invisibility) was important. He also expressed a shift in priorities sparked by his leave alone and the positive response from his colleagues, despite his initial worries (see chapter 3). He told me, 'I even got some messages um from senior people saying sort of "good on you" and "that's a, sort of, a good thing to, to do"' (interview 3). This shows the importance of a supportive relational network at work in disrupting gendered work norms. His sense of what it means to be a father is enabled and shaped by these interactions.

Tara and Tim's account suggests that SPL can shape the experience of parental role specialisation, reducing the difference that difference makes (Doucet, 2017). That is, despite the normative roles which they largely occupy (Tim as breadwinner and Tara as primary carer), these roles were not defining of their relationship with one another nor fixed for the future.

Future imaginings of work and family

Participants' visions of the future were largely differentiated according to gender, in similar ways to their current practices. First, men and women predicted little change in men's paid work lives. Men expected (and were expected) to continue within the same career and with the same full-time hours, with changes in seniority or employer the only potential variations mentioned:

I would hope to be more progressed in my career, so I imagine [that in] ten years' time I'd hope I'd be a lot more senior. Um, um so … I think we'd probably be living, you know, in our own house, probably a house not a flat.

Chidi, Interview 3

Katherine: So what do you think your lives will look like in nine years?

Peter: Um,what do I think it will look like? God [4 seconds], well I, I hope it would it would look and feel pretty much the same, in terms of work and home, just with, that's a terrible thing to say isn't it? [sighs] Well I, I would hope that we're all still happy and healthy, that would be kind of my number one. I hope that we would feel less, less pressured in certain ways, in, in, in terms of disposable income, in terms of time. I don't expect that will be that different ah in ten years' time. Um but, you know, it's a nice, it's a nice thought. Um [4 seconds]

Katherine: Will you be in the same job?

Peter: Will I be in the same job? Perhaps not in the same job, but something like it, yeah.

Katherine: Mmhmm=.

Peter: =I think so. I don't, I don't see a route out, you know, unless we upped sticks and left London and, you know, tried to live a, a simpler life. But um I don't, I don't, you know, we're, we're on a, a bit of a treadmill for as long as we want to stay in, in this house really, and so there needs to be an income to, to be able to, to pay, pay the mortgage, and I don't see how else that happens.

Peter, Interview 3

Katherine: What will your life look like in ten years' time do you think?

Victor: Pretty similar, I think. I will be working in the same area certainly. I love what I do so I'm really happy with what I do and the fact that what I want to do, I have to work these sort of hours, sort of, I'm okay with that.

Victor, Interview 3

In general, men discussed their future careers more than women did, and more than they discussed other aspects of their future lives. Moreover, as hinted in these accounts, the financial situation of their families was framed as reliant on the men and was expected to continue to be so in the future. For instance, Chidi said he expected to be more senior, 'so' they will have moved into a house rather than a flat by then. Peter, on the other hand, who was less enthusiastic about his career than other participants, said he was on a 'mortgage' treadmill which tied him to his job. These men communicated a sense of inevitability, even when they also expressed relative contentment with their situations.

In each interview, I additionally prompted the participants to discuss what their *preferred* family and work lives might look like. Most of the men said they would, in an ideal world, like to work part-time, but this scenario was written off as unimaginable and impossible, either because of their primary earner status within their families or, relatedly, because their employers did not or could not facilitate part-time work as an affordable career move, as expressed here by Riley.

> Katherine: Would it be possible for you to go part-time?
>
> Riley: No. I wouldn't choose to, I wouldn't choose to. I would, I would, I would love to do that, but there would have to be a general societal consensus for that sort of thing. I wouldn't, I wouldn't sacrifice my family's well-being for a, for going part-time.
>
> Riley, Interview 3

There is a sense of unfairness and resignation in his response. Riley went on to echo his original reasoning for his decision not to take any SPL: that one parent must focus on their career without any breaks to ensure the maximum financial benefit for the family. Since Rita took maternity leave, she became the person to take the career losses, which now is invoked to justify the long-term specialisation of roles between Riley and Rita. But women's take-up of all of the maternity leave was also narrated as inevitable, a 'forced choice' that cannot be deviated from. The available sociocultural narrative for this couple, solidified by work structures and negligible government support for childcare, is for women to take the bulk of the responsibility for children, first by taking all of the maternity leave and later by stepping back from their careers. The decision is preordained but also has consequences which further embed the gendered differences that Riley views and practises. The metaphor of the treadmill loomed large. Once you get on, no deviation is seen as possible. All roads lead to the same destination of role specialisation, from which it makes no (financial) sense to come off.

John was the only man in this group to say that, ideally, he would become a full-time parent, with Judy taking care of the financial provisioning. However, he identified many barriers to any changes in how they live their lives, chiefly that his earning prospects were higher than Judy's. His aim was to pay off their mortgage as soon as possible in order to ease the pressure to earn he felt himself to be under, and thus to become able at least to spend fewer hours in paid work (not part-time hours, just more 'reasonable' hours). Given his anxieties about money, he told me that he hoped that Judy would be back in paid work in 10 years' time, indicating a lack of agency over whether she does paid work or not, or perhaps a sense that it is not his place to interfere in her desire to be with their child.

In general, women's future in paid work was discussed in more uncertain terms than men's. Cara, for example, told me, 'I would probably still want to work, 'cause I do enjoy working', indicating a question mark over her future in paid work which was not seen in talk about men's work. This included whether women may continue in paid work as well as the hours they might work:

> I'll probably want to be part-time because if baby J is nine then we'll have a younger one who might be seven or whatever um and I think having ah a nine- and a seven-year-old walking home and walking to school alone is ridiculous, so I'd want to be there to, for the drop-offs and pick-ups.
>
> Judy, Interview 3

> So I do see Tara working at that point, although I, I, I don't know, ah she last had a, an office job five years ago and I think was, was happy to, to give it up. So I don't know whether um it would necessarily be something where she'd be working nine to five … Maybe more flexible or part-time hours? Um I do see myself working full-time.
>
> Tim, Interview 3

> I don't think Cara will be working at that time, in ten years' time, I imagine she'll be a, a full-time mum, but I'd probably put a probability of maybe, maybe seventy-five per cent chance, I think if the right career came, came along I think she would, she would

work full-time, if the right job came along. But, um, I think she would prefer to be a stay-at-home mum.

Chidi, Interview 3

I wanted to have [baby C] with me for more days than he was away from me, that's why I went back for three days and have him for four. But in the future I might feel different about that and I might go back to full-time earlier on, just because ... I think that would ... I'd probably get a lot of satisfaction from being able to do my job properly rather than, um, only being able to do half of it half of the time. So yeah, that was just my thinking, in ten years' time I imagine I'll be back full-time.

Cara, Interview 3

These extracts all indicate that women's careers are narratively linked to children's needs and school hours, and, although this was not discussed much, presumably also dependent on financial needs. Largely, participants' predictions of the future were in line with those of their partners, except in the case of Chidi and Cara: Chidi anticipated Cara leaving paid work and Cara predicted returning to work full-time. The repetition of 'might' indicates the uncertainty around her future paid work hours. Cara, like other mothers, told me about her children and how she has prioritised spending time with them while considering the future. In this way, she placed decisions about paid work in the context of her moral commitment to her children. These women already anticipated the challenges of balancing the time spent with their children with the time spent in their paid work, in a context in which their partners work long hours and are expected to continue to do so. Their current practices appear to rule out a future possibility of more shared paid and unpaid work responsibilities within the couples.

Conclusion

The couples in this chapter split earning and unpaid care responsibilities by gender, with men taking the role of breadwinner and women that of primary carer. Amongst all of these couples, the men worked full-time and anticipated doing so for the foreseeable future, while all the women worked part-time or had left paid work entirely. The finances of the family depended on the men's salaries, and the women's future engagement in paid work was portrayed as optional and contingent on the needs of the children and, to a certain extent, on the desires of the mother.

In line with the findings from Bonnie Fox's (2009) study of couples at the transition to parenthood in Canada, the separate lives which such role specialisation provokes can be difficult for couples to deal with. The diaries of women who worked part-time demonstrate the multiple and stressful demands of combining paid and unpaid work. They reported very full and long days dropping off and picking up children from childcare, completing housework and caring for young children. They lamented their inability to do their paid work 'properly' on a part-time contract, while appreciating the time they were spending with their young children. The high cost of childcare in the UK, along with discourses of its limited suitability for young children (in that a parent or other family member is often cited as 'best' for children's care), meant that parents were often trying to reduce the hours their children spent in formal childcare by working flexible hours or relying on family members. Full-time mothers (Tara and Judy) described difficulties in spending long hours at home without adult company. Meanwhile, their partners were working long hours to make up for their reduced paid work hours.

Empathy and appreciation from a partner for the work they were doing were key in how couples dealt with these challenges emotionally. Tara, for example, told me that she was satisfied that although she and Tim have a 'traditional' set-up, they were as fair as they could be, contributing to the family equally in their own ways. This view appeared to be strongly influenced by Tim's experiences of leave alone (he is the only father in this chapter that had taken SPL) and his recognition of the difficulties inherent in providing full-time care. Tim had reduced his work hours after SPL, apparently having had a reorientation towards paid and unpaid work after his leave. Their example shows the benefits of sharing leave even for couples who on the face of it practise traditional divisions of labour.

These gendered divisions of labour were set in motion at the time of the pregnancy (and sometimes even before that): the decision that the woman would take all the maternity leave consolidated preconceived ideas about the primacy of the mother for young children (Schmidt, Décieux et al., 2023; G. Wall, 2013). After this break in women's work, couples came to see women's careers as less critical for family finances, or perhaps just less important overall. Men on the other hand reported attributing new meanings to their earning, seeing it as being 'for the family' and therefore putting more effort into their paid work. They reported progressing in their careers during the maternity leave period and their expectations of progression in the next 10 years. In fact, all of the men, except Tim, were promoted, or changed to a more senior post with another employer, during the study period, while none of the women progressed at all in their careers and most of them reported that their maternity leave and subsequent part-time work had had a negative impact on their career progression. Their plans for the future were built on these foundations, with men's careers prioritised and women's paid work viewed as contingent on broader family needs.

7
Mothers as family managers

> I just feel like a sort of efficient worker in a, in a factory that's been nicely set up, if that makes sense? [...] She [Sarah] takes the lead on things like buying him [the baby] clothes, making sure we've got food for him, um [...] sort of more kind of managerial type stuff I suppose.
> Sam, Interview 3

In this second pattern, the distribution of practical aspects of paid and unpaid work within couples was largely even, but the mothers held the position of household or family manager, taking on the bulk of the 'thinking tasks' associated with this work. In recent years much academic and popular attention has been given to the 'mental load' or 'cognitive labour' and its gendered distribution (e.g. Daminger, 2019; Dean et al., 2022; Hogenboom, 2021; Twamley, Faircloth & Iqbal, 2023). This research shows that even in families with primary care fathers, mothers tend to retain the family management role (Brooks & Hodkinson, 2020; Doucet, 2006; Ranson, 2013), co-ordinating and leading decisions on the care of the child and housework. Participants were highly attuned to the concept of the 'mental load' and the potential for its uneven distribution. Helen, for example, sent me a link to a popular comic strip on the gendered nature of the mental load after our final interview together.[1] In their first interviews, many women participants had talked about this as a key concern of theirs, especially those that were keen to share leave (see chapter 3). In this chapter, I describe how this pattern works, the ways it emerged from leave experiences, and how such practices were already shaping the ways in which these participants envisaged their future work and family lives.

Parent practices a year after the baby is born

The diaries and interview transcripts from the parents in this group demonstrate the ways in which they managed different forms of labour. Everyday tasks were apparently divided equally, with participants describing a system of 'tag teaming' – for example one prepares the breakfast while the other dresses the baby – or 'turn taking' on a day-by-day basis as they manage their paid work and their household and childcare labour:

> Katherine: Okay. And can you describe a typical work day to me now?
>
> Henry: Erm, so then I will usually have him from sort of seven till like seven-forty-five in the morning, um, assuming that it's a regular day, and usually I'll just be kind of like, he's not that hungry first thing in the morning, so I used to try and feed him, now neither of us really bother unless he seems actively hungry, and that tends to be a slightly later in the day thing. So it's mostly just kind of like him having a bit of a wander round and us keeping him company and that sort of thing, and sometimes I'll try and eat breakfast and he's, he's now much more enthusiastic about any food we're eating than any food that's given to him, so I'll sit him on my knee and like I'll have cereal and I'll give him a tiny bit of cereal and he can't [laughs] he can't chew it or anything but he just swallows it [swallowing noise], just like this granola stuff I'm eating mostly for breakfast at the moment, just like [swallowing noise], and he quite likes the milk and I think that's it.
>
> Anyway, so about seven-forty-five I will hand him over either to Helen or to Helen's mum depending on the day, and then I just get ready for work, so from seven-forty-five until about eight-fifteen which is when I need to leave. Erm, I will then pop down to the train and I'll be in work for depending on transport somewhere between nine and nine-thirty, which is when my working day starts. So usually pretty busy day, client calls going back and forth, and I will get a bit of time for lunch, in theory I get an hour, in practice I usually get about half an hour

if I'm lucky. [...] I will then leave at about 6, sometimes it drags on a little bit longer, but I'm very very rarely later leaving work than 7.

Erm, I get the train back home and I will be back here for usually seven, seven-fifteen. And then food, erm, sometimes I will on a day when I'm working I will bring something back, usually I will be doing cooking at the weekend when I've got time to do food prep cause everyone's far too hungry by that point. Erm, usually then Helen does bath and then I do the getting into bed, and the getting into bed is, erm, getting baby H dressed, changed for bed after bath. Erm, sometimes I'll do his bath, if like Helen is having issues with like hip or things like that, or she's just exhausted, and then yeah, so yeah, getting him into bed, it's been like that was, I think that was pretty much a one bottle and straight down, that's a very new thing, usually that's sort of, sometimes it can be as long as an hour, with the ah, bottle of milk, sh, sh, sh, sh, sh, blah blah blah. Um, which isn't hard work but it's a nuisance and a faff, so I do that and Helen does bath is the, that sort of thing.

Then I'll do either, like sometime around that I'll do any combination of like taking out bins, taking out recycling, taking out cat litter, blah blah blah, erm, things like that, washing up, erm, baby bottles, making up the new bottles with the Gaviscon, which he needs for the reflux, so he's still going on that. Erm, then I get a bit of time for myself and I'll usually go to bed at about ten-ish, give or take. Er, and then like I said, then I have the overnight so that's, that's the normal working day.

Henry, Interview 3

Sarah: Monday morning I always drop baby S at nursery, ah Sam always picks him up. Tuesday I drop him off and pick him up and I do all the bedtime, bath time on Tuesday. Wednesday and Thursday I'm not around so Sam has to do everything. Friday I normally put baby S to bed as well, having picked him up. Sam would drop him in the morning, I would pick him up, and I put him to bed and feed him and all that stuff. And then at the

> weekend we share everything half, half. [...] So we do share things but it's pretty much the same sort of things we do, apart from, I suppose, like I said, those days in the week where it just depends on the day who's doing what.
>
> Katherine: Mmhmm.
>
> Sarah: Um but obviously because I'm away he, in the working week, those five days, he does do more than I do, just because I'm not around. But then there's other things, not to do with baby S, that, like I always do the Sainsbury's [supermarket] online shopping, I always do the laundry, I'm the person who does the paying and liaising with our cleaner and what she's got to do or whatever. I'm the one who tends to liaise with the nursery and pay all the bills and have the correspondence with them. Sam does everything to do with the car and the internet and the phone and, you know, he orders our wine and stuff from the Wine Society because he's interested in that and knows all about it. I tend to buy baby S's clothes and when he grows out of things I put them away in vacuum-seal bags and do it all and put it away in the attic, which Sam doesn't know about, or doesn't get involved with. So, so some of the bigger, maybe like strategic, not strategic, sort of [short laugh] [pause] directional things to do with baby S, like he should go to this nursery, that was my, my thing of 'We shouldn't send him to that first one, we should send him somewhere else'. Or, you know, 'We need to start moving him into this kind of bedding now that he's older' or 'He needs to start eating these kind of foods' I do. And all his food stuff I generally lead on. So whilst maybe he does a bit more day-to-day care like in the week, I think some of the bigger directional things I lead on more than him, if that makes sense.
>
> Sarah, Interview 3

These extended extracts give a flavour of how full the days, nights and weeks of parents were as they were juggling care work and paid work. From these extracts, it would seem on the face of it that the parents were sharing the various forms of work between them, and in many respects they were. The difference between fathers' accounts here and the accounts in chapter 6 is certainly striking.

However, there were hints, and later explicit explanations and further descriptions, that made it clear that the women in these couples were taking on the cognitive labour involved in care and housework. For example, Sarah told me that, although she and Sam split up the days of the week and various other household work in ways which she saw as fair, on the other hand she tended to make the 'strategic' and 'directional' decisions about baby S, such as what nursery he should attend and what kind of food he should eat. Sam agreed with this assessment, saying he felt like a 'factory worker' under Sarah's management (as shown in the opening quote of the chapter). Sarah and Sam appeared broadly content with this set-up, but even Sarah admitted some envy at Sam's ability to 'switch off' at times, while she is 'always on, always thinking about something' (interview 3).

Other women also expressed reservations. Helen told me that such a split is 'one hundred per cent the death of romance' (interview 3), while Winnie lamented having to 'nag' her husband Weston:

> I'm still the one that initiates things by saying 'Weston can you put, you know, a load of laundry on today please', because he, he might be working from home and I know that the laundry basket's bursting, or I might be 'Oh Weston can you go to the shop and pick up a few things?' and I'll write him a shopping list and he will go and do it. [...] I c-, I can't do it all, but because I'm very im- impatient, I have a tendency that if I see something that I want doing I will just do it myself, because that's easier than waiting for Weston to come home from work and then asking him to do it and then having to remind him to do it, and then having to nag him to do it. But Weston's um willing and, you know, to, to, to do more, so I'm taking advantage of that.
>
> Winnie, Interview 3

Winnie said that Weston was 'willing' to do more household and care work, which he spent considerable time discussing in his own individual interview, but she felt that his participation required work from her, to prompt him and oversee the work. Winnie's defining this as 'nagging' indicates her feelings about the set-up. The level of management work required in overseeing Weston's participation was a further persuasion for her to consider just doing it herself.

The general vision expressed by these parents was of shared responsibility for care work and paid work, not the specialisation of roles discussed in chapter 6. Indeed, no parent in this group gave up paid work and only Helen moved to part-time work after the leave period. (However, she was working one day every weekend, meaning that Henry had solo care of their child one day a week.) How is it, then, that the mothers were taking the principal role in managing household and care work?

My analysis of these data suggests that there are two main (and interlinked) factors which shape this division. On the one hand, parents in this group tended either to have shared leave or to now be settled into a pattern of work which meant that the fathers were spending at least a day a week at home alone with the children. The sharing of leave indicated prior engagement with ideas about gender equality and its importance for couple intimacy (see chapter 3). Fathers' experiences of giving care alone during or after the leave helped to shift the sharing of everyday house- and care work from ideal to practice, which led to the kind of 'tag teaming' described above. But enduring gendered cultural norms related to work and care stymied a more transformational change in the *moral responsibilities* of motherhood and fatherhood (Doucet, 2015). As I will show in the following stories, even when parents desire or 'are willing' (like Weston) to have a more equal division of responsibilities, societal structures work against them.

Let's return to the case of Sarah and Sam. Sarah took all of her maternity leave, telling me that she had always expected to do so and moreover felt 'deserving' of this leave after pregnancy and birth. Like other mothers, during maternity leave she took on the bulk of care and housework, becoming an 'expert' in her baby's care needs and establishing sleep and feeding routines. While she and Sam had previously taken a very degendered approached to their understanding of equality (telling me that gender per se did not figure in their structuring of their lives with one another), during her maternity leave Sarah noted that their lives had become divergent in ways they had not expected. Not only were they doing different things on an everyday basis (Sam mostly going to his paid work, Sarah mostly at home with the baby), but how they *felt* and experienced this time was very different. Sarah felt attached to the baby in ways Sam did not. She didn't feel capable of leaving the baby, even for short periods of time. In short, Sarah came to take the position of the primary carer, practically, emotionally and mentally (as discussed in chapter 4).

When the maternity leave ended Sarah negotiated with her line manager that she would work from home two days a week and spend the other three in the office. Since her office was in a different city from where she was living with Sam and baby S, she spent two nights a week away from their home. Coupled with her return to full-time work, this weekly absence shifted the balance of everyday tasks between her and Sam. A split in the mental load of care, however, remained. For Sam, the maternity leave was a key underlying factor in maintaining the mental-load split:

> She's, she's more engaged with that [decisions about baby S's care], as a hangover from maternity leave I suppose … and just maybe … because she's the mother [short laugh].
>
> Sam, Interview 3

It is interesting that despite his and Sarah's commitment to non-gendering in their roles (as described in chapter 2), he has come to a rather essentialised view of motherhood. This suggests that women's take-up of maternity leave structures women's mothering roles both through the repetition of responsibility and in how it begins to normalise women as primary carers.

Additionally, my reading of Sarah's diaries and interview data is that on the one hand the weekly divisions of care enabled more task-related equality, but on the other her weekly absence from the home encouraged her to take on the mental load of caring for baby S. She told me that she made sure to 'make up' for her weekly absences, largely by doing most of the care work while she was at home, but also, I argue, by taking on the cognitive labour in her household. She repeatedly told me in her final interview that her female friends and colleagues told her how shocked they are that she 'can stand' to spend regular time away from her son. Although she countered their normative perspectives on how a mother should feel about spending time away from her child, her taking on of the cognitive labour does seem to be part of an effort to embody ideas of 'good motherhood' despite her regular absences from home. Sarah has internalised, and now performs, a particular vision of good motherhood prompted by her relations with those around her. The family management role positions her clearly as 'mother', confirmed by Sam, who tells me that she makes the strategic decisions 'just because she is the mother', in a context where her absence throws into doubt her commitment to her child. Other research conducted with parents of older children finds that the systems and communities that surround parents reinforce the idea of the mother as primary carer, in part by excluding men (Doucet, 2006). For example, parent-and-baby clubs may shun fathers, or nursery staff ask for the mother instead of the father (Brooks & Hodkinson, 2020). Such instances weren't reported by my participants, perhaps because they had had fewer interactions with such institutions (their children had only just started in formal childcare by the end of the data collection, for example). Rather, the maternity leave experiences, and indeed the policy, have already been enough to solidify these differences, which are seen to have repercussions beyond the leave period.

Similar processes were seen with Debbie and David. Like Sarah, Debbie took all the maternity leave, becoming an 'expert' in caring for baby D over the course of her leave. Once the leave period was over, she reflected on the repercussions for David as a father:

> Like this evening he was going to put her to bed and she was just so knackered from nursery that she just ended up crying, so I just went up and took over, and as soon as I go in she calms down, and I think he finds that hard. Like I think he wants to be as involved as possible and, you know, do things fifty–fifty, and I just think that's, you know, he hasn't been there as much as me so it's totally natural that she's got like a main person that's me. But I think he would, he'd like, that's, I think that's what he finds difficult and a bit, probably a bit frustrating, but he doesn't get like outwardly frustrated about it.
>
> Debbie, Interview 3

On the other hand, David and Debbie were both spending a day a week at home alone with baby D, since they have both moved to a condensed four-day working week. They reported that David's time alone with the baby, along with protracted discussions about Debbie's wish to share the mental load (as seen in chapter 2), have resulted in a greater balance in care work between them:

> I think on a Monday my go-to is that we just need to have fun and enrich her experiences and go places, but I've consciously tried to more in the evenings or towards it, afternoon evenings, like think, 'What do I need to do in the house as well?' So cooking, cleaning, like checking things are done, do some admin, particularly when she's asleep. Um but it's just finding that balance, because I think my go-to is just I need to do all the fun things with her.
>
> David, Interview 3

Debbie agreed and specifically attributed this shift to David's time alone with the baby:

> He's doing like an awful lot more um with her, and I think he's kind of thinking of things like, 'Oh, make sure the water's been on so she

can have a bath', or think about what she's going to have for dinner tonight, which like he would do if I asked him before but it wouldn't necessarily be in his mind as well. I think, so I think, and also that's probably because he's spending days with her when I'm not there at all, so he's kind of planning things out a bit more and anticipating things a bit more. So yeah I think it would probably look more, more equal, though not quite equal.

Debbie, Interview 3

Although David and Debbie observed that they had made some progress towards establishing a shared division of responsibilities, Debbie was still taking on the bulk of the mental load. This was bolstered by their differing orientations towards work and family. For David, his paid work is part of his identity as a father:

> I'm not really bothered about a flash car or anything like that. But I do want to be able to say take them scuba diving or travel places. So underpinning and driving me forward in the career, is I want to earn enough money to be able to do those things. I'm quite ambitious, I really want to progress in my career and earn good money and kind of give my kids lots of opportunity and I just enjoy what I'm doing and I know where I want to be in my role. And it's kind of marrying that to being a good father, being present, and obviously being a good husband and supporting my partner.

David, Interview 3

David wants both to be present for his children and to earn sufficient to give his children 'lots of opportunity'. For him and other fathers in this group, breadwinning was an aspect of his care for his partner and child (as also discussed in relation to fathers in chapter 6, and see Schmidt, 2018). Debbie earned a similar amount to David, but did not discuss her earning or financial providing in this way; nor did any other woman in this study. Such gendered orientations to earning may be different in other class and racialised groups (Duncan et al, 2003; Gillies, 2008; Hamilton, 2023).

David did, however, express some ambivalence about how to 'marry' being a provider with other aspects of being a good father and husband. His wife, Debbie, was clearly influential in this regard, stressing to David (and to me) that his attention to their son was important for how she viewed him as a father and partner:

> Debbie: I would say with that as well, with the relationship, I think I, I've grown like more, even more fond of him watching him become a really good dad, whereas I think he, he knows that I'm a really good mum but he doesn't see that as part of our relationship, whereas I, like that colours my, like how I perceive him. It's like he's baby D's dad and that's, like and I just see all the nice things he does with her, and that really, it makes me feel closer to him the closer I see him being to baby D.
>
> Katherine: Have you discussed this with David?
>
> Debbie: Yes, and it's funny, he doesn't see it that way, towards me I mean.
>
> Debbie, Interview 3

The differing perspectives of Debbie and David relate to the sense of gifting within couples (Hochschild, 2003). In this economy of gratitude, hands-on care from fathers to children is appreciated by women, while such care between mothers and babies is expected and supported in a variety of ways. Because of the moral responsibility for earning men felt, male participants attempted to reconcile the intimate and earning elements of contemporary ideas of appropriate fatherhood as best they could, which often meant taking on care tasks, but not the thinking about and management of such care tasks.

In the case of the couples who had shared leave, the fathers in this group had seemingly sufficient time to establish the sharing of everyday house- and care work during the leave period, but not enough to shift the mothers' position as the primary carer. For this (partial) shift in care divisions, the timing and the length of leave were significant. For instance, Filip took six months of SPL at the same time as his wife Faria. During his leave, their diaries and interviews indicated that they shared decisions and different aspects of the care of their baby (as described in chapter 5). But in his final interview he explained that Faria's time alone after he went back to paid work was pivotal in establishing her as the 'expert' in baby F's care and therefore her take-up of managerial control in similar ways to Sarah and Debbie:

> I think since baby F, the slight imbalance has come because Faria had that six months at home on her own doing everything for baby F during the day and has got so good at it and so organised and it's sort of her system and she knows what food is in the freezer and what baby

F likes on particular days if she's looking sort of under the weather and that kind of thing. Which I probably wrongly haven't made the effort to learn, and haven't been forced to do, 'cause there hasn't, Faria has been here and, erm, and it hasn't needed to be me. […] So it needs me to be a bit more proactive and push my way in. Erm, but then you feel a bit kind of like a klutz 'cause you come in and try and do something and you get the food wrong or you, er, forget what time the nap is supposed to be, erm, or give her the wrong, Calpol at the wrong time or something so it perks her up just before a nap.

Filip, Interview 3

Filip reflected that Faria's time off had given her a greater connection to and knowledge of their child. Research conducted in other settings has uncovered similar outcomes of fathers' leave being taken at the same time as the mother. For example, in Norway Brandth and Kvande (2003a and b) compared fathers who had taken leave alone with fathers who had taken leave with the mother. They found that those who had cared for the child alone had a higher level of care competence as well as a stronger perceived connection with the child. These examples suggest that to shift the ingrained historical gendered moral responsibilities related to parenthood, fathers need extended time alone with their children.

The accounts of these couples show how moral discourses around motherhood and fatherhood differ, even amongst couples who aspire to equality in parenting. Few couples were more committed to a symmetrical division of labour than Helen and Henry. Over the course of the leave period, however, the different gendered moral pressures they were under clashed with their ideals and understandings of equality. Helen engaged in discourses of intensive motherhood in ways similar to mothers who gave up paid work entirely. She spent considerable time in her interviews emphasising the importance of parent care for a child and stressing that she only used formal childcare as a last resort. She 'displays' (Finch, 2007) her good mothering through examples of self-sacrifice which position her as a devoted parent who will do anything to meet her child's needs. For instance, she told me about the lengths she went to to shorten her commute so that she can get home as early as possible to see her son:

I had an hour-and-twenty-five-minute commute, do you know what I mean, and I was literally calculating, you know, I, I stopped taking the easiest way and I started taking the fastest way, which, you know, from [town in London] was two buses and three trains, and I had to run between each connection to make sure I would be making up that time, getting back a few minutes earlier.

Helen, Interview 3

Helen positioned herself in this small story as the self-sacrificing mother who goes to great lengths to be there for her child. She told me that work had become 'meaningless' to her since her child was born, even though she previously found her career valuable in her life. The men in this chapter did not present themselves in similar ways. Henry, for example, detailed the sacrifices he was making in spending long hours at the office and searching for a better-paid job to provide for the family. These differing pressures, illustrated by these narratives, are compounded by the perceived impossibility of sharing care while both partners are pursuing careers. As Helen told me in her final interview,

> I wish that, what I mostly wish is that I wish we lived in a society where it would be acceptable and okay for us both to work four days a week now, and it is just not.

Helen is not wrong. Part-time work, even though, officially, all working parents can request it, is more likely to be granted to women and is shown to inhibit career progression (Cook et al., 2021; Gatrell & Cooper, 2016). Helen said that it was important that at least one of them worked part-time, and that it was her because she was earning less than Henry. The difference in their work hours is later drawn upon by Helen to justify their differing levels of engagement in cognitive labour, though it is clear that she was dissatisfied with this division.

In other cases, couples started the study with similar earnings, but the men improved their career trajectories over the course of the study, which meant that initial plans to share things equally were modified over time. For instance, Winnie and Weston started the study in similar jobs in the same field and with the same level of earnings. Over the course of the study, Weston was promoted twice (despite taking SPL for two months), while Winnie did not get any promotion. (Indeed, no woman in the study was promoted, and only Helen changed her job, staying at a similar level but with a shorter commute.) In her final interview, Winnie told me she would like to change jobs, but now that Weston had been promoted she would have to compromise:

> Given the fact that Weston and I do similar things, kind of the next step for me would be to, in my career, would be to take a job similar to what, the job that Weston has, and just feasibly that's not possible um which is [pause] frustrating, but it's, but it's no fault of Weston's. Um, he had the job first, I'm sensible enough not to ask him to give up a well-paying secure job just so that I can try and find something that suits my fancy a bit more.
>
> Winnie, Interview 3

We know from other research that men's careers tend to flourish at the transition to parenthood (the fatherhood or 'daddy' bonus; see for example Hodges & Budig, 2010), meaning it is more likely that the man's career will be treated as the priority if it is deemed that two careers cannot realistically be supported. Research also shows that women tend to give more active support for their partners' careers, while men tend to support with words and not deeds (Wong, 2023), thus perpetuating this dynamic.

The idea that one career must be prioritised is related to 'greedy work' norms (Goldin, 2021), as discussed in chapter 2, which are often a key driver in the role specialisation of earner and carer within couples. Olly and Olivia faced a similar position when Olly was promoted to firm partner just two weeks after their baby was born. Olivia reflected on the repercussions for her career and for their family:

> I know the friends that are renting our flat they've done shared parental leave but his job is really, I mean he walks to work in London and he leaves at five and he doesn't really have, it's not like a high [pause] and he took a pay cut, he used to work at [law firm] with Olly but he took that active decision to take a different kind of job, and as a family we have not done that. So obviously that puts different pressures on us and I think it does, you know, it does affect, does it affect my career, what I've done? Maybe I would've gone into transaction services if, if he didn't have, but then actually would I really have enjoyed that? I probably still would've missed baby O and have been travelling more and working longer hours, so I probably still would've ended up where I was anyway.
>
> Olivia, Interview 3

Olivia's ambivalence concerning career 'choices' and the complex emotions and trade-offs they involve is evident. While she communicated a sense of frustration about her stalled career advancement and the higher share of household labour she was shouldering, she also acknowledged the upsides. These included the time spent with her daughter and a respite from the relentless pressures associated with professional life. Moreover, these advantages were made possible, at least in part, by the financial benefits accrued through Olly's elite career. Her story highlights the ways in which women's and men's career (and care) trajectories are tied to those of their partners.

Helen made similar observations about the tied nature of parenthood. In her final interview, she likened the shift to parenthood as one in which she and Henry must share 'one pie', referring to the ways in which they must now divide their time and energy:

> It's like suddenly there was just one pie, and however big a slice you took it was depriving somebody else from that pie, and normally in life that's not like that and I don't even think in partnership it is, but I think in childrearing, particularly in the first year it definitely is.
>
> Helen, interview 3

Here she is referring to her dependence on Henry to care for baby H or complete housework so that she can do something else (such as see a friend or catch up on paid work). Since this mutual dependence is heightened by the dependency of an infant, it could conceivably shift over time, but, as seen in the last chapter, future plans have already been set in motion by decisions made and practices followed during leave.

Olivia's account also demonstrates how family practices are shaped by personal value judgements about the kind of life that is desirable, and of course possible. Her mixed feelings about her and Olly's divisions of labour point to broader societal discourses about the relative values of different forms of work. The low social value accorded to care and housework has long been documented in feminist and care literature (Folbre, 2011; Oakley, 1974). At the same time, men and women are beholden to different moral discourses about work and family, in that men are under more pressure to earn and women to care (Duncan et al., 2003; Schmidt, 2018), as seen most starkly in chapter 6. This backdrop likely influenced Olivia's own perceptions and assessments of her role, both in the professional sphere and within her family, relative to Olly's. We also hear echoes of Orgad's (2019) research on highly educated women who left their careers after becoming a mother. Orgad found that even when such women told of social forces of inequality which pushed them out of paid work, they ascribed their decisions to leave work to individual failures to be sufficiently ambitious or confident. What my study adds is the relational dimension. Female participants viewed themselves as less confident and ambitious than their male partners (without taking account of how these men's careers have been supported by gendered work inequalities and the care and housework which women take up), and so concluded that it 'makes sense' within the couple to focus on his career over hers.

Mothers managing in the future?

Looking over the visions of future life described by these parents, I notice that the men featured in this chapter gave much more detailed accounts of how they imagined their future family lives than the fathers in chapter 6, who tended to focus on their future careers. Here I give two (shortened) examples to illustrate the kinds of issues which these men discussed:

> Katherine: So what, what do you think your life will be like in nine years' time?
>
> Filip: Nine years' time, er, we would hope to have a second child with us. […] By then I think we'll have moved away from central London here, I think we'll be out in the country more. That's going to be a compromise and quite a tricky one to pick, 'cause I, I mean I grew up in the countryside and do really want to move back and would love our kids to grow up somewhere where you don't worry so much about them being outside and the, like a green space isn't one with a tarmac path across it, it's just a field, that kind of countryside. I don't think we're ever going to get, I don't think we're going to get kind of my idyllic countryside view, especially if it does end up with me stopping work and Faria carrying on 'cause, um, it's unfair her having to commute back in that long. [Pause] Erm, nine years would be, so baby F would be four or five years into school maybe … We'll probably try and pick somewhere, unsurprisingly again, that has decent schools. Ideally decent state schools. […] Yeah, so I think based on the few weeks that [Faria] has been back at work, my guess would be in nine years' time Faria is still the breadwinner and working and I'm still at home with no immediate plans to return to work or anything.
>
> Filip, Interview 3

> Katherine: So as Helen mentioned I plan to be coming back in about nine years' time when baby H will be ten, so what do you think your lives will look like when I come back at that / stage?
>
> Henry: /Ooh, well I think we'll still be here. Erm ... We may or may not have a second child. Erm, that depends, that's a whole other discussion. Erm [sighs] Yeah, I don't know, I think it will be not dissimilar from what we're doing now. I mean like by that age, I expect to have a bit more of a life back. Like once children are a bit older and a little bit more independent and like don't need constant vigilance, then I think that's a bit more plausible. It'd be nice to do family holidays, by the age of ten I can start introducing him to the sort of stuff that interests me, which'll be really, really nice. Erm, and there's loads of stuff that I remember from childhood really enjoying that I would really like to introduce him to, which is like silly things, like I want to take him at some point to this tram museum, which is a museum in Derbyshire. Just loads of trams, that's it, and you get on the trams, the trams go places, and they come back from those places, you can put a token on and they go down a different route, just trams, so I really loved that, so things like that. Erm, and yeah, erm ... I don't know really, like I don't know, in terms of other, other spheres of life, like career-wise, I know Helen is umming and ahing about a career change but I'm not sure how, I'm not sure if she's got a particular set direction or particular route planned to that.
>
> Henry, Interview 3

These men's visions of the future reflect the ways in which they are already embedded and invested in everyday family life, in ways that the breadwinner fathers in chapter 6 were not. This demonstrates how integration in everyday family life shapes the ways in which men imagine their future lives. The current everyday practices are the available narratives on which participants build an image of the future.

On the other hand, most of the participants in this group (men and women) envisioned a shift away from their current situation of mostly sharing care and paid work (other than the mental load) towards a future in which one parent will take primary responsibility for care and the other for paid work, as shown in these examples:

> Katherine: So um if I do manage to track you down [short laugh] /in nine years' time / what do you think your life will look like in terms of work and family and where you're living and what you're /doing?
>
> David: /Yeah. /Yeah. / Nine years' time, I'll be forty years old. Um, because I think we've talked a lot about it's probably not sustainable for us to both work full-time if we have another child or two children more. […] We have to look at who does what and how that set-up occurs. Um but that'll have to play out and we'll have to look at money and experiences and what we want for the children, but I certainly think Debbie's thinking about maybe working part-time in the future, and I think we've definitely had a conversation of 'See how you go after six months being back', and then definitely if we have the other child like for Debbie to look to go to maybe three days, proper three days like normal hours, and um it's kind of less pressure on the evenings and stuff. Um, yeah I suppose that's what I'm hoping for.
>
> David, Interview 3

> Katherine: What about your work in nine years' time?=
>
> Olivia: =Work-wise? Oh I don't know, um I think it depends if we have three kids or two kids. Ah I think, well, hmm. Partly I'm working now just to keep my toe in the water so that when you have kids and they get a bit older I've then got a flexibility to go back to work. My mother has said to me on a number of occasions, she says actually having had three girls she actually thinks that when they're teenagers that almost they need their mother at home more then than when they're kids, which I always thought was quite interesting. So it might mean actually that in nine, ten years' time um maybe I think now that I'm doing it so I can go back to work when they're a bit older, but actually maybe they'll want more stabili-, you know, maybe they'll need more ah, yeah I think that would be me over my husband. I kind of, I don't think

it will be him that will be the, making that life choice, for sure. I think that's um well unless he, everything goes really badly in this job [both short laugh]. [...] Yeah I don't know, I don't know if I'll be working or not. I'd like to think I would be but it doesn't, I think it's a difficult balance, so yeah there's a, I guess there's a bit of a question mark as to what will happen. [...] Ultimately in our decision about who the carer will be would come down to money and who had the more money, and he would earn more money.

Olivia, Interview 3

It'll be interesting because it depends how much they sort of, your children need you. At the moment I'm finding working five days very difficult because I think baby W's developing some separation anxiety. So for example he now cries in the morning from the moment I put his shoes on until I drop him off at the childminder [...] The practicalities are that, you know, they go to school and as they get older they develop their own life as well, and you need to, you know, encourage that and embrace that, and it's very important to me that baby W is an independent individual, and so I wouldn't want him to feel as though he has to spend time with me. So maybe actually working from home or working part-time wouldn't be a good thing. But anyway so yeah, so I think, I think the reality is, is that ah Winston's career, at least for the time being, it's going to sort of primarily drive how um the childcare um and work, the childcare, working life balance gets split.

Winnie, Interview 3

The relational and emotional nature of these visions is apparent, as parents considered what their children and partner might do or need in the future (Lebano & Jamieson, 2020). These parents viewed a dual full-time working household as unlikely to be compatible with care for children, although this is how most of them are currently functioning. Participants' future lives are not fixed, of course, but the imagined needs of children and partners are figuring in their plans, and participants reported having already had discussions about how women may adapt their working hours in the future.

I see the apprehensions of parents regarding the management of both paid and unpaid labour in the future as rooted in their experiences of exceptionally demanding days. These experiences were perceived as unsustainable and unappealing in the long term and likely to be constrained by existing work norms. As parents anticipated the possibility of having more children and encountering increased professional responsibilities because of career advancement, they expressed doubts about the feasibility of distributing responsibilities equitably within the partnership. At present, the disproportionate burden of the 'mental load' falls on women, exacerbating their concerns about balancing full-time employment with caregiving. This dynamic reinforces the perception amongst women that sustaining full-time professional commitments alongside caregiving responsibilities is not realistic, which may encourage them to consider stepping back from paid work in the future while their partners continue full-time. The experiences of participants to date suggest that this will lead to longer work hours for men as they attempt to progress in their careers to make up for the women's fewer work hours, meaning more divergence in their everyday lives.

As with the plans described by participants in chapter 6, women's future involvement in paid work is portrayed as unstable and contingent. For example, Olivia said that whether she would continue in paid work and how many hours she would work would depend on what would be best for the kids and how Olly was doing in his paid work. And Winnie's work hours were envisaged as depending on what was best for baby W, which may be full-time rather than part-time hours. Men's higher earning (potential) was framed as integral to these decisions (and already framed Helen's fewer working hours). Of course, many UK parents could not afford anything less than dual full-time work, which highlights the relative privilege of this cohort.

Two contrasting couples in this group help us untangle the factors which lead to this dominant imagining of the future. As described previously, Sarah (lawyer) and Sam (surgeon) both work full-time and share the everyday care of baby S, but Sarah takes on a greater proportion of the mental load. This set-up is in part facilitated by Sarah's weekly stay in another city for her job. As they look to the future, Sam said he pictures himself in the same job, working the same hours, but both he and Sarah are less sure about what Sarah's future work life will be like:

> It depends whether Sarah stays working in London, which she might do, we haven't decided. I don't think I'll change my job. […] You know, I think I've got a very good balance. […] I think sometimes, you know, we think, or I think, it would be nice if Sarah lived in [city where they live] and had a job in [city where they live], but it would have to be a job that she found rewarding, as rewarding as her job

in London, and I don't think we're quite there yet. So, I d-, I don't really mind the time, you know, it's quite nice to look after him on my own and to be, have that time on my own. I think if I had lots of weeks like the one I described and it was just really exhausting then I would want her to come back for that sort of practical reason. But if it can not be that most of the time and just very occasionally like that, then I think it's, it's quite a good set-up because it's nice for her to have that foot in another camp professionally and um we'll see. But she may well get a job in [city where they live], I don't know. […] I think she's aware that she'd take a massive cut in income. And I suppose she might worry about how that would affect her sort of position in the family or how it would affect our family finances and how it would affect, you know, how I would have to do a lot more work and that might affect the, you know, she might get a great work–life balance and I'd get a totally useless work–life balance, and I think that might worry her.

Sam, Interview 3

Sarah and Sam's case highlights the deeply relational nature of work and care negotiations. At the time of the final interview, Sam noted that they are both fulfilled professionally and he felt capable of taking regular sole responsibility for baby S. The future of Sarah's paid work, however, is unclear (which Sarah also attested to). Although Sam identified his ability to cope with regular solo care as one factor to consider in Sarah's future work, there are other factors, including the degree to which she finds her work fulfilling. He says 'we haven't decided' about the future of her paid work, indicating that Sarah's work is a joint decision, with implications for them all, including his own paid work hours.

In this example, less than in others already discussed, the work and family lives of both partners are discussed in the round without an a priori assumption that Sarah will take on more care work than Sam. In their first interview, they (in part) attributed their 'non-gendered' approach to dividing housework to their similar earnings. This parity continued to frame their discussions. Sam explained that a shift in Sarah's earnings in the future might alter their divisions of work. Studies often frame being the higher earner as a means for men to bargain their way out of care and housework; here it is clear that Sam is not keen to work longer hours, but he suggests that his doing so would shift other divisions of care and housework. This complicates straightforward readings of couple behaviour which draw on 'bargaining theory' (Brines, 1994; Evertsson & Nermo, 2004; Ross, 1987) by considering how individuals may work together relationally in their assessment of the balance of paid and unpaid work for shared goals related to financial security. It is notable nonetheless that women repeatedly voiced a lower attachment to their careers than men (something Sarah put in motion before she even met Sam: see chapter 2); women often also portrayed their work as being 'fulfilling', rather than for breadwinning.

In the case of Faria (lawyer) and Filip (business consultant), Faria earns significantly more than Filip and this is envisioned as the deciding factor in how they will arrange paid and unpaid work between them, with Faria working full-time and Filip becoming a stay-at-home father. Like other couples in this group, they felt that one parent should be focused on care and the other on paid work.[2] This division 'makes sense' in the same way that other couples said it 'makes sense' for the mother to reduce her work hours when the father earns more. However, this future is not 100 per cent certain; Filip told me that Faria has 'first refusal' on being the stay-at-home parent:

> Filip: We're comfortable with the idea of having a nanny for now but we think when she [baby F] gets to about school age and it's kind of helping with homework time, that kind of stage in her development probably [laughs] it may always change but that's the time when we'd like one of us to be at home with her, to be at home full-time. And the plan has always been and I think will continue to be that my wife would have sort of first refusal on being that person, but if she likes being back at work and she can find a nice balance where she feels like she has enough time at home with our baby as well as working, I'd be more than happy to give it a go and retire, and be a househusband.
>
> Katherine: And why would Faria get first refusal, how did that decision come about?
>
> Filip: Um, it's a good question 'cause I know yeah, my, sort of following my philosophy through to its logical conclusion there shouldn't be any inequality there, so I guess that's kind of the last vestiges of some kind of gender roles in my head. But, um, yeah, I've never really questioned why I would have thought about it that way. I don't, even if it wasn't something that was a traditionally for one gender rather than the other I'd, not sure, I think I probably

would still give her first refusal just 'cause that's the way our relationship works. But undoubtedly there's probably an element of ... mum should get first refusal on whether she wants to be the one at home with the baby in my mind. Erm ... Yeah. I'm just trying to think, 'cause I've never interrogated why I kind of thought that. Erm, yeah. I think generally I've always, generally I'm normally kind of 'after you' for everything in terms of making the relationship work. Erm, but I think there probably is an element of if mum wanted to be at home with the baby and I kind of fought her on it because I felt like I wanted to be at home with the baby I'd feel like it wasn't the right thing to do. Erm, yeah.

Filip, Interview 3

It is clear that Filip had not interrogated this assumption of 'first refusal' before my prompting, which indicates the ingrained nature of gendered ideologies. Such views were clearly shared by Faria:

Let's put it this way, if he was in my job and I was in his job I think it would be kind of a no-brainer that he continued his job earning three times as much as I do, um, and, erm, having more flexibility. Earning more and having more flexibility, it would be a no-brainer that he does it. It's only at all an issue because I'm a woman, and therefore have more of an instinct, natural instinct I feel, even, in spite of the fact that he's so fatherly, natural instinct to be around the baby more. Erm, erm, and therefore it's more of a question whether it should be me or him. But I think financially and just practically it makes far more sense for it to be me who continues working than him, just 'cause of the jobs we have.

Faria, Interview 3

Faria recognised that gender was structuring their decision-making, but unlike Filip, who felt that this went against his general philosophy on gender, Faria affirmed essentialised ideas of gender and care, claiming that she had a more 'natural instinct' to be with their baby than Filip did, despite the fact that he was very keen to be a stay-at-home dad.

Moreover, Faria's narration of being the main earner in the family was markedly different from that of male breadwinners in that she did not narrate her earning as part of her caring for the family:

> I think I definitely see career as more of a means to an end now, and I, having spoken to more people with varying levels of seniority, I'm, I'm pretty convinced that when I'm sixty and I look back on my life I'm not going to remember whether I took on a case or didn't take on a case or who the client was or what the point of law that we argued was, but I think I will remember if I, you know, I never make it to one of the school events or parent–teacher meetings or that I've missed significant events in Filip's life or in our life as a family, I think I would really remember that. So I don't think I'm ambitious in the sense of achieving career at the cost of family. I think my main thing is to do my work as best as I possibly can and to be proud of whatever leaves my desk.
>
> Faria, Interview 3

In that moment, Faria was evidently still connected to her career, and stated her aspiration to be good at what she did, but whereas male primary earners said their earnings were important for the lives of their children (and sometimes their partners), Faria focused on reducing her ambitions to ensure that she does not compromise on 'being there' for her children. This shows how the available narratives of mothering and fathering differ, provoking different orientations to work and care even amongst higher-earning mothers.

Filip's deferral to Faria and her preferences despite her higher earnings can also be seen to be part of the relationship work Filip engaged in within their marriage, which here is upholding gendered parenting roles. Such gender-affirming acts of relationship work have been seen in other research, which shows men refusing to 'take away' women's access to maternity leave or even to gender-neutral parental leave lest their partners be upset (McKay & Doucet, 2010; Twamley, 2019). Faria and Filip's case demonstrates the limits of using earning differentials alone to explain gendered divisions of paid and unpaid work. While men earn more, they are likely to continue to take primary responsibility for providing, but women's higher or similar earnings are not *necessarily* going to shift such divisions.

Conclusion

Within this group of couples, participants described very full and demanding days in which both parents juggled paid and unpaid work, often through a system of 'tag teaming' in which one parent does one thing (such as feeding the baby) while the other does another (such as washing the dishes). However, in all of these couples the mother took the role of the family manager, taking on the bulk of the 'mental load' (Dean et al., 2022) or 'cognitive labour' (Daminger, 2019) in the household.

In part these final divisions were shaped by differing moral discourses on what it means to be a mother. For example, Sarah took on the bulk of the mental load in order to conform to an ideal of the good mother despite her regular absences from the home. But it is also clear that couples' experiences of leave were formative in their final division of labour. These parents had either taken SPL at the same time, or had not taken SPL but had used some other flexible-working policies to enable the father to spend some limited time caring for their child alone. These experiences helped to establish the sharing of everyday housework and care, but were not enough to shift mothers' position as the primary carer with overall responsibility for household management. These findings are supported by other research conducted in the UK with primary care fathers of older children. Brooks and Hodkinson (2020) found that even when fathers gave up paid work entirely to look after their children, the mothers who remained in paid work continued to manage the household. The authors considered this lingering division of the mental load to be a result of the expertise developed by women during maternity leave. I also observed that, according to their parents, children themselves contributed to this process, for example by expressing a preference for the mother, with whom they were more familiar, and thus reifying discourses of the primacy of the mother in young children's lives.

Since in most of these cases both parents were working full-time at the time of the final interview, and sometimes working long hours (over 35 hours a week), they struggled to keep up with the multiple demands of paid and unpaid work. Women in particular reported tiredness and frustrations, which isn't surprising given their greater responsibilities. These experiences of struggle shaped parents' visions of the future, in which both women and men (mostly) expected that the woman would step back from paid work in order to meet these multiple demands more effectively. Whether this is what happens will be revisited when the children turn 10.

Notes

1. Emma, 'The gender wars of household chores: A feminist comic'. *The Guardian*, 26 May 2017. https://www.theguardian.com/world/2017/may/26/gender-wars-household-chores-comic. Accessed 8 April 2024.
2. This wouldn't necessarily mean a shift in the home-managerial role, as demonstrated in other research with primary care fathers (see Brooks & Hodkinson, 2020; Doucet, 2006).

8
Parents sharing responsibilities of paid and unpaid work

> So I'd say that Baby K is completely split. I can't say one of us does more than the other at all. If I had to pinpoint one thing I'd say it's probably the fact he took leave that makes him more involved. And then house stuff we were always pretty even, but I'd say there's things that, like I used to do the Ocado [supermarket] shop more and now Keith is more involved in that because he was doing it more when he was off. And I think washing was always my thing and he's more involved in washing now. So I'd say, yeah I think it's pretty much even.
>
> Kate, Interview 3

Five couples in this study reported sharing the work and responsibilities of family life. Their diaries and interview data show not only the kinds of everyday tag teaming seen in chapter 7, but also that no one partner seemingly 'manages' the other. At the same time, not all the couples in this group did the same tasks to the same degree, which indicates the difficulties of divvying up discrete care tasks completely symmetrically (Orloff, 2009). For example, while most participants in this chapter worked the same number of paid work hours as their partner, Kate worked four days a week and Keith worked five days a week. And while Gina and Gerald did work the same number of paid work hours, Gina appeared to have slightly more responsibility for care and Gerald for housework. Overall, however, it was difficult to identify amongst these participants consistent patterns of inequality, in which one partner described undertaking more work or responsibility than the other. These couples self-identified as 'equal' and described themselves as attentive to potentially fluctuating participation, indicating their ongoing vigilance against 'slipping' into more traditional gendered divisions of labour.

In the first section I describe what this sharing looks like on an everyday basis and to what degree it relates to participants' leave experiences. In the second section, I examine their future plans and imaginings in order to consider whether and how they envision similar practices in relation to work and care in the future.

Parent practices a year after the baby is born

Monday 30th April

This morning baby B was not feeling well and she stayed at home. She didn't have a nice weekend. She felt sick and had a belly problem. yesterday she seemed better but this morning she had a temperature so we decided to keep her at home. we don't have alternatives but staying at home with her. so Beth stayed at home in the morning and i came back at 2. the weather was miserable so we stayed at home. we played a bit with the clothes, she was moving around the living room quite independently, then we played with colours. we did a mess with the coloured paint for kids, but she had fun. then, we had an afternoon snack, but she felt sick immediately after, so another change straight after. poor girl. towards the evening she looked better and she had plain pasta. mum came back at 7ish. mum stopped breast feeding in the evening last friday, so i am putting her in bed. i quite enjoy it actually. i find it really relaxing. i give her milk and then i read a story and it's super sweet seeing her falling asleep softly in her bed. after dinner i needed to work (marking) and then i went to bed after midnight quite destroyed.

Bart, Diary 4 (baby 13 months old)

Monday 30th April

Baby B had again temperature in the morning. We were hoping that she would go to nursery but it was too high. I do not know what is going on this time. She barely ate her breakfast. I stayed at home. Calpol worked and she was in better mood. She even ate a bit of biscuits and drank some milk. We stayed at home because the weather was just awful, too cold.

She was again not herself at lunch time and she did not eat anything. I was so frustrated and as always when I am tired, I lost it a bit. I shouted. At least she drank some milk just before she fell asleep.

I quickly tidied up the most necessary thing, had lunch and managed to do outstanding items on my list, and then she woke up after an hour and half. Just before Bart came home to exchange me.

I went to work by train because of the weather. I am a bit stressed on the amount of work and with an insufficient team. I was in the office thill [until] 18:30 and then I ran home.

I could not wait to see baby B and Bart. I suffer when she is not well. Bart said that she had temperature again and she also vomited a bit. Despite all these odds she ate her dinner and one whole banana. We did bath and Bart put her in bed. Fourth day without breastfeeding. She seems ok with it. I probably miss it more than her.

Beth, Diary 4 (baby 13 months old)

These diary extracts show how Beth and Bart shared the responsibility for the care of their daughter. When she was ill, as reported here, neither parent's job took priority, and both worked together to consider how to look after her. (Bart says 'We decided to keep her at home' and Beth 'We were hoping that she would go to nursery but it [her temperature] was too high'.) Beth and Bart had both shifted to four-day weeks for six months after the birth of their child by working compressed hours. This meant that their daughter was only in nursery for three days a week. The other two days they split, usually one working in the morning and the other in the afternoon. (The autumn after she turned one, they both returned to a five-day working week, but otherwise their practices remained the same.)

Beth and Bart were unusual in this group, in that they were the only couple that had *not* shared leave. The other four couples shared leave quite extensively: Keith took three months of leave alone, Edward two months of leave alone, Mark 10 weeks of leave alone plus six weeks with Mary, and Gerald and Gina took nine months of leave together (they took no leave separately). These couples were clear that the experience of SPL was fundamental to achieving their shared approach to paid and unpaid work, as we can see in these extracts:

> Katherine: You say you're glad that you took SPL, why is that?
>
> Keith: For a few reasons. Because I think that I'm much closer to baby K as a result of it and I feel completely confident looking after him, so we have a much more, now that we're both back at work we have a very equal, well I feel like we have a very equal, distribution of, of parental responsibilities, certainly compared to other people that

> I know. And I will be just as likely to do something as Kate um, and he will be just as likely to come to me as he will to Kate in most cases. So the, so I think that that whole setting the groundwork for the rest of his life is well worth the three months.
>
> Keith, Interview 3

> Now I've done the shared paren-, such a long stint of shared parental leave I think Mary's very confident in, or says she is anyway [short laugh], is very confident in my abilities as a parent, and she's, well she obviously hasn't minded me being sole carer for ten days while she's been away. So I feel very, that's felt very good as well. I've felt just, actually yeah just, I suppose, yeah just feel very, more and more confident I would say, the, the journey has been until now ... Yeah I just feel sort of total confidence in how to look after him and how to do it on my own, and, yeah, yeah it's just been great and um, I think we share, share everything quite well when, when we're both around. Yeah so I suppose that would be my, the theme has been sort of growing confidence on my, my side.
>
> Mark, Interview 3

> Katherine: And so you said one of your motivations to take SPL was that you wanted Edward to take responsibilities in the same way that you saw that mothers usually do. Do you think that has happened?
>
> Emily: Without a doubt, like absolutely without a doubt. Um he's exac-, he's just as good as I am at, he's just as likely to forget the bottle of milk as I am, or remember it [short laugh]. Um and I can't be sure that's because he had time off on his own with her but, like obviously I can't know but I'm as sure as I can be. Um like it really, really changed in those couple of months. I would be amazed, there'd be days in those weekends where I'd say 'Oh, you know, we've got to give her her teatime um it's five o'clock already', and he'd say 'No Emily teatime's five-thirty at the moment' [short laugh], you know? And just, like he's just, you know, just brilliant, yeah, and I, I'm sure, because, you know, having a full-time responsibility for a baby does make you think differently. Um so yeah I think it's, from that perspective I think it's

really worked really well. I don't know what it would've been like [short laugh] but I think it worked really, really well.

Emily, Interview 3

As is apparent, the idea that fathers build confidence in caring while on leave was repeated by mothers and fathers in this group. We see a gaining of expertise parallel to that reported by women during their maternity leave, and that this confidence has shaped how they care for their children once the leave is over. If we compare this confidence with Filip, where in chapter 7 he called himself a 'klutz' in relation to baby F's care after his wife took the final six months of maternity leave alone, the importance to fathers and mothers of this gained expertise becomes apparent.

These quotes also denote a high level of satisfaction and celebration. Fathers compared themselves favourably with other fathers (as do their partners). There is a sense of achievement, which suggests that participants were aware that their expertise runs contrary to popular discourses of mothers as naturally better parents (Schmidt, Décieux et al., 2023). Keith, for example, explicitly mentioned that their child was 'as likely to come to me as he will to Kate', indicating the importance he places on this bond between himself and his son, as well as the perceived unusualness of such a relationship between child and father.

Fathers reported how their orientation to work and care had shifted as a consequence of SPL, and on the bond that had developed during this time with their child:

I don't think I realised how much being um being a sort of, a dad would become part of, sort of my main bit of my, I don't know what the word is, maybe a bit pretentious, sort of identity sort of thing. I thought I'd be a person who had a child and I would be a dad sort of thing, but after the ten weeks of leave I thought very much like, 'Oh I could easily give up work and just have the little one as my job'.

Mark, Interview 3

It's really, it's very, very strange now um, you know, when I last saw you from then until now I'm very happy just spending an entire weekend hanging out with baby E and yeah when, you know, even like a year ago that would've been, I would've seen that as like, probably like a really boring thing to do, as like a, as a man, like hanging out with a baby. I just, I used to see like guys like pushing their babies around in the park and be like 'Poor guy. God I'm glad I'm not him', and now I am that guy and I'm, I couldn't be happier! It's quite bizarre how ah your like opinions on these sorts of things change so quickly.

Edward, Interview 3

These findings illustrate how parental leave can play a role in changing gendered orientations to paid and unpaid work.

The shared nature of what parents had gone through, each having extended periods of parental leave, was experienced as beneficial for the intimacy of the couples, as they had hoped (as was reported in chapter 3):

> I think it also, it's good that I have done a bit of the SPL because it is a bit that I can like see what she went through, to a certain extent. Um, you know, looking after a child, making sure that they, you know, are fed and watered and cleaned and clothed every day. And so I think our like sort of partnership of shared responsibility has been strengthened, yeah I'd say we are like a stronger partner after the year of like raising a child. I'd say that's definitely strengthened our relationship.
>
> Edward, Interview 3

Edward was initially one of the fathers least keen to share leave, and had reported reservations about taking SPL. In his first interview he appeared to repudiate the idea of taking SPL to strengthen gender equality with his wife (see chapter 3). After the leave, however, he used language similar to his wife's about 'shared responsibility', and celebrated both his bond with their child and the ways in which the sharing of responsibilities improved his relationship with Emily. This example gives credence to the idea that fathers' take-up of leave can shift the parenting perspectives and practices 'even' of men who are circumspect about its benefits, and who explicitly dissociate themselves from egalitarian goals.

Other fathers were more ambivalent about their experiences of SPL. Keith, for example, is committed to sharing responsibilities with his wife, and celebrated his close relationship with her and his child, but on the other hand he noted that his life is more challenging than that of his male colleagues who had not taken leave:

> Keith: I can't do what I used to do and all the rest of it directly stems from the decision to be more involved, and I think that it throws up a whole lot of new challenges where

um [pause] if I hadn't made that decision and didn't take that approach it would be much easier to balance a whole lot of these things, because I just would force all responsibility onto Kate. But it just makes things, I don't personally think that that's fair.

Katherine: Mmhmm.

Keith: Um and the consequence of that is that it leads to other challenges that I feel like I've got more responsibility, because I do.

Keith, Interview 3

This recognition that sharing responsibilities is difficult speaks to what men give up, as well as gain, when they take on more care and housework. In his final interview, Keith told me that, although he was happy he took SPL, he was unlikely to have a second child, since that would require another extended leave period and even further sacrifices of his personal and career time. As Schwartz (1994) noted in her study of mixed-sex 'peer marriages' in the 1980s, for equality to flourish within a couple, career progression must take a back seat. This may result in 'identity costs' for men, as they are less likely to fulfil masculine expectations of career progression (and similarly women may not fulfil feminine expectations of intensive motherhood). Such losses are consolidated by policies and work norms which do not support the combination of caregiving and career progression (Cook et al., 2021; Goldin, 2021; Schwartz, 1994). Andrea Doucet (2016) observed similar losses amongst primary care fathers who prioritise caregiving, and notes that feminist scholarship has failed to take such losses seriously.

One couple, Gerald and Gina, reported that SPL had not brought them closer as a couple. In chapter 5, I described how tensions arose during their extended nine months of SPL together, when Gina took on the more hands-on care role with the baby, leaving Gerald to a more supportive role. After the leave period, both reduced their work hours to spend more time with baby G. Their diaries indicated a sharing of responsibilities that they equate to a fifty–fifty division, but Gerald's responsibility was greater in housework and Gina's in hands-on care of their baby. For example, both described how Gerald sometimes struggled to help baby G to fall asleep at night, and that the baby had more than once called out for his mother instead of his father on these occasions. On the other hand, Gerald takes almost all responsibility for food shopping and cooking. This couple, then, do not provide a neat example of *symmetrical* sharing as others do. But it is clear that overall they divide paid and unpaid labour responsibilities evenly between them and neither feels that there is a 'manager' in the relationship, as Gerald explained in relation to baby G:

> So we learnt together [to care for baby G], and both opinions are respected I think. That makes me happy. I'm glad that has happened. It gi-, it feels like it gives me, the shared parental leave has given me a bit of a, a right to, to express that opinion and, because we're equal in that sense, and that's good. Yeah.
>
> Gerald, Interview 3

As Gerald himself attested in his final interview, it is likely that he would have a more independent relationship with baby G had he taken some SPL alone, while Gina would perhaps have taken more responsibility for housework if she had experienced some leave alone. This shows the different repercussions of leave taken together or separately when the leave period is over, even within a couple who were highly committed to gender equality in their relationship and family life, and who took SPL for this reason.

So far I have discussed how sharing leave impacted on the division of labour in this group of parents. However, as mentioned at the beginning of this chapter, one couple – Beth and Bart – did not share leave but nonetheless forged shared responsibilities once the maternity leave was over. Bart reported that during his first two weeks of paternity leave he engaged in paid work (at the time of the birth) and was assisted by his mother during the second two weeks (nine months later when baby B was settling in at nursery).[1] Given the limited nature of this leave, neither attributed their current division of labour to Bart's experiences of leave. My reading of their data is that their similar orientations to work were formative in their final sharing of paid and unpaid work responsibilities. Beth is a senior member of staff in a small firm and Bart is a postdoctoral researcher at a top university in the UK. Both are passionate about their jobs, but feel their positions are precarious and highly demanding. As immigrants to the UK (they are both Italian), they are very dependent on one another, without any local family support. They often discussed in their interviews the high cost of living in the UK, particularly in relation to childcare and housing. They were renting a flat in London and speculated that they would never buy somewhere if they continued to live in London. Along with this, Bart's work situation was very flexible, which contributed to his reluctance to share leave, since he argued that he could be present anyway when Beth needed him and catch up on work later (and indeed in his diaries he often recorded spending time with Beth and baby B and then working late into the night). Bart 'hid' his absences from work in ways that Beth could not: for example, she explicitly negotiated a temporary work pattern of compressed hours, while Bart also worked compressed hours but did not officially negotiate this with anyone. Thus, neither felt inclined to reduce their paid work hours given the high cost of living, their aspiration to buy a home and their ambition to progress in their respective careers. Bart's work flexibility was key to helping them manage paid and unpaid work, since he could step in when Beth was unavailable and more often did nursery pick-ups, since he could more easily leave work at a reasonable hour. Their account shows that parental leave is not indispensable for more gender-equal relations, and how flexible working patterns can potentially facilitate such relations (Chung, 2022). However, the precarious nature of their jobs was part and parcel of the reasoning and context in which they worked together to provide for their family financially, and such work patterns may not be sustainable in the longer term.

Plans for the future

The accounts of the men and women featured in this chapter show that most of them anticipated a continuation of their current set-up, in which both take responsibility for paid and unpaid work. This group narrated the least gendered differences in terms of expectations, though gendered differences in orientations to the future are still discernible. Mary and Mark, for example, told me that they expected to be in the same jobs, perhaps at a slightly more senior level. He said, 'I don't think either of us are massively ambitious', and so they will focus on maintaining a work–life balance rather than on career progression. He thought they would both be working full-time by the time their child turns ten but Mary thought they might both stick with a four-day week. Meanwhile, Beth and Bart expressed strong doubts about their ability to predict the future, which reflected their anxieties about the precarious nature of their jobs. Nonetheless, they anticipated a set-up largely similar to their current situation. But Beth identified her gender as an extra barrier that she must face in her career:

> Katherine: So I just wondered what you think your life ah as a family or whatever, and your work as well /will look like in nine years' time?

Beth: [sighs] No idea, seriously no idea, because nine years, it's really a long time. I've been here in London for, it will be nine years exactly, so, and how much happened, I mean in terms of work actually [laughs] not that much, because I'm pretty much eight years in the same office. So ah yeah, I don't know. [...] I'm not sure whether we would have a second kid, because it was very difficult for us to get one [short laugh], ah in terms of health problems. Ah so maybe we will be just still three of us. Um [pause] I don't know, I could just say probably what I hope for rather than what, obviously I don't know what it will be, but ah I hope that we will still be together and that we will be able to, to maintain our relationship as, as a couple, so that it's still, that really we will like each other's company basically. [...] It worries me whether I will be able to maintain my position, as a woman unfortunately, yeah ah because I don't want to have my own group, because I just, I, I tried it and I just don't have the capacity to deal with that, with the level of stress ah which that brings. And so therefore I don't want that, and um I'm happy to stay in, in one place for long if, if it provides me enough ah joy, ah let's say, ah and reasonable salary. But yeah, I am a bit worried. [...] So yeah, so that's a little bit pfft, because we don't see so many older women in, in my industry. But hopefully it will change.

Beth, Interview 3

We can see in this illustrative account that women identified more difficulties in combining work and care in the future than men. As detailed in chapters 2 and 3, women are more attuned to and expectant of career penalties linked to their motherhood status and caring role.

Career progression was not a central focus for these couples in the ways described by (mostly) men in previous chapters. Edward, for example, focused on how he is likely to take more responsibility for childcare than his wife Emily when he spoke of the future:

Edward: So I think, in ten years' time I think there'll be a lot more flexibility to work from home. So that would probably be what I'd be doing I'd say. Just like help with

> like pick-up and drop-off to school and that sort of thing I think would be very helpful.
>
> Katherine: Mmm=.
>
> Edward: =And it would allow Emily to stay at her firm, be a partner if she wanted to be. I could, I could be the sort of, you know, the the parent who does picks ups and drops offs and that sort of thing.
>
> Katherine: Mmhmm.
>
> Edward: And I would be very happy to do that.
>
> Katherine: Mmhmm. And ah do you think you'll be working full-time?
>
> Edward: Yes, I think so. I don't work very long hours anyway and I enjoy my job.
>
> Edward, Interview 3

Edward expected more specialisation in roles in their family, given Emily's expected long working hours, and his expectation was no doubt influenced by her higher earnings. For him, however, his greater care role will be compatible with full-time work. This future is not certain, however, as Emily expressed some doubt about her future career plans:

> Yeah, hopefully we're just having a nice like, I think probably I'll still be working um full-time. Well maybe, I mean hopefully I'd be working four days a week by then, somewhere, probably not in my current job. I think it'd probably be too busy to carry on forever. […] My current job is one where they would either make me partner in about four or five years' time or I would have to leave basically. Um and it, it might be that I want to be a partner there and they want me to be um […] I sort of suspect that we'd sit down and think, it's such a big commitment and time commitment that it's not right. Um but I don't know, that might, so that's an option. Um I think if I, ah my career doesn't follow that path then I would try and find an in-house job um at like a kind of big like pharmaceutical or tech company um somewhere that basically has lots of um investigations um or litigation work, and I would hopefully have a kind of relatively senior um litigation job there, I guess is what I'd hope to do.
>
> Emily, Interview 3

Note how Emily brought Edward into her career decision-making in the future ('we'd sit down and think ...'). Like the women in chapter 7, Emily's career is contingent on family needs, though given her primary earning status in the couple and Edward's relative flexibility and shorter working day (even if Emily doesn't become a partner), it seems likely that Edward will take more responsibility for childcare than Emily. There may also be a certain amount of 'display' (Finch, 2007) of good motherhood in her narration, as Emily positions her family as more important than her career. Either way, her account demonstrates the narrative possibilities of the future available to her and how these shape decisions about career and family.

One other participant in this group anticipated a move to role specialisation: Keith. As we discussed above, Keith lamented the impact of SPL on his career, although he reported that, overall, the benefits of SPL for him and his family outweighed the disadvantages. At the time of the final interview, he and Kate shared responsibility for paid and unpaid work, earning similar amounts and with no 'family manager' in place. When they talked about the future, however, differing *moral* responsibilities relating to parenthood came into focus. For example, Keith talked about his attachment to his career and a sense that he was ultimately responsible for family finances:

> Katherine: So did you say you expect to work longer hours in the future?
>
> Keith: Yes I think this is, for [...], again with, with no hubris at all the um the sort of level that I'm at and the, and the sort of jobs that I would look to take would be jobs that, that expect a level of commitment that um that you will always get the work done and you will always find a way to make sure that, that your job is, is, is done. Now here in my current company that is achievable within um core business hours plus a little bit now and again, but I think that that's unusual. I think that most places where I was doing a senior role, that I would be looking to do, would require me to work longer hours than I work here.
>
> Katherine: So would it be possible to find a job with similar work hours to what you do now?
>
> Keith: I think for me finding the right job is more important, or, I need to caveat that, I think that other things around career development, progression, significance those

sorts of things, are more important to me than working hours, and so it's highly likely that, that were I faced with a, a choice of places where I had to work longer hours um for a job that I thought was better for us all um [pause] – and I know that that is itself a mixed statement – then, then I would be attracted to that job even if it meant that I wasn't going to be home to be involved in the evenings the same amount as I am here.

Katherine: So what, what, what's better for us? What do you mean by that?

Keith: So I think the, uh, in terms of, of giving us access to um better quality of living um and earning more money, getting more progression um having more job satisfaction for me, that that, that obviously affects the family as well. And I think that for me it's quite important to feel like I'm making a difference at a wider scale, and so […] there's a lot of personal objectives in there but they overflow very directly into […] our ability to do things that, that Kate in particular likes. So the ability to have holidays and not really have to worry about money and those sorts of things.

Keith, Interview 3

In this case, Keith's experiences of SPL, which were the most negatively summarised (see chapter 5), did not reorient his attitude to work. He remained ambitious for his career, tying such advancements to family needs and desires ('what Kate in particular wants') in ways similar to more traditional fathers (reported in chapter 6). In tandem, he anticipated that Kate would prioritise the care of their child over career progression, perhaps because she was already working part-time. For her part, Kate told me that she expected to be back in full-time work when their son was 10, and to be more focused on her career, 'almost having a bit of a resurgence in my career perhaps' (interview 3). While it's true that Kate was working part-time at the time of the final interview, she had previously told me that this is the norm in her (female-dominated) workplace and that she did not anticipate that this temporary reduction of hours would have major long-term consequences for her career advancement. Thus, the future of this couple's sharing of paid and unpaid work remained the least certain.

Conclusion

In this chapter I have detailed the experiences of couples sharing responsibility for paid and unpaid work, where each parent takes on the everyday practical tasks of this work and the associated 'mental load' (Dean et al., 2022) in managing it. I find that fathers' leave alone was an important factor in establishing this sharing, both from the perspectives of the participants themselves and also from my observation of their practices over time. In particular, it was notable that fathers developed confidence in caring for their children 'in their own way' during leave alone. When the leave period was over, they continued to hold responsibilities for childcare and housework, and their relationship with their children had also developed in such a way that their son or daughter did not express a preference for the mother (as we saw in previous chapters). On the other hand, one couple in this group, Beth and Bart, did not take SPL. Their shared perspective on care and work, along with Bart's access to flexible working, shaped their shared responsibilities. It is also possible that Bart's avoidance of SPL, despite Beth's encouragement, has resulted in him 'compensating' by making sure that he participates fully in childcare and housework. Either way, their example shows that men's participation in parental leave is not 'indispensable' for more gender-equal relations (see also O'Brien & Wall, 2017) and that a shared ideology and access to other work–care reconciliation policies can also play a role.

As these couples look to the future, most of them anticipate similar patterns of sharing paid and unpaid work responsibilities. However, gendered differences in orientations to the future were still discernible: women were more likely than men to envision challenges in combining a career with care responsibilities, because of their own previous experiences in paid work and those of their female colleagues (as discussed in chapters 2 and 3). It is also notable that most of the fathers in this chapter expressed less career ambition than fathers in previous chapters, which supports other research which has found that sharing of responsibilities is more likely when career progression is not prioritised (Schwartz, 1994). Bart and Keith were the exceptions, with Keith envisaging a future switch to more role specialisation in his family. So even in couples who share the responsibilities of paid and unpaid work after the leave period, we can see that gendered orientations to and experiences of work and care shape the constraints and opportunities they envisioned in their future family lives. How such visions of the future play out will be examined when their children turn 10 years of age.

Note

1 Unusually, Bart's employer offered four weeks of fully paid paternity leave.

9
Does shared parental leave live up to its promise? Concluding thoughts

Before I began this study, well before I wrote this book, I had my own experience of sharing leave with my husband. I took leave in this way because I believed that it would lead to more equal parenting between us. This is the 'promise' of SPL, as outlined in the original policy statements (Department for Education & Department for Business, Innovation and Skills, 2013) and often promoted in popular feminist texts (e.g. Asher, 2011) and by scholars of social policy and division of labour studies (see Gornick & Meyers, 2003). But what does 'equality' mean? A dominant understanding is that a fifty–fifty division of paid and unpaid work is the *most* 'equal' option (Doucet, 2015; Orloff, 2009). This is the 'symmetrical' division of tasks which sharing couples in this study often aspired to. However, even putting aside the practical (and analytical) difficulty of accounting for and splitting every household or care task, greater parity between these tasks may not mean more 'equality' – nor disparity mean less equality. Reflecting on her research with stay-at-home fathers, for example, Doucet (2015) notes a sharp division in paid and unpaid work (albeit not along traditionally gendered lines), which is coupled with egalitarian practices concerning, for instance, the sharing of decision-making in the family.

Moreover, without a shift in the value accorded to paid work and care work, a symmetrical division of labour could also lead to what Nancy Fraser (1994, 2013) calls a 'universal breadwinner' model, in which traditionally masculine norms of the ideal worker prevail. In this scenario, both parents have similar participation in different forms of labour, but their lives are dominated by paid work, with family and leisure time squeezed out. Such work and care divisions are likely to be propped up by paid domestic services, often provided by racialised and migrant workers (Prattes, 2022). This does little to shift societal gendered role specialisation, since the outsourced care is often itself deeply gendered in terms of who undertakes which tasks (men doing handiwork and women cleaning; see Prattes, 2022) and in that it is often the mother that manages such outsourced help (Brooks & Hodkinson, 2020).

I have also found that not all individuals will conceive or narrate 'equality' in this symmetrical way (Twamley & Faircloth, 2023). As we have seen in this study, other couples may aspire to a sense of 'fairness' in their divisions of paid and unpaid work. While this often resulted in a traditional gender split (the mother taking primary responsibility for care and the father for earning), some couples said they equally appreciated and respected both roles. In these cases, adopting different roles did not necessarily result in uneven power relations more broadly in the relationship (such as in key decision-making, or in one partner consistently making compromises for the other), or in less intimacy and closeness within the couple relationship. But, as other scholars have long noted, when practices at the couple level are replicated across a population, the pattern becomes itself a gendering structure. The gendered separate spheres which can follow mean that individuals are inhibited from achieving their full range of capabilities (Nussbaum, 1997) and are closed off from alternative possibilities. For example, while there may be much joy in caring for children, if it is seen as compulsory for women to take on a primary role it can become a source of frustration, sadness and regret (Donath, 2015; Mauthner, 2002). Expectations that women will take on an intensive mothering role and prioritise care above paid work can also contribute to gendered discrimination in the workplace and to the gender pay gap (Goldin, 2021; Sullivan, 2019). The difficulties of combining a career with motherhood may push women out of a career path or paid work entirely, to their possible later regret (Orgad, 2019). Meanwhile men are potentially locked out of a close and intimate relationship with their child, spending increasing time in a job which they may or may not find fulfilling. These deeply ingrained gendered narratives of motherhood and fatherhood were apparent across the study and were upheld by work norms and social policies (including SPL) that do not support flexibility in parents' negotiations of work and care, but, rather, often seem to reinforce these gendered narratives.

A better model, according to Fraser, is the 'universal caregiver model' (1994, 2013) in which care responsibilities are foregrounded and shared by men and women. The hope is that bringing men into care could challenge the demanding nature of work cultures and encourage men to break away from traditional masculine norms (Elliott, 2016). There are signs that parental leave can be part of this landscape of change: earlier research has shown that when men care for children they begin to value the skill involved in care work and question normative work structures (Doucet, 2006). In the next section, I consider what the present study tells us about how the UK leave system can be part of this process of change.

What difference does fathers' take-up of leave make?

The current menu of parental leave options in the UK, of which SPL is a part, frames the transition to parenthood of men and women. First, paternity leave is an individual right for fathers (or partners of the mother/second parents), which gives up to two weeks of (low-paid) leave, usually taken at the time of birth. As documented in Part II, the two weeks of paternity leave was considered too short to offer effective support for new mothers or for fathers to establish care routines with their new baby. Mothers detailed severe challenges when men returned to paid work, even describing the end of paternity leave as 'traumatic'. Women who had experienced a difficult birth or had a child with health issues reported the most challenges. This experience at the transition to parenthood has lingering impacts on the rest of the maternity leave and is recalled a year later with much sadness. The innovative use of the diary exposes the difficult experiences of mothers on leave alone, highlighting the individualised nature of contemporary mothering and the heightened sense of risk associated with caring for a newborn (Lee et al., 2023).

Parents' accounts of the maternity leave period also demonstrate how influential women's leave is in establishing mothers as primary caregivers. Women reported the challenge of being (or feeling) solely responsible for their children's health and development, which they saw as hinging on a 'correct' way of parenting. The more time they spent with their babies, the more confident they grew in meeting their children's needs, and the more children began to express a preference for the mother over the father. Men's time with their babies was much more limited and their expertise correspondingly lower. Over time, women's increasing expertise affirmed available narratives about the importance of mothers to their children as well as about their biological superiority in nurturing.

Where fathers used SPL or another employer-supported leave to increase the length of leave at the time of birth, usually to between four and six weeks, this made a tremendous difference to mothers and fathers. The transition to parenthood was described in much more positive terms and mothers reported a sense that parenting was a 'shared endeavour'. However, four fathers did not take even their two weeks of paternity leave, or worked through part of their leave. Since they all reported that their leave would have been fully paid, this decision was not due to financial constraints. Nonetheless, given the large numbers (at the national level) of fathers that take this leave (Chanfreau et al., 2011), this study indicates that an increase in paternity leave entitlement would be very beneficial for the well-being of families.

Leave taken together does not, however, appear to shift gendered norms of parenting responsibilities. Couples who took their leave at the same time, no matter how long they took, did not report the same shifts as couples in which the father took leave alone. As detailed in Part II, during leave together fathers and mothers often worked collectively in upholding the mother's primary care role. Such findings have been observed in other settings (Karu, 2012). This pattern of leave tended towards a symmetrical sharing of everyday care tasks, but with mothers taking an overall 'family manager' role after the leave period was over. 'Family-managing mothers' recounted severe struggles in maintaining all the family mental load alongside paid work, which translated into an expectation that they would step back, further or entirely, from paid work in the future. Other research has demonstrated the detrimental impact on women's mental health of this uneven distribution of the mental load (Reich-Stiebert et al., 2023).

When fathers were on leave alone, this was seen to have a greater impact on couples' practices in relation to paid and unpaid work and, importantly, on perceived *responsibilities* for paid and unpaid work. These fathers built up confidence in their care abilities over long periods of leave alone (two months or more), in similar ways to women on leave alone. In the words of the mothers and the fathers, men learned to care 'in their own way', thus developing an independent relationship with their child. They also took on responsibilities in housework, not just care work, meaning there was a shift in gendered practices overall, not just in relation to care work or more involved fathering. Importantly, there were couples in this group that had not started the study with a particularly egalitarian perspective, which indicates that sharing leave can *change* men and women's gendered perspectives and practices. In a contrasting case, one father, Tim, took a period of leave alone but the eventual practices of the couple were 'traditional' in that his wife Tara gave up paid work, thus taking on the bulk of the responsibility for care, and Tim took the responsibility for earning. However, Tim reported a reorientation to care and paid work, and the couple's daily accounts emphasised a sharing of domestic work, as far as was feasible given Tim's full-time work. This example shows the benefits of sharing leave 'even' for couples who on the face of it practise traditional divisions of labour. In line with research conducted in Canada and Sweden (Doucet & McKay, 2020; Duvander et al., 2017), I have found that when men take parental leave alone, they disrupt 'masculine work norms' and begin the process of shifting broader 'social, public, and cultural narratives' (Somers, 1994:614, quoted in Doucet & McKay, 2020).

SPL is not, however, a magic bullet which will transform gendered relations in the UK. For a start, many more men need to be able to take it for any societal shift to occur. In the next section, I bring together the findings from this study to consider what shapes why and how people take parental leave in the UK, their experiences of leave and of the period after it ended. In the final section I return to a consideration of what changes to the current UK parental leave system would be needed to address these factors and effect more change.

What shapes UK parents' decisions on and experiences of leave?

The workplace

Across the period of the study, from pregnancy right through to participants' plans for the future, 'greedy work' (Goldin, 2021) looms large in the everyday lives of participants. Greedy workplaces rely on 'ideal workers' (Acker, 1990) who prioritise their paid work over all other commitments. These workplaces penalise those who work part-time or use flexible work policies, and disproportionately reward those who put themselves entirely at the disposal of their employers (Goldin, 2021). This type of work culture is most commonly found in white-collar jobs and professions, and is at its 'greediest' in high-stress, high-demand sectors such as finance, law and technology (Goldin, 2021; T. A. Sullivan, 2014), in which several of my participants worked. Such workers typically perceive long work hours as *legitimate* (Byun & Won, 2020; Williams et al., 2013), which can place indirect limits on fathers' leave-taking (Haas & Hwang, 2019).

In the first round of interviews, before the babies had even been born, greedy work shaped the decisions that participants made about SPL. They told me that only one career could realistically be supported in the household, and since parental leave was likely to be (more) detrimental to men's careers, men should forgo SPL. For example, Debbie initially encouraged her husband David to take six months of SPL, to support his wish to be an involved father and to establish equal parenting of their daughter. David told me that he was enthusiastic at first, but later felt that this was 'too long' a time to take out of his career and would likely inhibit his career progression. He then considered taking one month's leave, but worried that even this amount of time off work might impact on his career, and ended up not taking any SPL at all. What is interesting in David's case is that he decided against taking SPL even though he reported support from colleagues, his line manager and his wife. This shows that greedy work is manifested not only in explicit discouragement from taking SPL by co-workers or line managers (of which some was reported by participants; see also Atkinson, 2023), but in a fundamental understanding of employee–employer responsibilities which David had internalised, interpreting even supportive statements in ways which ultimately convinced him not to take SPL. He described imagining what might be said by others behind his back (and indeed his own hypothetical response to another colleague considering SPL), indicating the intersubjective relational nature (Burkitt, 2016) of decisions about leave.

The reach of greedy work is seen most explicitly in fathers' practices concerning paternity leave. Although the two weeks off from paid work is a well-established right in the UK (having been introduced in 2003), some fathers in this study reduced their paternity leave or continued to work through it. Wider statistics indicate that most fathers take leave around the time of birth, but not all take paternity leave (Chanfreau et al., 2011: 200). Since the leave is so poorly remunerated, some fathers forgo their two weeks of paternity leave entitlement and choose to take annual leave instead. Even when fathers take paternity leave, as found in this study, some may continue to undertake paid work during their leave. Participants did not regard their lack of take-up of paternity leave as the fault of unsupportive greedy work contexts, but, rather, as par for the course in contemporary professional work. In fact, some fathers, such as Bart (university postdoctoral researcher), expressed *gratitude* at the flexibility he was afforded by his employers, which meant he could continue to work during his paternity leave. This signals the sociocultural narratives of work and care prevalent in the UK: the latter is seen as a private familial responsibility, and little consideration is given to how employers might facilitate employees' care (or other) responsibilities. Such a sentiment was expressed again later by Bart in accounting for his decision not to take SPL: that is, since he can effectively decide his work hours anyway, he can be present for his wife and children without taking SPL. This aligns with Heejung Chung's insight of the 'flexibility paradox' (2022): she suggests that greater control over their work schedules can paradoxically lead to employees working more hours than their contracts stipulate. Here we see that it may also impact on men's take-up of leave. As Burkitt (2016) reflects, participants such as Bart do not necessarily deliberate reflexively on how to respond to an external structure such as the workplace, but are embedded within the everyday relationships of that structure, so that they respond in non-reflexive ways. That is, their experiences and relationships within the workplace have shaped the ways in which they feel and think about leave from work.

For those that did share leave, greedy work influenced the amount of time they planned to take off: they kept their total SPL length to a (seemingly arbitrary) shortish term, usually less than a third of what their partners took, or took their leave in periods when they were unlikely to be busy (see also Atkinson, 2023). These participants are conforming to the logic of their work contexts, even if they are breaking with established norms in which men do not take SPL at all. The fathers who took the longest leave were those that rejected the ideal of personal career progression entirely, envisaging fatherhood as likely to offer a more fulfilling future. Mark, for example, who took six months of leave, told me that he had no ambition to achieve a senior position at work, which would only impact negatively on his personal and familial goals and well-being.

During the maternity leave period, greedy work affected men's ability to spend time with their partners and children. Men reported struggling to get home before the baby had been put to bed, or getting home but working late into the night to catch up. Bart, who lauded his work flexibility, repeatedly reported in his diaries his stress over meeting work deadlines while also trying to be present for Beth and baby B. These struggles were greater for men who were the primary or only breadwinner in the family. Such men reported a perceived responsibility to provide, and worked harder and longer for greater financial rewards and job security than men who were able to share the role of provider with their partners.

Work precarity heightened anxieties about earning. This is a growing facet of contemporary work, and it feeds into ideal worker norms by encouraging 'ideal' workers to work increasingly long hours in order to avoid redundancy. The expansion of the gig economy, in which worked hours directly correlate with earnings, will mean that lower-earning parents are likely to experience similar or heightened pressures to those of higher-earning parents. In other research, men's increased earnings after becoming fathers have been called the fatherhood or 'daddy' bonus: quantitative studies show that men who become fathers often experience an acceleration in their careers (Hodges & Budig, 2010; Koslowski, 2011). What is lost in this moniker is the loss experienced by men and their families, namely time with their newborn baby and partner. This was often sorely regretted in men's diaries and later interviews, though without a concomitant criticism of UK work structures. As Adam told me in his first interview, 'it's just what successful people do' (see chapter 3).

Women and men narrated the impacts of greedy work in different ways. While women were more likely to opt out of or take time out from their careers, men spent considerable time describing their deliberations and struggles with high workloads and career ambitions. In part, this is down to decisions about whose career will be prioritised, as described in the first interviews when the women were pregnant, as well as men's positioning as the breadwinner (and the gendered sociocultural narratives available to mothers and fathers, which are discussed further in the next section). The difference also reflects long-standing expectations of (or resignation to) the motherhood penalty on the part of women. That becoming a parent will impact on women's careers is well established in research (Goldin, 2021) and well understood amongst female participants. Along with wishes to be active and involved mothers, women reported choosing careers or career paths which would be more compatible with having a family long before becoming pregnant. Studies which examine young people's aspirations for the future report similar findings (Grunow & Evertsson, 2016; Cantó-Milà & Seebach, 2015; Patterson & Forbes, 2012). That is, women are more likely than men to step back from or opt out of paid work and ambitious career dreams.

Such stepping back is encouraged by women's (and men's) understandings of gendered discrimination, as evidenced in the gender wage gap (Cukrowska-Torzewska & Lovasz, 2020). Although discrimination against men that take parental leave was a greater focus in many of the interviews, such worries were grounded in an understanding of historical discrimination against carer-employees, who typically have been (and continue to be) women. As reported in chapters 2 and 3, fear of career repercussions figured prominently in men's accounts of decisions about SPL. There is a lack of evidence on the impact of men's take-up of parental leave on their careers or earnings. Research in Germany found that the majority of fathers that take leave report a negligible impact on their career progression, regardless of the length of leave taken (Samtleben et al., 2019), while women's length of leave is associated with a career penalty (women's *shorter* leave provoked the penalty) (Hipp, 2018; Samtleben et al., 2019). The men in this study who took SPL did not report any substantial penalty from having done so, and several of them were promoted or moved to a better job after having taken it. No woman at all was promoted over the course of the study, and just one changed job (staying at the same level). While this is a small sample, it is consistent with wider quantitative research on the motherhood penalty (Goldin, 2021). Thus, it does appear that broader structures tend to support men's careers, even when they take extended parental leave. Then, if one parent's career needs to take precedence, all too often it 'makes sense' that it should be the man's. More extensive projects of large-scale research are needed, however, on how taking extended parental leave may impact on men's career advancement.

These decisions about paid work had lasting effects. In the final round of interviews, when the parental leave period was over, most fathers were working full-time and most mothers were working part-time or had left paid work. It is rare for mothers to leave paid work entirely, but the 1.5 working household is the dominant pattern amongst parents of young children in the UK (Connolly et al., 2016; ONS, 2021). The parents who had shared leave were more likely to be working similar hours, often part-time. Overall, the reach of work culture into the decisions and experiences of leave highlights the importance of 'eliminating masculine work norms' (Williams, 2012:128) if the full potential of parental leave is to be realised (see also Moss & Deven, 2015; Doucet, 2023).

'Families we live by'

> This Saturday as he [Riley] wants to carry on working, I go with baby R to the park. It feels weird as on the weekends all buggies are pushed by mum and dad. I wonder if people notice that we are without dad in the park. I text Riley and ask if he is done with the work he wanted to do and say that he should come to the park and that we should go for an ice cream. He joins us later, we walk and talk while baby R is sleeping. This is mostly the only couple time we have since baby R was born.
>
> Rita, Diary 2 (baby 6 months old)

'Families we live by' (Gillis, 1997) refers to images and expectations, often idealised, of family life that influence family practices (D. H. J. Morgan, 2011) and how we display family (Finch, 2007). In 'families' I include couples, and indeed couple display was seen clearly across the study. Here I am referring to the means through which participants construct and project a particular vision of their intimate or family life, and how these are incorporated into their leave narratives. The understandings of family or couple life which participants draw on come from shared sociocultural narratives apparent in various media (television, advice books and so on), threaded through government policies, and handed down from generation to generation. They are also drawn from memories of our own childhoods and the stories we tell about them (Gillis, 1997). As the extract from Rita's diary shows, individuals may reflexively negotiate these visions of family in their everyday life. In this study, participants were often seen to have an emotional attachment to particular ideas of family, and to attempt to (re-)create these visions through their everyday practices. Rita, for example, recorded that she felt 'weird' being without her partner. In other entries, she expressed sadness when her idea of family, and her and her partner's practices, didn't match. Such ideals of what it means to be or practise family are arguably *more* influential at the point of transition to parenthood, as participants attempt to work out the ways in which they are and do family, as for example Rita, who asks Riley to join her after observing other families around her on her walk.

Parental leave, or more precisely maternity leave, which was introduced in the UK in 1973, figures in normative visions of the transition to parenthood in ways that men's extended leave does not (at least in the UK). Sarah, for example, talked about how she had always anticipated taking all of her maternity leave. She reported having had various discussions with her (female) friends about what maternity leave would be like and about her plans for various activities while on leave. This is the predicted and normative transitional pathway to motherhood in the UK, as is the two weeks of paternity leave for fatherhood. As a historical norm it ties in with available narratives on the primacy of the mother in young babies' lives (Hays, 1996), and reinforces the idea of the maternity leave period as morally belonging to the mother. This is further enshrined in the make-up of SPL, which functions through a maternity leave transfer mechanism whereby the mother must go through administrative procedures in order to give part of her leave to the father of the child. Thus, some couples in this study did not discuss sharing leave at all, but just assumed that the mother would take all the leave. Even when mothers did encourage their partners to take SPL, some men expressed reluctance to 'take her leave', as was the case with David and Debbie (see chapter 2) (see also Stovell, 2021; Twamley, 2019). Colleagues and friends reinforced this assumption, telling participants, for example, 'My wife would never let me take her leave', which highlights the moralised context in which parents navigate decisions about SPL.

The differing pressures on men and women in relation to leave reflect the wider gendered hegemonic norms of intensive parenting prevalent in UK society (Lee et al., 2023). Scholars have noted that, while the number of mothers in paid work has increased, so have the demands placed upon them. The 'intensive mother' is positioned as responsible for all aspects of a child's physical and emotional development, to be substituted by no one else, not even the father (Hays, 1996; Lee et al., 2023). She should be ever-present, always prioritising the needs of the child, no matter the cost to herself, since the future well-being of her child rests on her shoulders (Wolf, 2011). Ideals of intensive mothering were certainly visible amongst the participants in this study and fed into decisions about leave and later employment. Judy, for example, spent considerable time explaining to me the importance for the development of her child of her being a full-time mother at home, and how this led her to give up paid work entirely. In fact, most of the women in the study reduced their paid work hours or left employment after the leave period. As discussed in the previous section, couples felt that only one 'greedy' career could be facilitated. This is due to both the nature of paid work *and* the 'greedy' nature of intensive parenting. Even when couples had set aside career progression as a goal, as Mary and Mark did, the idea that a parent needed to be present shaped their work hours because they wanted to avoid formalised childcare as far as possible.

Such discourses of intensive motherhood also shaped mothers' experiences of the leave period. As documented in chapters 4 and 5, women described high levels of anxiety during the initial months of their maternity leave. In their accounts, mothers presented themselves as uniquely placed to care for their babies, even as they understood themselves to be still learning how to care. As Sarah told me in her second interview, 'The challenge [of maternity leave] is being responsible but learning at the same time.' Even when others were present, as in Helen's case when her mother moved in with her, or in Cara's case, whose sister lived nearby, this help was appreciated but did not shift the overwhelming sense of individual and personal responsibility that mothers expressed for their newborn infants. Therefore, women agonised over tiny shifts in weight and nap schedules, complaining that their partners did not take their concerns sufficiently seriously. The more time alone they spent with their babies during extended maternity leave, the more they learned to care for them, thus gaining more expertise than anyone else, which fed into narratives about the indispensability of mothers to their young children and ensured that in the majority of cases care responsibility stayed firmly on their shoulders.

Some women were seen to take on ideals of intensive mothering over the course of the leave period. Gina, for example, had initially been very forthright in her belief in the importance of the equal participation of men and women in parenthood. During her initial interviews she had rejected essentialised ideas of motherhood and fatherhood and anticipated a 'fifty–fifty' division of all care tasks between herself and her partner Gerald. However, once her baby arrived, she expressed anxieties about her ability to mother properly, many centred on breastfeeding, which she increasingly came to see as a measure of 'how good a mother' she was. By her own account, the moral pressure to breastfeed was so strong that she put the health of baby G at risk by refusing to switch to formula feed even when his weight dropped worryingly low. The apparent ideological shift in her understanding of motherhood after the birth of her child is testament to the powerful discourses surrounding the primacy of motherhood and its links to breastfeeding (Faircloth, 2013, 2021). This shift demonstrates that *becoming* and living as a mother, and the exposure to ideals of motherhood that comes with such a transition, can shape women's experiences of motherhood as much as previously received ideas of motherhood. For Gina, there were few other (apparent) available narratives of good motherhood for her to draw on after she 'failed' in what she saw as one of the most vital elements (breastfeeding). In response, she took on ever more responsibility for their child, much to her partner Gerald's frustration, who was keen to be an equal or even primary parent.

As documented in chapter 1, scholars have noted shifts in understandings of fatherhood over the last 30 years (Brannen et al., 2023; Dermott & Miller, 2015), of which the introduction of SPL can be seen as a symptom (and potential accelerator). The shifts in understanding point to the dynamic nature of family life ideals. Increasingly, fathers are expected to be 'involved' in the hands-on care of their children in ways their fathers before them were not (Brannen et al., 2023). Indeed, time-use studies demonstrate an upward trend in the time fathers spend with their children since about 2000 (Sullivan, 2019). However, as is reflected in the findings presented here, men's involvement in care is often negotiated with their responsibilities in paid work. There often is no clear dichotomy for men between being a 'good carer' and a 'good provider' (Shirani et al., 2012a; Yarwood, 2011), certainly less so than for women. Breadwinning clearly remains a key aspect of fathering for the men in this study. Several men reported an increased sense of responsibility for financial provisioning after the birth of their children. This was heightened in families where women were planning to leave or reduce their paid work. In these cases, breadwinning could be perceived as care for both children *and* partner, in that the father was supporting the mother's wish to be the primary caregiver. However, these 'care' practices of breadwinning did not necessarily conform to Elliott's (2016) tenets of caring masculinity, in which men should 'embrace care *and* reject domination' (Roberts & Prattes, 2023:9, emphasis original), in the ways that women earners did. For instance, we saw examples of higher-earning women who explicitly de-emphasised the importance of earning in negotiations of leave, in an apparent bid to counteract potential power differentials. In contrast, some men, such as Riley, centred earning differentials in negotiating his way out of unpaid labour in the household.

Not all men embraced the role of breadwinner, and some experienced deep conflict between their wish to be present in their children's lives and the felt need to work long hours in order to support their family financially. As discussed by Brooks and Hodkinson (2020), men's greater involvement in paid work than women is often assumed to be an advantage which men enjoy, since paid work offers career rewards and financial autonomy. The benefit of financial autonomy cannot be denied (not all fathers will experience 'career rewards' per se), but we should be mindful not to overlook the challenges men experience in their role as providers (Townsend, 2002), which they must balance against ideals of (and their own desires to be) involved fathers. This was most poignantly seen in the case of John, who experienced high levels of stress as he attempted to provide for his family while also being present for his wife Judy and their daughter (see chapter 6).

Unlike Andrea Doucet (2018) in her research with couple parents in Canada, I did not observe that mothers and fathers both felt they were responsible for caring and financial provisioning. Women in this study did not articulate providing as part of their responsibility as a mother or towards the household more generally. This is perhaps because of the moment in participants' lives at which this study was conducted, at the transition to parenthood, when gendered orientations to family are at their peak (Faircloth, 2021; Yavorsky et al., 2015) and perhaps because of the class background of the participants (it was possible for some of the couples to rely almost entirely on one salary). Instead, I found women's orientations to provisioning to be markedly different from men's. Women did not discuss responsibility for 'breadwinning' in the same way as men, even when they earned similar amounts to, or more than, their partners, which ties in with earlier research which shows that earning is not a sufficient condition to be perceived as a breadwinner (Nadim, 2016; Schmidt, 2018). Given these different orientations to breadwinning, men's time with children tended to be accommodated to work responsibilities, while women's paid work was more often accommodated to care responsibilities (see also Miller, 2005, 2010).

Perhaps it is not surprising that SPL does not always figure in conceptualisations of good fatherhood, especially when we consider the ways in which SPL defies the logics of UK work culture (as described in the previous section). This narrative absence was notably the case amongst non-sharers. Ian, for example, wrote in his initial survey that his plan to take two weeks of paternity leave and no SPL would ensure that he and Ivy would be 'involved parents' (see chapter 2). Ian's perspective appears to reflect conceptions of what Esther Dermott (2008) calls the 'intimate father'. She writes that contemporary fathering ideals in the UK often idealise a father who is emotionally close to his child, but that such closeness is not necessarily predicated on intensive time demands in the way that good mothering is.

On the other hand, such an understanding – of leave from work as incidental to involved fatherhood – stands in strong contrast to sharers' perspectives. For these couples, SPL was central to fathers' imagined (future) close relationship with their child, as well as the couples' intimate relationship (discussed further below). Moreover, going against ideals of intensive mothering, fathers in these couples were often narrated as (potentially) equally responsible with women. The inclusion of these fathers in this study affords an examination of the conditions under which couples decide to arrange paid and unpaid work in ways that differ from the norm. As I discussed in chapter 3, a number of factors were necessary to support these couples in 'going against the grain', including a less gendered perspective on parenting and family life.

This brings me to the next point, that alongside ideals of family are those of couple intimacy, in which equality between partners is frequently understood as key (Jamieson, 2011; Twamley, 2012; Van Hooff, 2011). In this study, all the women and most of the men expressed some sense of equality as an important element of their relationship. A minority of men saw equality as a secondary matter or were primarily concerned with equality in divisions of childcare (and not housework). Similar findings from Finland and Spain suggest that this is not unique to the UK (Eerola, Närvi, Terävä & Repo, 2021; Romero-Balsas et al., 2013). Couples' narration of themselves as 'equal' inflected their leave narratives, so that for non-sharers, for example, leave was positioned as impossible, or as unnecessary for equality. I call these 'intimate negotiations' to highlight the relational couple context in which they occur, but also to emphasise that these narratives are constructed in accordance with the ideals and desires the couples hold for their intimate relationships. These shape how they narrate and construct decisions about leave, as they project, for themselves and to me, their (preferred) understanding of their relationship.

While equality and intimacy were linked for participants, narrations of what equality meant were not uniform (Twamley & Faircloth, 2023). Non-sharers tended to take an approach centring 'fairness', in which the partners may have different levels of involvement in paid and unpaid work, but this is expressed as resulting from personal preferences or abilities, rather than as being due to gendered structures. This perspective echoes discourses of 'choice feminism', in which little attention is paid to gendered structural constraints on choices (Budgeon, 2015; Gill et al., 2016). It is then the responsibility of the individual (usually the woman) to address any resultant dissatisfaction with divisions of labour, or it may lead her to blame herself for not being sufficiently ambitious or clever to progress in paid work (see Orgad, 2019). Sharers, on the other hand, tended to express a desire for symmetry, that is, both partners doing the same tasks to the same degree. Therefore, both partners taking SPL was considered a key aspect of practising equality in their relationships.

Between fairness and symmetry, only symmetry lives up to policy and scholarship ideals which present a fifty–fifty split as the normative goal (Orloff, 2009). This split is the most difficult configuration to achieve, both because of the attention and monitoring it requires and because current employment and policy structures do not readily facilitate such an arrangement. Moreover, couples seeking symmetry were most likely to identify their division of labour as unequal, since the bar was higher and was more visible when it wasn't reached. This is concerning, since a gap between spouses' ideals and practices of gender equality leads to a higher risk of partnership dissolution (Oláh & Gähler, 2014).

As noted in previous research, so embedded is the notion of equality as intrinsic to intimacy that couples may avoid identifying and discussing gendered inequalities (Orgad, 2019; Twamley, 2012). This was particularly notable amongst the non-sharers in this study. In chapter 2, I posited that this dynamic evolves in response to notions of feminism or appeals for equality as 'cold' and thus incompatible with loving relations. The result is an avoidance of explicit negotiations concerning parental leave, at least as it relates to equality or fairness, and an absence of any discussion about why SPL may be helpful in or necessary to the setting up of more equal parenting. A particularly memorable example of this was observed between Cara and Chidi. Cara expressed a strong desire for Chidi to take SPL but told me that after extended discussions they realised it was not financially possible, since he earned more than she did. In response, he revealed that in fact his company provided full pay for SPL, which meant not only that it would be affordable but that they would be better off if he took some of the SPL (since Cara's maternity leave pay was capped at the statutory level). Nonetheless, they appeared to work together within the interview to obfuscate the possibility of SPL in a process which I call collaborative gatekeeping (inspired by Miller's writing (2010) on the connected nature of so-called maternal and paternal gatekeeping). In contrast, amongst sharers, whose attitudes to feminism were in general much more positive than those of non-sharers, SPL was posited as a means to establish practices of equality, so that later negotiations (or 'nagging') were less likely to happen. We can see, then, that both sets of parents were keen to avoid discussing divisions of labour, but that for sharers SPL was understood as establishing norms that would avoid such negotiations, which were seen as harmful to intimacy.

'Families we live with'

Gillis (1997) distinguished 'the families we live by' from 'the families we live with', the latter representing the realities of family lives. Although they are defined separately, they are interconnected; idealised perceptions of family ('the families we live by') impact everyday practices and interactions. In using the term 'families we live by' here, I also wish to emphasise the relational nature of everyday family life (Twamley, Doucet & Schmidt, 2021), and how family and relationship practices are negotiated with real (and imagined) others (Burkitt, 2016; Holmes et al., 2021). Those that consider taking SPL navigate work, gender and family norms and ideals in their discussions with one another, with me, and with those around them, such as colleagues, friends and wider family. Participants' parents questioned whether SPL was a good idea and encouraged their sons to take fewer weeks of SPL (interestingly, discouragement from parents transferring maternity leave to their partners was not reported by mothers in the study). Meanwhile, friends and colleagues reportedly gave a more mixed picture: some actively supported participants' decisions to take SPL, but in a way which reinforced the idea that taking SPL was a 'risky' decision; for example, Keith's friends said things like 'I wouldn't do it, but good for you!', and Mark's manager warned him that SPL might be detrimental to his career progression. This is an example of the 'emotive gendering imposed by significant others' (Holmes et al., 2021:745) which was incorporated reflexively into how participants interpreted the possibility of taking SPL. It shaped how participants viewed and practised SPL, and increased the commitment necessary to go against the grain and take it.

At the couple level, it cannot be denied that the relative earnings of each parent shaped negotiations concerning divisions of paid and unpaid work. Previous research has shown that when the woman earns more her partner is more likely to take parental leave (Beglaubter, 2017; Valentova, 2011; Wood et al., 2023; Yarwood & Locke, 2016). This pattern was partially reflected in this study. Sharing couples were more likely to have the mother earning more than the father, while non-sharing couples were more likely to have the father earning more. In previous research, higher-earning mothers are commonly interpreted as having more bargaining power to negotiate their way out of care and housework. The findings of this book demonstrate a more complex situation; if women's earnings are higher than or similar to their partners', this gives men the opportunity to take a greater role in fatherhood. Some men, for example, reported long-held dreams of being an 'involved' or even a stay-at-home father; their attraction to their partner was increased by her complementary career ambition (this was the case with Gina and Gerald, for instance). In other cases where women earned more, this did not figure as an explicit reason for men to take SPL and was often even denied to have any relevance. This refusal to discuss women's higher earnings as a reason to share leave serves to downplay women's (potential) role as breadwinners in families. Indeed, being the higher or an equal earner was not a sufficient or automatic criterion to define a mother as a breadwinner (as discussed in the previous section). In contrast, where men earned more, this fact was cited as a barrier to men's take-up of SPL; participants told me that the financial impact of the father's SPL led them to decide against it. In some cases, such as that of Cara and Chidi, there was no apparent financial penalty from men's taking SPL, but couples still managed to rationalise barriers to men's take-up. Kaufman (Kaufman, 2018; Kaufman & Almqvist, 2017) and Stovell (2021) made similar observations in their research with fathers taking extended parental leave in the UK, concluding that constraints (such as affordability) are negotiated within the moral responsibilities of motherhood and fatherhood. This demonstrates that affordability is not sufficient motivation to shift parental leave practices, though it may well contribute.

Whatever the relative earnings, the decision to take SPL was most often framed as the *father's* choice. This is surprising given the maternity transfer mechanism through which SPL functions. This deferral to men's prerogative maintains heterosexual scripts of the man as active decision-maker, and the woman as passively reacting to him. Ellen Lamont (2014) argues that such dynamics emerge from gendered courtship conventions. Focusing on marriage proposals between US couples, she found that women who lead proposals are seen as coercive towards men and as taking a step too far in transgressing gender roles. Therefore, women encourage marital proposals or make their enthusiasm for marriage known, but the official proposal is set up to be made by men, which symbolically upholds gendered roles in the relationship. These findings concur with Schmidt, Rieder et al.'s (2015) research on couples' decision-making about leave in Austria. The authors argued that decisions for and against sharing leave were father-centred, and that framing the sharing of leave in this way reaffirmed hegemonic masculine ideals. Likewise, in her research with mixed-sex couples in which the woman earned more than the man, Tichenor notes that 'Instead of using their substantial resources to make claims to power, wives often defer to their husbands in the decision-making process. Even if wives disagree with husbands, they often seem reluctant to resist their husbands' wishes, or make their own opinions more clearly known' (2005:200).

These negotiation practices demonstrate how the relationship work engaged in by couples can reinforce normative gendered identities and positions. Gabb and Fink (2015:24) define relationship work as 'the everyday practices that couples do to sustain their relationships and the material conditions that shape their personal lives'. Women in this study upheld narratives of men as breadwinners and decision-makers in negotiations about leave. To frame this as 'relationship work' is to recognise that women (and men) may collude in hegemonic norms in a bid to support their partner and their intimate relationship with them. The loving care with which individuals negotiated difficult decisions about paid and unpaid work is an example of this work. In couple and individual interviews and diaries, participants showed the ways in which they are attuned to the difficulties that partners may experience in transgressing normative practices. This is shown in Emily and Edward's negotiations about leave, as observed in their first interview. Emily told me that she had been very keen for Edward to take leave so that they might establish more equal parenting responsibilities. Edward was more ambivalent and described the anxieties he felt about taking SPL. He said SPL was an 'alien' concept to him and that he worried both about what other people would think of him if he took SPL and about the repercussions at his workplace. Emily demonstrated sympathy towards his reluctance to take leave and told me that she left the decision to him; if he did not take the proposed two months of SPL, she would take it instead (as maternity leave). As Emily was earning considerably more than Edward, her taking the full maternity leave period would have come at a substantial financial cost (since the two months they were discussing were during the unpaid period of leave). The financial aspect is downplayed, which diffused potential power differentials within the couple and reduced the pressure

Edward might have felt to take SPL. In the end Edward did take two months of SPL, in part because he realised that the leave would fall in his least busy period of work.

In an article in which I focused on Emily and Edward's negotiations of parental leave, I posited that such gender-conforming negotiations were unlikely to lead to more egalitarian practices after the leave period (Twamley, 2021). In fact, as expanded upon in chapter 8, Edward's experiences while on leave were narrated as having a transformative impact on their relationship and family practices. He and Emily described how Edward built confidence in his ability to parent and experienced unexpected joy in his parenting over the course of SPL. In the final interview, they both reported sharing responsibilities of paid and unpaid work, care work and housework. Like other couples in that chapter, they attributed their shared parenting practices to Edward's period of leave alone. Their case is particularly notable given how circumspect Edward initially was towards SPL, and towards goals of gender equality more generally. These findings extend previous retrospective research which suggested that fathers' leave alone could transform men's orientation to paid work and care (O'Brien & Wall, 2017). By following fathers from pregnancy, I have been able to disentangle previous egalitarian attitudes and practices from those which emerged over the course of the leave. Through Edward's example, we can see that fathers' take-up of leave can shift the parenting perspectives and practices 'even' of men who are sceptical about its benefits, and who explicitly dissociate themselves from feminist or egalitarian goals.

In cases where men initiated the idea of SPL, this was apparently taken up without much resistance from women, though sometimes the length of the leave was debated. For example, Keith attended a talk at his workplace given by a man who had taken SPL. He told me in the first interview that the talk inspired him to take SPL, a key motivator being the potential for a close relationship with his future child. Kate had not considered SPL before but told me she was immediately happy to support Keith's proposal. She told me that she thought SPL would be good for their couple relationship, by helping to establish equal parenting roles and by improving empathy between her and Keith. Holmes (2004) argues that women are more attuned than men to the compromises that are needed to make relationships work, and are therefore more likely to make concessions. This may help explain women's reported acquiescence to share leave: women like Kate are demonstrating care for their partner through their willingness to share leave. But I also observed that women were more likely than men to see value in SPL, which didn't dramatically alter their own experience of leave (since most men propose to take a moderate two to three months of the 12 months' maternity leave). That is, the *starting points* for men and women are often demonstrably different; men perceived SPL as risky to their identities, women less so. This is confirmed by other research which finds different perceptions of leave take-up according to the sex of the person taking the leave (Petts, Mize & Kaufman, 2024; Petts, Kaufman & Mize, 2023).

On the flip side, some men were seen to prioritise what they perceived to be their partners' needs and desires related to caregiving, for example by avoiding SPL or working long hours to support a stay-at-home mother, even when this did not appear to align with their own preferences (see the case of John, for example). As Kaufman and Grönlund (2021:225) observe, 'displaying good fatherhood could mean engaging fully in paid work to support the mother's part-time work'. I might also add displaying 'good' intimacy, as individuals attempt to support their partner's preferences and desires as best they can. Stovell (2021) reported similar findings, writing that a 'fear of creating tension' (p. 236), heightened at the transition to parenthood, may lead couples to avoid potentially uncomfortable conversations related to shifting care-work practices. In these cases, care may be expressed through not sharing leave. This work, then, highlights the various meanings which may be attributed to leave: it may be an opportunity not just to look after one's child, but also to contribute to broader couple and family goals, or even to be a 'gift' to one's partner (O'Brien & Twamley, 2017).

This observation has relevance beyond negotiations about SPL, as some couples were seen to compromise ideals of equality in order to support their intimate relationship. For example, Helen and Henry expressed a strong commitment to a symmetrical division of labour in their first interview with me. Over the course of the study, however, they struggled to realise this vision. In her final interview Helen reflected on the uneven division of labour between herself and Henry:

> So it's like you have to constantly sometimes … be … you know, marking on a curve basically if you want to be happily married, you know? You could be right, you could be 'equal' or trying to be, or you could be happy, pick one. I wanna be happy, so I think, you know, yeah …
>
> Helen, Interview 3

Helen concluded that she must make compromises in the ideal of equality she had hoped for in their relationship, given the reality of the situation in which they were living. She and Henry made a valiant attempt to forge equal relations, but their different orientations to and responsibilities for paid and unpaid work, along with a context hostile to shared parenting, compromised their ability to do so. As Goldin (2021, p. 217) notes in her research exploring the impact of greedy work on couples' division of paid and unpaid work, at some point couples ask themselves how much they are willing to pay for equity. Here she is referring primarily to the shared career sacrifices and everyday difficulties in meeting children's care needs that come about when both partners pursue a career. The present study also reminds us of the toll on the couple relationship when people try to pursue equality in a social and policy environment which does not support it (see also Faircloth, 2021). In response, Helen tried to reconfigure her desire to be 'happy' rather than 'equal'.

Beyond couple's relative earnings, it is also clear that total earnings influence the ability of participants to forge more equal parenting practices. As I have already said in relation to 'greedy work', those who felt most precarious in their work or whose earnings did not cover their costs (this was most likely when women reduced their paid work hours), tended to work the longest hours. This impacted on (usually) men's ability to provide hands-on care for their wives and children. For some couples, this constraint on men's ability to engage in care work (beyond provisioning) clashed with the ideal of a symmetrical division of labour, which provoked mutual resentment and disappointment. Lower earners were also less able to meet nursery costs after the leave period, which pushed some women to reduce their paid work hours to take care of their children (where earnings were lower than nursery fees). As well as a low-paid parental leave scheme, the UK has one of the costliest childcare systems in OECD countries (OECD, n.d.), with costs rising year on year (Jarvie et al., 2023). Under the current childcare policy, no free childcare hours are provided for most families between the end of the statutory maternity leave period and a child's third birthday. The gap in provision has become the focus of significant media and political interest (Morton, 2019; Topping, 2022); this has led to an announcement of expanded free childcare hours from September 2024 (HM Treasury, 2023), but a clear plan as to how this expansion might be delivered is lacking. Childcare thus constitutes a significant financial burden for many households, especially for couples with more than one child, ranking just below mortgage or rent payments (Harding et al., 2017). Sometimes local family could provide this support, but often grandparents did not live nearby or were occupied with their own jobs. That participants in this study, most of whom earned above the national average wage, experienced such difficulties suggests that these pressures are greater for lower earners.

Additionally, as shown by the survey conducted for this study, knowledge of and eligibility for SPL are correlated with higher socioeconomic status (Twamley & Schober, 2019). Similar associations for eligibility to paid maternity and paternity leave were uncovered by O'Brien, Aldrich et al. (2017). They argue that inequalities and divisions between parents with and without access to parental leave are likely to grow as employment contracts diversify further, including through zero hours contracts and a rise in the number of self-employed individuals (ONS, 2016). Since the data were collected, a series of social crises (including the COVID-19 pandemic and the Ukraine war), coupled with years of government-imposed austerity measures, have provoked a cost-of-living crisis, which is such that even earners in the top 10 per cent are feeling the impact (González Hernando & Mitchell, 2023). These crises are likely to compound the stress experienced by parents who are struggling to make ends meet, and increase their collusion with ideal worker norms and gendered role specialisations, given the gaps in childcare provision.

Such challenges were compounded in families where children needed extra support. As Doucet (2023) notes, studies which explore couples' negotiations of paid and unpaid labour rarely consider the impact of the individual child on these negotiations and their outcomes. It was clear to me, however, that the baby (or babies) could strongly shape couples' experiences and the ways in which they could arrange paid and unpaid work. Helen and Henry stand out in this regard. Their son, baby H, suffered from reflux, which was not diagnosed until he was almost 6 months old. Before his diagnosis, he struggled to sleep and (unbeknown to his parents) was in severe pain when put down on his back to sleep (as per SIDS guidance in the UK[1]). Since Helen was on maternity leave, it was she that bore the brunt of the sleepless nights. Henry meanwhile was searching for a better job which would improve their family finances, but this entailed working late at night making job applications and networking to hear about new opportunities. During the period of baby H's illness, Helen recorded the following in her diary:

> I love Henry so much and he's trying so hard to support me and I desperately need that support but I feel bad for leaning on him when it runs him down so much faster. It's like sometimes with the sleep

thing, we are both exhausted swimmers in the ocean and we need to balance leaning on each other without accidentally dragging the other one down.

Helen, Diary 1 (baby 4 weeks old)

Because of these difficulties, they increasingly diverged into separate roles – Helen as the carer and Henry as the earner.

These examples demonstrate the multiple mechanisms which are needed to support equal parenting, beyond access to and support for SPL, and show the importance of attending to social and material differences in families' circumstances.

How can SPL be improved?

At the heart of the UK shared parental leave policy is a contradiction. The policy aims to offer parents 'more choice and freedom over how they share the care of their child' (Gov.uk, 2014) but, as I have shown, 'choice' cannot be exercised in such a straightforward and individualised way as this statement implies. That this is the case for a subset of relatively well-off parents indicates that many of the issues are likely to be even more salient for lower-earning parents. On the other hand, previous research shows that parents' ideas about what is morally right in terms of paid and unpaid work differ by class as well as by gender (Duncan et al., 2003). I acknowledge, therefore, that the findings here may be most applicable to highly educated, white, mixed-sex couples, and further research with more diverse couples is needed to understand how different intersections, for example of sexuality, ethnicity and class, may influence the findings. Nevertheless, the results here demonstrate that even couples with heightened forms of capital experience constraints on their ability to 'choose' SPL and on the ways in which they can manage leave. These constraints in turn impact on how care (for partner and child) is conceptualised and manifested. Overall, I conclude that the UK is an environment hostile to the sharing of leave and, more generally, to the sharing of care. In this chapter I have discussed the most salient of the factors that work against sharing, relating to how work and family life are conceived and experienced by men and women. I have shown that fathers' taking leave alone can have an impact on parents' orientations to paid and unpaid work, and argued that it can support a transformation of the structural systems which hold parents back from realising non-normative gendered practises. In this section I make proposals for how the UK parental leave system should be adjusted to take more effective account of the context in which parents deliberate on and experience parental leave.

1. Eligibility for and access to parental leave. As uncovered in the survey conducted as part of this study, around a third of parents are not eligible for SPL (Twamley & Schober, 2019; see also Department for Business and Trade, 2023). There are a number of reasons for this, including the timing of pregnancy in relation to employees changing jobs, one partner being out of employment, and parents being self-employed or on zero-hour contracts. These were not covered extensively in this study, since all the participants were recruited as eligible for leave, but it stands to reason that greater access to leave is necessary if we wish more parents to take SPL. However, another important aspect of eligibility relates to who 'owns' the leave. SPL as it currently stands functions through a maternity leave transfer mechanism, which acts as a barrier to take-up in multiple ways. First, it reinforces normative ideas of the mother as the primary carer and the default parent to take leave. Many parents (and their employers) just assume that mothers will take all the maternity leave. Second, some fathers express apprehension about 'taking away' their partner's leave and narrate that part of being a good partner and father is supporting the mother to take as much leave as possible. Third, participants felt that employers view fathers' taking leave as a choice *against* paid work (see also Petts, Mize & Kaufman, 2022). An individual right to leave which will be lost if not taken, sometimes called a 'daddy quota', would be less likely to be perceived in this way. To address these barriers, an individual entitlement to parental leave for fathers should be introduced in the UK. This means extending paternity leave and introducing fathers' parental leave. As outlined in the opening section of this chapter, the evidence from this study is that longer paternity leave with the mother (or primary parent) at the time of birth would reduce anxiety and stress at this time, and that leave alone, of at least eight weeks, would enable changes in gendered parenting practices.

2. Remuneration. The relationship between earnings and leave take-up was observed not to be straightforward in this study. Higher remuneration will not act as a magic bullet, but in combination with a 'daddy quota' it would signal broader social support for men's leave uptake, which many felt was lacking in the current context. A higher

remuneration for men's leave would also improve its affordability for families in which the father earns more than the mother (at present, fathers tend to take SPL when it is unremunerated or paid at the (low) statutory level). This should also reduce inequalities in access, since at present it is higher-paid employees who have access to paid leave and who are more likely to receive enhanced parental leave pay from their employers (Koslowski & Kadar-Satat, 2019; O'Brien, Aldrich et al., 2017).

3. Access to high-quality part-time and flexible work. Parents in this study described contexts of 'greedy work' *and* 'greedy' parenting norms. It is difficult to shift such cultural norms of paid and unpaid work, but their outcomes could at least be better managed. As I have shown, women anticipated and later experienced struggles in juggling paid and unpaid work, which prompted decisions to reduce paid work hours after the maternity leave or a shift in career even before pregnancy to ensure a greater capacity to meet these demands (see also Orgad, 2019). Parents' visions of the future suggest it is likely that women will continue to reduce paid work to meet their families' care needs. Part-time work as it is managed in the UK and abroad inhibits career progression (Gatrell et al., 2014; Yerkes, 2009). But, as the case of Bart and Beth shows, flexible working can be a means by which parents forge more equal parenting (see also Chung, 2020). Employers need to do more to support part-time workers (men and women) in their career progression.

The introduction of SPL created opportunities for some parents to forge more equal relations with one another. But changes are needed. At present, SPL fails to take account of the very real gendered differences in understandings and expectations of mothers and fathers. It draws on an idea of individualised rational choices that parents are able to make about their divisions of paid and unpaid work. As I have argued, in reality parents' choices are made and practices followed in relation to and with those around them (including one another) and the work and family norms within which they live. An effective leave design will take into consideration the relational agency (Burkitt, 2016) of parents as they negotiate leave. I have outlined three key changes to family and work policies which could enable parents to tread a different path within this context. These are in line with recommendations made by other scholars and advocates who have drawn on research from a range of contexts (Brandth & Kvande, 2020; Deven & Moss, 2002; Kaufman, 2020). Given the entrenched nature of gendered practices, transformations are unlikely to happen overnight. However, if we are serious about enabling parents to live up to their full capabilities (Nussbaum, 1997) as well as giving children access to both parents (O'Brien, 2009), these recommendations should be taken seriously.

Note

1   UK public health guidance is that babies should be put to sleep on their backs to reduce the risk of sudden infant death syndrome (SIDS), also known as cot death. See 'Reduce the risk of sudden infant death syndrome (SIDS)' (NHS): https://www.nhs.uk/conditions/baby/caring-for-a-newborn/reduce-the-risk-of-sudden-infant-death-syndrome/#:~:text=To%20reduce%20the%20risk%20of%20SIDS%3A,no%20higher%20than%20their%20shoulders (accessed 10 April 2024).

Appendix: analysis methods

As set out in chapter 1, I applied Andrea Doucet's (2006, 2018) version of the 'listening guide' approach to the data in interpreting the accounts of the participants. This is a narrative method of analysis which is underpinned by a relational understanding of people, and therefore suited to the epistemological framing of this study. Doucet outlines different 'listenings' or readings of the data, listening in a different way each time. I adapted the approach to my own purposes and research questions, combining it with a thematic analysis approach, which I outline here.

First, for four sets of parents, selected for their diverse experiences and rich, complete data sets, I conducted three reading-listenings of interview transcripts and diary entries. The first was a reflexive reading, attending to the 'emplotment' of stories or narratives from the participant, and to how I guided or provoked such emplotment. 'Emplotment' refers to the narrative plot of the account; the term emphasises the active and fluid nature of this process. Here I attended to how the account was structured and the key messages that participants were communicating through their narrations. At the same time, I considered my own reactions in the moment of 'listening' and how they shaped the interaction and my interpretation. I attended to how I responded emotionally to the data being presented, to what extent I linked what the participants are saying to my own biography, and how the latter shaped my response (Doucet, 2018).

In the second reading, the focus is on the participant's narrated identity, that is, how the participant refers to herself or himself, or to the couple. I examined when and how they spoke of themselves and what this could tell me about how they saw themselves or wanted to be seen within that moment. Given my interest in choice and agency, I used the movement of pronouns (from 'me' to 'you' to 'we', and so on) to explore how decision-making was presented or enacted; this includes such aspects as who appears to dominate or lead particular perspectives or decisions, or what is presented as a universal or obvious 'choice' or practice to be enacted, for example 'You always take as much leave as you can.'

The third reading sought out the sociocultural and political narratives that were drawn upon by the participants (and myself in asking questions), and how these narratives related to the structural context in which the participants live. Such narratives include those of gendered responsibilities of financial provisioning and care, and stories about state responsibility for childcare provision as related to the UK context, in which the state takes very little responsibility for young children.

The diaries could not be 'listened to', as they were text- (and image-) based, but I similarly conducted three readings of the diary entries and of the interview transcripts. In addition, I reduced diary entries to 'I-poems'. This involved copying all the 'I' statements from the diary and pasting them into a separate document. Each week of diary entries was made into one 'poem', with a day represented by a single 'stanza', and each 'I' statement occupying one line. Gilligan and colleagues (2003) developed the I-poem method to examine the ways in which participants understand and speak about themselves, and in particular how these subjective understandings or portrayals of self may change over time. This fitted my own aim of understanding whether and how participants' perceptions of themselves as parents shifted over the period of the study. Edwards and Weller (2012) contest the claim that the 'I-poem' can be used to access an authentic pre-analytical self of the participant. It was not with this intention that I used the method. I took the I-poems to be relational in their communication, between the writer and reader, and between the writer and the 'person in the head' to whom the participant was writing. They helped me to pick apart in my readings both the descriptions of everyday behaviour and the ways in which the participants were portraying themselves in their parenting (which is what the diaries were about). They 'provided a valuable angle' (Edwards & Weller, 2012:216) for attending to the emotional and sometimes conflictual concerns of the participants.

While conducting these multiple listenings and readings, I drew up codes based on my interpretations with detailed memos. Once I was happy with the list of codes, I applied them to the data that came from the remaining participants. I then went back to the data from each couple and wrote up stories drawing on the codes I had been applying. Finally, I 'read' these stories to examine the 'ontological narratives' I was telling through their creation, in order to unpack how my own concerns and concepts were shaping the data (Doucet, 2018). Thus, the analysis was a combination of a 'listening guide' approach and a thematic analysis approach. I hoped that this approach would help me to attend to the stories created (and my role in creating them) and to examine any patterns across the different participants (men and women, sharers and non-sharers).

References

Acker, J. (1990). Hierarchies, jobs, bodies: A theory of gendered organizations. *Gender and Society*, 4(2), 139–58. https://doi.org/10.1177/089124390004002002.

Ahmed, S. (2010). Feminist killjoys. In *The Promise of Happiness*, pp. 50–87. Durham, NC: Duke University Press.

Alaszewski, A. (2006). *Using Diaries for Social Research*. London: SAGE Publications.

Almqvist, A.-L. & Duvander, A.-Z. (2014). Changes in gender equality? Swedish fathers' parental leave, division of childcare and housework. *Journal of Family Studies*, 20(1), 19–27. https://doi.org/10.5172/jfs.2014.20.1.19.

Almqvist, A.-L., Sandberg, A. & Dahlgren, L. (2011). Parental leave in Sweden: Motives, experiences, and gender equality amongst parents. *Fathering*, 9(2), 189–206. https://doi.org/10.3149/fth.0902.189.

Alsarve, J. (2021). Parental leave – and then what? A study of new parents' negotiations about work, care and parental leave. *Families, Relationships and Societies*, 10(1), 83–98. https://doi.org/10.1332/204674320X15998282224893.

Andersen, S. H. (2018). Paternity leave and the motherhood penalty: New causal evidence. *Journal of Marriage and Family*, 80(5), 1125–43. https://doi.org/10.1111/jomf.12507.

Andysz, A., Jacukowicz, A., Stańczak, A. & Drabek, M. (2016). Availability and the use of work-life balance benefits guaranteed by the Polish Labour Code among workers employed on the basis of employment contracts in small and medium enterprises. *International Journal of Occupational Medicine and Environmental Health*, 29(4), 709–17. https://doi.org/10.13075/ijomeh.1896.00745.

Arendell, T. (2000). Conceiving and investigating motherhood: The decade's scholarship. *Journal of Marriage and Family*, 62(4), 1192–1207. https://doi.org/10.1111/j.1741-3737.2000.01192.x.

Asher, R. (2011). *Shattered: Modern motherhood and the illusion of equality*. London: Harvill Secker.

Atkinson, J. (2023). Reconciling the ideal worker norm and involved fatherhood: New fathers' experiences of requesting Shared Parental Leave in UK organizations. *Community, Work and Family*, 1–24. https://doi.org/10.1080/13668803.2023.2274276.

Back, L. (2015). Why everyday life matters: Class, community and making life livable. *Sociology*, 49(5), 820–36. https://doi.org/10.1177/0038038515589292.

Baird, M. & O'Brien, M. (2015). Dynamics of parental leave in Anglophone countries: The paradox of state expansion in liberal welfare regimes. *Community, Work and Family*, 18(2), 198–217. https://doi.org/10.1080/13668803.2015.1021755.

Ball, S. J., Vincent, C., Kemp, S. & Pietikainen, S. (2004). Middle class fractions, childcare and the 'relational' and 'normative' aspects of class practices. *Sociological Review*, 52(4), 478–502. https://doi.org/10.1111/j.1467-954X.2004.00492.x.

Banister, E. & Kerrane, B. (2022). Glimpses of change? UK fathers navigating work and care within the context of Shared Parental Leave. *Gender, Work and Organization*, 31(4), 1214–1229. https://doi.org/10.1111/gwao.12813.

Barker, G., Burrell, S. & Ruxton, S. (2021). COVID-19 and masculinities in global perspective: Reflections from Promundo's research and activism. *Men and Masculinities*, 24(1), 168–74. https://doi.org/10.1177/1097184X211000385.

Beglaubter, J. (2017). Balancing the scales: Negotiating father's parental leave use. *Canadian Review of Sociology/Revue canadienne de sociologie*, 54(4), 476–96. https://doi.org/10.1111/cars.12173.

Benjamin, O. & Sullivan, O. (1999). Relational resources, gender consciousness and possibilities of change in marital relationships. *Sociological Review*, 47(4), 794–820. https://doi.org/10.1111/1467-954X.00196.

Berdahl, J. L., Cooper, M., Glick, P., Livingston, R. W. & Williams, J. C. (2018). Work as a masculinity contest. *Journal of Social Issues*, 74(3), 422–48. https://doi.org/10.1111/josi.12289.

Birkett, H. & Forbes, S. (2019). Where's dad? Exploring the low take-up of inclusive parenting policies in the UK. *Policy Studies*, 40(2), 205–24. https://doi.org/10.1080/01442872.2019.1581160.

Blood, R. O. & Hamblin, R. L. (1957). The effect of the wife's employment on the family power structure. *Social Forces*, 36(4), 347–52. https://doi.org/10.2307/2573974.

Blum, S., Dobrotić, I., Kaufman, G., Koslowski, A. & Moss, P. (eds.) (2023). *19th International Review of Leave Policies and Related Research 2023*. https://www.leavenetwork.org/annual-review-reports/review-2023/ (accessed 10 April 2024). https://doi.org/10.25365/phaidra.431.

Boase, J. & Humphreys, L. (2018). Mobile methods: Explorations, innovations, and reflections. *Mobile Media and Communication*, 6(2), 153–62. https://doi.org/10.1177/2050157918764215.

Brandth, B. & Kvande, E. (1998). Masculinity and child care: The reconstruction of fathering. *Sociological Review*, 46(2), 293–313. https://doi.org/10.1111/1467-954X.00120.

Brandth, B. & Kvande, E. (2001). Flexible work and flexible fathers. *Work, Employment and Society*, 15(2), 251–67. https://doi.org/10.1177/09500170122118940.

Brandth, B. & Kvande, E. (2002). Reflexive fathers: Negotiating parental leave and working life. *Gender, Work and Organization*, 9(2), 186–203. https://doi.org/10.1111/1468-0432.00155.

Brandth, B. & Kvande, E. (2003a). Father presence in child care. In A. M. Jensen & L. McKee (eds.), *Children and the Changing Family: Between transformation and negotiation*, pp. 61–75. London: Routledge Falmer.

Brandth, B. & Kvande, E. (2003b). 'Home alone' fathers. *NIKK magazine*, 3, 22–5.

Brandth, B. & Kvande, E. (2020). *Designing Parental Leave Policy: The Norway model and the changing face of fatherhood*. Bristol: Bristol University Press.

Brannen, J. (2013). Life story talk: Some reflections on narrative in qualitative interviews. *Sociological Research Online*, 18(2), 48–58. https://doi.org/10.5153/sro.2884.

Brannen, J., Faircloth, C., Jones, C., O'Brien, M. & Twamley, K. (2023). Change and continuity in men's fathering and employment practices: a slow gender revolution. In C. Cameron, A. Koslowski, A. Lamont & P. Moss (eds.), *Social Research for Our Times: Thomas Coram Research Unit past, present and future*, pp. 227–42. London: UCL Press.

Brines, J. (1994). Economic dependency, gender, and the division of labor at home. *American Journal of Sociology*, 100(3), 652–88.

Brooks, R. & Hodkinson, P. (2020). *Sharing Care: Equal and primary carer fathers and early years parenting*. Bristol: Bristol University Press.

Brown, L. & Gilligan, C. (1992). *Meeting at the Crossroads: Women's psychology and girls' development*. Cambridge, MA: Harvard University Press.

Brown, L. M. (1999). *Raising Their Voices: The politics of girls' anger*. Cambridge, MA: Harvard University Press.

Budgeon, S. (2015). Individualized femininity and feminist politics of choice. *European Journal of Women's Studies*, 22(3), 303–18. https://doi.org/10.1177/1350506815576602.

Budig, M. J. & England, P. (2001). The wage penalty for motherhood. *American Sociological Review*, 66(2), 204–25. http://dx.doi.org/10.2307/2657415.

Burkitt, I. (2012). Emotional reflexivity: Feeling, emotion and imagination in reflexive dialogues. *Sociology*, 46(3), 458–72. https://doi.org/10.1177/0038038511422587.

Burkitt, I. (2016). Relational agency: Relational sociology, agency and interaction. *European Journal of Social Theory*, 19(3), 322–39. https://doi.org/10.1177/1368431015591426.

Bygren, M. & Duvander, A. Z. (2006). Parents' workplace situation and fathers' parental leave use. *Journal of Marriage and Family*, 68(2), 363–72. https://doi.org/10.1111/j.1741-3737.2006.00258.x.

Bytheway, B. (2012). The use of diaries in qualitative longitudinal research. Timescapes Methods Guides Series, 7. Economic & Social Research Council. https://timescapes-archive.leeds.ac.uk/wp-content/uploads/sites/47/2020/07/timescapes-bytheway-use-of-diaries.pdf (accessed 10 April 2024).

Byun, S.-Y. & Won, S.-Y. (2020). Are they ideological renegades? Fathers' experiences on taking parental leave and gender dynamics in Korea: A qualitative study. *Gender, Work and Organization*, 27(4), 592–614. https://doi.org/10.1111/gwao.12410.

Cantó-Milà, N. & Seebach, S. (2015). Desired images, regulating figures, constructed imaginaries: The future as an apriority for society to be possible. *Current Sociology*, *63*(2), 198–215. https://doi.org/10.1177/0011392114556583.

Carter, J. (2013). The curious absence of love stories in women's talk. *Sociological Review*, *61*(4), 728–44. https://doi.org/10.1111/1467-954X.12082.

Carter, J. (2022). Traditional inequalities and inequalities of tradition: Gender, weddings, and whiteness. *Sociological Research Online*, *27*(1), 60–76. https://doi.org/10.1177/1360780421990021.

Chambraud, C. & Chanrai, K. (2018). Equal lives: Parenthood and caring in the workplace. Business in the Community. https://www.bitc.org.uk/report/equal-lives-parenthood-and-caring-in-the-workplace/ (accessed 10 April 2024).

Chanfreau, J., Gowland, S., Lancaster, Z., Poole, E., Tipping, S. & Toomse, M. (2011). *Maternity and Paternity Rights Survey and Women Returners Survey 2009/10*. London: Department for Work and Pensions & Department for Business Innovation and Skills. https://assets.publishing.service.gov.uk/media/5a7c76a1ed915d6969f450bf/rrep777.pdf (accessed 10 April 2024).

Christopher, E. (2021). Capturing conflicting accounts of domestic labour: The household portrait as a methodology. *Sociological Research Online*, *26*(3), 451–68. https://doi.org/10.1177/1360780420951804.

Chung, H. (2020). Gender, flexibility stigma and the perceived negative consequences of flexible working in the UK. *Social Indicators Research*, *151*(2), 521–45. https://doi.org/10.1007/s11205-018-2036-7.

Chung, H. (2022). *The Flexibility Paradox: Why flexible working leads to (self-)exploitation*. Bristol: Policy Press.

Collins, C. (2019). *Making Motherhood Work: How women manage careers and caregiving*. Princeton: Princeton University Press.

Connell, R. W. (1995). *Masculinities*. Cambridge: Polity Press.

Connolly, S., Aldrich, M., O'Brien, M., Speight, S. & Poole, E. (2016). Britain's slow movement to a gender egalitarian equilibrium: Parents and employment in the UK 2001–13. *Work, Employment and Society*, *30*(5), 838–57. https://doi.org/10.1177/0950017016638009.

Cook, R., O'Brien, M., Connolly, S., Aldrich, M. & Speight, S. (2021). Fathers' perceptions of the availability of flexible working arrangements: Evidence from the UK. *Work, Employment and Society*, *35*(6), 1014–33. https://doi.org/10.1177/0950017020946687,

Corte Rodríguez, M. de la (2018). Child-related leave and women's labour market outcomes: Towards a new paradigm in the European Union? *Journal of Social Welfare and Family Law*, *40*(3), 376–93. https://doi.org/10.1080/09649069.2018.1493657.

Costa Dias, M., Joyce, R. & Parodi, F. (2020). The gender pay gap in the UK: Children and experience in work. *Oxford Review of Economic Policy*, *36*(4), 855–81. https://doi.org/10.1093/oxrep/graa053.

Cukrowska-Torzewska, E. & Lovasz, A. (2020). The role of parenthood in shaping the gender wage gap: A comparative analysis of 26 European countries. *Social Science Research*, *85*(January), art. no. 102355. https://doi.org/10.1016/j.ssresearch.2019.102355.

Cukrowska-Torzewska, E. & Matysiak, A. (2020). The motherhood wage penalty: A meta-analysis. *Social Science Research*, *88–9*(May–July), art. no. 102416. https://doi.org/10.1016/j.ssresearch.2020.102416.

Daminger, A. (2019). The cognitive dimension of household labor. *American Sociological Review*, *84*(4), 609–33. http://dx.doi.org/10.1177/0003122419859007.

Daminger, A. (2020). De-gendered processes, gendered outcomes: How egalitarian couples make sense of non-egalitarian household practices. *American Sociological Review*, *85*(5), 806–29. http://dx.doi.org/10.1177/0003122420950208.

de Laat, K., Doucet, A. & Gerhardt, A. (2023). More than employment policies? Parental leaves, flexible work and fathers' participation in unpaid care work. *Community, Work and Family*, *26*(5), 562–84. https://doi.org/10.1080/13668803.2023.2271646.

Dean, L., Churchill, B. & Ruppanner, L. (2022). The mental load: Building a deeper theoretical understanding of how cognitive and emotional labor *overload* women and mothers. *Community, Work and Family*, *25*(1), 13–29. https://doi.org/10.1080/13668803.2021.2002813.

Department for Business and Trade (2023). Shared Parental Leave: Evaluation report. BEIS/DBT Research Paper Series, 2023/10.

Department for Education & Department for Business, Innovation and Skills (2013). Children and Families Bill 2013. https://www.gov.uk/government/publications/children-and-families-bill-2013 (accessed 1 May 2024).

Dermott, E. (2008). *Intimate Fatherhood: A sociological analysis*. Abingdon: Routledge.

Dermott, E. & Miller, T. (2015). More than the sum of its parts? Contemporary fatherhood policy, practice and discourse. *Families, Relationships and Societies*, 4(2), 183–95. https://doi.org/10.1332/204674315X14212269138324.

Dermott, E. & Pomati, M. (2016). 'Good' parenting practices: How important are poverty, education and time pressure? *Sociology*, 50(1), 125–42. https://doi.org/10.1177/0038038514560260.

Deutsch, F. M. & Gaunt, R. A. (eds.) (2020). *Creating Equality at Home: How 25 couples around the world share housework and childcare*. Cambridge: Cambridge University Press.

Deven, F. & Moss, P. (2002). Leave arrangements for parents: Overview and future outlook. *Community, Work and Family*, 5(3), 237–55. https://doi.org/10.1080/1366880022000041766.

Donath, O. (2015). Regretting motherhood: A sociopolitical analysis. *Signs: Journal of Women in Culture and Society*, 40(2), 343–67.

Doucet, A. (1998). Interpreting mother-work: Linking methodology, ontology, theory, and personal biography. *Canadian Woman Studies/Les cahiers de la femme*, 18(2/3), 52–9.

Doucet, A. (2006). *Do Men Mother? Fathering, care, and domestic responsibility*. Toronto: University of Toronto Press.

Doucet, A. (2015). Parental responsibilities: Dilemmas of measurement and gender equality. *Journal of Marriage and Family*, 77(1), 224–42. https://doi.org/10.1111/jomf.12148.

Doucet, A. (2016). Is the stay-at-home dad (SAHD) a feminist concept? A genealogical, relational, and feminist critique. *Sex Roles*, 75(1–2), 4–14. https://doi.org/10.1007/s11199-016-0582-5.

Doucet, A. (2017). The ethics of care and the radical potential of fathers 'home alone on leave': care as practice, relational ontology, and social justice. In M. O'Brien & K. Wall (eds), *Comparative Perspectives on Work–Life Balance and Gender Equality: Fathers on leave alone*, pp. 11–28. Cham: Springer Open.

Doucet, A. (2018). *Do Men Mother?* 2nd edn. Toronto: University of Toronto Press.

Doucet, A. (2023). Care is not a tally sheet: Rethinking the field of gender divisions of domestic labour with care-centric conceptual narratives. *Families, Relationships and Societies*, 12(1), 10–30. https://doi.org/10.1332/204674322X16711124907533.

Doucet, A. & Klostermann, J. (2024). What and how are we measuring when we research gendered divisions of domestic labor? Remaking the Household Portrait method into a Care/Work Portrait. *Sociological Research Online*, 29(1), 243–63. https://doi.org/10.1177/13607804231160740.

Doucet, A. & Mauthner, N. S. (2008). What can be known and how? Narrated subjects and the Listening Guide. *Qualitative Research*, 8(3), 399–409. https://doi.org/10.1177/1468794106093636.

Doucet, A. & McKay, L. (2020). Fathering, parental leave, impacts, and gender equality: What/how are we measuring? *International Journal of Sociology and Social Policy*, 40(5/6), 441–63. https://doi.org/10.1108/ijssp-04-2019-0086.

Druedahl, J., Ejrnæs, M. & Jørgensen, T. H. (2019). Earmarked paternity leave and the relative income within couples. *Economics Letters*, 180, 85–8. https://doi.org/10.1016/j.econlet.2019.04.018.

Duncan, S. (2015). Women's agency in living apart together: Constraint, strategy and vulnerability. *Sociological Review*, 63(3), 589–607. https://doi.org/10.1111/1467-954X.12184.

Duncan, S., Edwards, R., Reynolds, T., and Alldred, P. (2003). Motherhood, paid work and partnering: values and theories. *Work, Employment and Society* 17 (2): 309-330. https://doi.org/10.1177/09500170030170020

Duvander, A.-Z., Haas, L. & Thalberg, S. (2017). Fathers on leave alone in Sweden: Toward more equal parenthood? In M. O'Brien & K. Wall (eds.), *Comparative Perspectives on Work–Life Balance and Gender Equality: Fathers on leave alone*, pp. 125–45. Cham: Springer Open.

Edwards, R. & Weller, S. (2012). Shifting analytic ontology: Using I-poems in qualitative longitudinal research. *Qualitative Research*, 12(2), 202–17. https://doi.org/10.1177/1468794111422040.

Eerola, P., Närvi, J. & Lammi-Taskula, J. (2022). Can fathers' leave take-up dismantle gendered parental responsibilities? Evidence from Finland. *Journal of Family Research*, 34(3), 958–82. https://doi.org/10.20377/jfr-723.

Eerola, P., Närvi, J., Terävä, J. & Repo, K. (2021). Negotiating parenting practices: The arguments and justifications of Finnish couples. *Families, Relationships and Societies*, 10(1), 119–35. https://doi.org/10.1332/204674320X15898834533942.

Elliott, K. (2016). Caring masculinities: Theorizing an emerging concept. *Men and Masculinities*, *19*(3), 240–59. https://doi.org/10.1177/1097184X15576203.

Equality and Human Rights Commission (2015). *Pregnancy and maternity-related discrimination and disadvantage: summary of key findings, BS/16/145*. https://assets.publishing.service.gov.uk/media/5a749756e5274a410efd0d40/BIS-16-145-pregnancy-and-maternity-related-discrimination-and-disadvantage-summary.pdf.

Evertsson, M. & Nermo, M. (2004). Dependence within families and the division of labor: Comparing Sweden and the United States. *Journal of Marriage and Family*, *66*(5), 1272–86. https://doi.org/10.1111/j.0022-2445.2004.00092.x.

Eydal, G. B. & Rostgaard, T. (eds.) (2016). *Fatherhood in the Nordic Welfare States: Comparing care policies and practice*. Bristol: Policy Press.

Faircloth, C. (2013). *Militant Lactivism? Attachment parenting and intensive motherhood in the UK and France*. New York: Berghahn.

Faircloth, C. (2014). Intensive parenting and the expansion of parenting. In E. Lee, J. Bristow, C. Faircloth & J. Macvarish (eds), *Parenting Culture Studies*, pp. 25–50. Basingstoke: Palgrave Macmillan.

Faircloth, C. (2021). *Couples' Transitions to Parenthood: Gender, intimacy and equality*. Cham: Palgrave Macmillan.

Faircloth, C. (2023). Intensive fatherhood? The (un)involved dad. In E. Lee, C. Faircloth, J. Bristow & J. Macvarish (eds.), *Parenting Culture Studies*, 2nd edn, pp. 241–65. Cham: Palgrave Macmillan.

Faircloth, C., Hoffman, D. M. & Layne, L. L. (2013). Introduction. In C. Faircloth, D. M. Hoffman & L. L. Layne (eds.), *Parenting in Global Perspective: Negotiating ideologies of kinship, self and politics*, pp. 1–17. Abingdon: Routledge.

Finch, J. (2007). Displaying families. *Sociology*, *41*(1), 65–81. https://doi.org/10.1177/0038038507072284.

Floro, M. S. & Meurs, M. (2009). *Gender Equality at the Heart of Decent Work*. Geneva: International Labour Office.

Folbre, N. (2011). The invisible heart. In H. Bertram & N. Ehlert (eds.), *Family, Ties and Care: Family transformation in a plural modernity*, 189–194. Opladen: Barbara Budrich Publishers.

Folbre, N. (2021). Quantifying care: Design and harmonization issues in time-use surveys. UN Women. https://data.unwomen.org/sites/default/files/documents/Publications/Quantifying%20Care.pdf (accessed 10 April 2024).

Fox, B. (2009). *When Couples Become Parents: The creation of gender in the transition to parenthood*. Toronto: University of Toronto Press.

Fraser, N. (1994). After the family wage: Gender equity and the welfare state. *Political Theory*, *22*(4), 591–618. https://doi.org/10.1177/0090591794022004003.

Fraser, N. (2013). *Fortunes of Feminism: From state-managed capitalism to neoliberal crisis*. London: Verso.

Friedman, M. (2014). Relational autonomy and independence. In A. Veltman & M. Piper (eds), *Autonomy, Oppression, and Gender*, pp. 42–60. New York: Oxford University Press.

Furedi, F. (2001). *Paranoid Parenting: Abandon your anxieties and be a good parent*. London: Allen Lane.

Furedi, F. (2012). Why the 'couples where women do more housework stay together' study isn't shocking. *The Independent*, 1 October. http://www.independent.co.uk/voices/comment/why-the-couples-where-women-do-more-housework-stay-together-study-isnt-shocking-8192069.html (accessed 11 April 2024).

Gabb, J. (2008). *Researching Intimacy in Families*. Basingstoke: Palgrave Macmillan.

Gabb, J. & Fink, J. (2015). *Couple Relationships in the 21st Century*. Cham: Palgrave Macmillan.

Gatrell, C. J., Burnett, S., Cooper, C. and Sparrow, P. (2014). Parents, perceptions and belonging: Exploring flexible working among UK fathers and mothers. *British Journal of Management*, *25*(3), 473–487.

Gatrell, C. & Cooper, C. L. (2016). A sense of entitlement? Fathers, mothers and organizational support for family and career. *Community, Work and Family*, *19*(2), 134–47. https://doi.org/10.1080/13668803.2016.1134121.

Gaunt, R. (2013). Breadwinning moms, caregiving dads: Double standard in social judgments of gender norm violators. *Journal of Family Issues*, *34*(1), 3–24. https://doi.org/10.1177/0192513X12438686.

Geisler, E. & Kreyenfeld, M. (2011). Against all odds: Fathers' use of parental leave in Germany. *Journal of European Social Policy*, *21*(1), 88–99. https://doi.org/10.1177/0958928710385732.

Gheyoh Ndzi, E. (2021). The devastating impact of gender discrimination on shared parental leave in the UK. *International Journal of Law and Society*, *4*(4), 254–61. https://doi.org/10.11648/j.ijls.20210404.13.

Gill, R. (2011). Sexism reloaded, or, it's time to get angry again! *Feminist Media Studies*, *11*(1), 61–71. https://doi.org/10.1080/14680777.2011.537029.

Gill, R., Kelan, E. K. & Scharff, C. M. (2016). A postfeminist sensibility at work. *Gender, Work and Organization*, *24*(3), 226–44. https://doi.org/10.1111/gwao.12132.

Gillies, V. (2008). Childrearing, class and the new politics of parenting. *Sociology Compass*, *2*(3), 1079–95. https://doi.org/10.1111/j.1751-9020.2008.00114.x.

Gillies, V. (2009). Understandings and experiences of involved fathering in the United Kingdom: Exploring classed dimensions. *Annals of the American Academy of Political and Social Science*, *624*(1), 49–60. https://doi.org/10.1177/0002716209334295.

Gillies, V., Edwards, R. & Horsley, N. (2017). *Challenging the Politics of Early Intervention: Who's 'saving' children and why*. Bristol: Policy Press.

Gilligan, C., Spencer, R., Weinberg, M. K. & Bertsch, T. (2003). On the Listening Guide: a voice-centred relational method. In P. Camic, J. Rhodes & L. Yardley (eds), *Qualitative Research in Psychology: Expanding perspectives in methodology and design*, pp. 157–72. Washington, DC: American Psychological Association.

Gillis, J. R. (1997). *A World of Their Own Making: Myth, ritual, and the quest for family values*. Cambridge, MA: Harvard University Press.

Goldin, C. (2021). *Career and Family: Women's century-long journey toward equity*. Princeton: Princeton University Press.

González Hernando, M. & Mitchell, G. (2023). *Uncomfortably Off: Why the top 10% of earners should care about inequality*. Bristol: Policy Press.

Gornick, J. C. & Meyers, M. K. (2003). *Families that Work: Policies for reconciling parenthood and employment*. New York: Russell Sage Foundation.

Gornick, J. C. & Meyers, M. K. (2009). Institutions that support gender equality in parenthood and employment. In J. C. Gornick & M. K. Keyers (eds.), *Gender Equality: Transforming family divisions of labor*, pp. 3–64. London: Verso.

Gov.uk (2014). Parents can now apply for Shared Parental Leave and pay. https://www.gov.uk/government/news/new-shared-parental-leave-regulations-come-into-effect (accessed 18 June 2024).

Grunow, D. & Evertsson, M. (eds.) (2016). *Couples' Transitions to Parenthood: Analysing gender and work in Europe*. Cheltenham: Edward Elgar Publishing.

Gunnarsson, L. (2016). The dominant and its constitutive other: Feminist theorizations of love, power and gendered selves. *Journal of Critical Realism*, *15*(1), 1–20. https://doi.org/10.1080/14767430.2015.1136194.

Haas, L. (1992). *Equal Parenthood and Social Policy: A study of parental leave in Sweden*. Albany, NY: SUNY Press.

Haas, L. & Hwang, C. P. (2008). The impact of taking parental leave on fathers' participation in childcare and relationships with children: Lessons from Sweden. *Community, Work and Family*, *11*(1), 85–104. https://doi.org/10.1080/13668800701785346.

Haas, L. & Hwang, C. P. (2019). Policy is not enough: The influence of the gendered workplace on fathers' use of parental leave in Sweden. *Community, Work and Family*, *22*(1), 58–76. https://doi.org/10.1080/13668803.2018.1495616.

Hamilton, P. (2020). *Black Mothers and Attachment Parenting: A black feminist analysis of intensive mothering in Britain and Canada*. Bristol: Bristol University Press.

Hamilton, P. (2023). Swings and merry go rounds: Transgression and opportunities for fatherhood in pandemic Britain. *Women's Studies International Forum*, *101* (November–December), art. no. 102838. https://doi.org/10.1016/j.wsif.2023.102838.

Harding, C., Wheaton, B. & Butler, A. (2017). Childcare survey 2017. Family and Childcare Trust. https://www.familyandchildcaretrust.org/childcare-survey-2017 (accessed 11 April).

Hardyment, C. (2007). *Dream Babies: Childcare advice from John Locke to Gina Ford*, rev. edn. London: Frances Lincoln.

Harper, D. (2002). Talking about pictures: A case for photo elicitation. *Visual Studies*, *17*(1), 13–26. https://doi.org/10.1080/14725860220137345.

Hays, S. (1996). *The Cultural Contradictions of Motherhood*. New Haven, CT: Yale University Press.

Heaphy, B. & Einarsdottir, A. (2013). Scripting civil partnerships: Interviewing couples together and apart. *Qualitative Research*, 13(1), 53–70. https://doi.org/10.1177/1468794112454997.

Hipp, L. (2018). Damned if you do, damned if you don't? Experimental evidence on hiring discrimination against parents with differing lengths of family leave. *SocArXiv Papers*, August. https://doi.org/doi:10.31235/osf.io/qsm4x.

HM Treasury (2023). Spring budget 2023 factsheet: Labour market measures. Policy paper, 15 March. https://www.gov.uk/government/publications/spring-budget-2023-labour-market-factsheet/spring-budget-2023-factsheet-labour-market-measures (accessed 11 April 2024).

Hobson, B., Lewis, J. & Siim, B. (2002). *Contested Concepts in Gender and Social Politics*. Cheltenham: Edward Elgar.

Hochschild, A. R. (2003). *The Managed Heart: Commercialization of human feeling*, 20th anniversary edn. Berkeley: University of California Press.

Hochschild, A. R. & Machung, A. (2012). *The Second Shift: Working families and the revolution at home*, 2nd edn. New York: Penguin Books.

Hodges, M. J. & Budig, M. J. (2010). Who gets the daddy bonus? Organizational hegemonic masculinity and the impact of fatherhood on earnings. *Gender and Society*, 24(6), 717–45. https://doi.org/10.1177/0891243210386729.

Hodkinson, P. & Brooks, R. (2023). Caregiving fathers and the negotiation of crossroads: Journeys of continuity and change. *British Journal of Sociology*, 74(1), 35–49. https://doi.org/10.1111/1468-4446.12980.

Hogenboom, M. (2021). The hidden load: How 'thinking of everything' holds mums back. *BBC Worklife*, 18 May. https://www.bbc.com/worklife/article/20210518-the-hidden-load-how-thinking-of-everything-holds-mums-back (accessed 11 April 2024).

Holmes, M. (2004). The precariousness of choice in the new sentimental order: A response to Bawin-Legros. *Current Sociology*, 52(2), 251–7. http://dx.doi.org/10.1177/0011392104041811.

Holmes, M., Jamieson, L. & Natalier, K. (2021). Future building and emotional reflexivity: Gendered or queered navigations of agency in non-normative relationships? *Sociology*, 55(4), 734–50. https://doi.org/10.1177/0038038520981841.

Illouz, E. (2007). *Cold Intimacies: The making of emotional capitalism*. Cambridge: Polity.

Illouz, E. (2012). *Why Love Hurts: A sociological explanation*. Cambridge: Polity.

Jackson, S. (1993). Even sociologists fall in love: An exploration in the sociology of emotions. *Sociology*, 27(2), 201–20. https://doi.org/10.1177/0038038593027002002.

Jamieson, L. (2011). Intimacy as a concept: Explaining social change in the context of globalisation or another form of ethnocentricism? *Sociological Research Online*, 16(4), 151–63. http://dx.doi.org/10.5153/sro.2497.

Jarvie, M., Shorto, S., Kunwar Deer, L. & Goddard, E. (2023). Childcare survey. Coram Family and Childcare. https://www.familyandchildcaretrust.org/sites/default/files/Resource%20Library/Childcare%20Survey%202023_Coram%20Family%20and%20Childcare.pdf (accessed 11 April 2024).

Jensen, T. (2010). Warmth and wealth: Re-imagining social class in taxonomies of good parenting. *Studies in the Maternal*, 2(1), 1–13. https://doi.org/10.16995/sim.86.

Johnson, P. (2005). *Love, Heterosexuality and Society*. Abingdon: Routledge.

Jones, C., Wells, J., Imrie, S. & Golombok, S. (2021). Transitions into and out of work: Stay-at-home fathers' thoughts and feelings: A brief report. *Journal of Men's Studies*, 29(3), 373–83. https://doi.org/10.1177/10608265211032097.

Karu, M. (2012). Parental leave in Estonia: Does familization of fathers lead to defamilization of mothers? *NORA – Nordic Journal of Feminist and Gender Research*, 20(2), 94–108. https://doi.org/10.1080/08038740.2011.601466.

Kaufman, G. (2018). Barriers to equality: Why British fathers do not use parental leave. *Community, Work and Family*, 21(3), 310–25. https://doi.org/10.1080/13668803.2017.1307806.

Kaufman, G. (2020). *Fixing Parental Leave: The six month solution*. New York: New York University Press.

Kaufman, G. & Almqvist, A.-L. (2017). The role of partners and workplaces in British and Swedish men's parental leave decisions. *Men and Masculinities*, 20(5), 533–51. https://doi.org/10.1177/1097184X17727570.

Kaufman, G. & Grönlund, A. (2021). Displaying parenthood, (un)doing gender: Parental leave, daycare and working-time adjustments in Sweden and the UK. *Families, Relationships and Societies*, 10(2), 213–29. https://doi.org/10.1332/204674319X15683716957916.

Kaufman, G., Petts, R. J., Mize, T. D. & Wield, T. (2024). Gender egalitarianism and attitudes toward parental leave. *Social Currents*, 11(2), 181–99. https://doi.org/10.1177/23294965231175824.

Kelland, J., Lewis, D. & Fisher, V. (2022). Viewed with suspicion, considered idle and mocked: Working caregiving fathers and fatherhood forfeits. *Gender, Work and Organization*, 29(5), 1578–93. https://doi.org/10.1111/gwao.12850.

Kiger, G. & Riley, P. J. (1996). Gender differences in perceptions of household labor. *Journal of Psychology*, 130(4), 357–70.

Koslowski, A. S. (2011). Working fathers in Europe: Earning and caring. *European Sociological Review*, 27(2), 230–45. https://doi.org/10.1093/esr/jcq004.

Koslowski, A. & Kadar-Satat, G. (2019). Fathers at work: Explaining the gaps between entitlement to leave policies and uptake. *Community, Work and Family*, 22(2), 129–45. https://doi.org/10.1080/13668803.2018.1428174.

Kvande, E. (2007). *Doing Gender in Flexible Organizations*. Bergen: Fagbokforlaget.

Lammi-Taskula, J. (2008). Doing fatherhood: Understanding the gendered use of parental leave in Finland. *Fathering*, 6(2), 133–48. https://www.researchgate.net/profile/Johanna-Lammi-Taskula/publication/247897052_Doing_Fatherhood_Understanding_the_Gendered_Use_of_Parental_Leave_in_Finland/links/5d8cb596a6fdcc25549b54d1/Doing-Fatherhood-Understanding-the-Gendered-Use-of-Parental-Leave-in-Finland.pdf.

Lamont, E. (2014). Negotiating courtship: Reconciling egalitarian ideals with traditional gender norms. *Gender and Society*, 28(2), 189–211. https://doi.org/10.1177/0891243213503899.

Lamont, M. (1992). *Money, Morals, and Manners: The culture of the French and American upper-middle class*. Chicago: University of Chicago Press.

Lebano, A. & Jamieson, L. (2020). Childbearing in Italy and Spain: Postponement narratives. *Population and Development Review*, 46(1): 121–44.

Lee, E., Bristow, J., Faircloth, C. & Macvarish, J. (2023). *Parenting Culture Studies*, 2nd edn. Cham: Palgrave Macmillan.

Leshchenko, O. & Chung, H. (2023). Homeworking and division of domestic work: The role of gender role attitudes in Germany. *SocArXiv Papers*, October. https://doi.org/10.31235/osf.io/85b23.

Lundberg, S. & Pollak, R. A. (1996). Bargaining and distribution in marriage. *Journal of Economic Perspectives*, 10(4), 139–58. https://doi.org/10.1257/jep.10.4.139.

Lynch, K. (2007). Love labour as a distinct and non-commodifiable form of care labour. *Sociological Review*, 55(3), 550–70. https://doi.org/10.1111/j.1467-954X.2007.00714.x.

Lynch, K. & Walsh, J. (2009). Love, care and solidarity: what is and is not commodifiable. In K. Lynch, J. Baker & M. Lyons (eds.), *Affective Equality: Love, care and injustice*, pp. 35–53. Basingstoke: Palgrave Macmillan.

Mason, J. (2004). Personal narratives, relational selves: Residential histories in the living and telling. *Sociological Review*, 52(2), 162–79. https://doi.org/10.1111/j.1467-954X.2004.00463.x.

Mauerer, G. & Schmidt, E.-M. (2019). Parents' strategies in dealing with constructions of gendered responsibilities at their workplaces. *Social Sciences*, 8(9), art. no. 250. https://doi.org/10.3390/socsci8090250.

Mauthner, N. S. (2002). *The Darkest Days of My Life: Stories of postpartum depression*. Cambridge, MA: Harvard University Press.

Mauthner, N. S. & Doucet, A. (2003). Reflexive accounts and accounts of reflexivity in qualitative data analysis. *Sociology*, 37(3), 413–31. https://doi.org/10.1177/00380385030373002.

May, V. & Nordqvist, P. (eds.) (2019). *Sociology of Personal Life*. London: Bloomsbury Academic.

McAndrew, F., Thompson, J., Fellows, L., Large, A., Speed, M. & Renfrew, M. J. (2012). *Infant Feeding Survey 2010*. Health and Social Care Information Centre. https://sp.ukdataservice.ac.uk/doc/7281/mrdoc/pdf/7281_ifs-uk-2010_report.pdf (accessed 11 April 2024).

McKay, L. & Doucet, A. (2010). 'Without taking away her leave': A Canadian case study of couples' decisions on fathers' use of paid parental leave. *Fathering*, 8(3), 300–20. https://www.academia.edu/4900480/McKay_L_and_Doucet_A_2010_Without_taking_away_her_leave_A_Canadian_Case_Study_of_Couples_Decisions_of_Fathers_Use_of_Paid_Parental_Leave_2010_

McMunn, A., Bird, L., Webb, E. & Sacker, A. (2020). Gender divisions of paid and unpaid work in contemporary UK couples. *Work, Employment and Society*, 34(2), 155–73. http://dx.doi.org/10.1177/0950017019862153.

McQueen, F. (2023). The new feeling rules of emotion work in heterosexual couple relationships. *Emotions and Society*, 5(1), 85–99. https://doi.org/10.1332/263169021X16541387415753.

Meil, G. (2013). European men's use of parental leave and their involvement in child care and housework. *Journal of Comparative Family Studies*, 44(5), 557–70. https://doi.org/10.3138/jcfs.44.5.557.

Miller, T. (2005). *Making Sense of Motherhood: A narrative approach*. Cambridge: Cambridge University Press.

Miller, T. (2010). *Making Sense of Fatherhood: Gender, caring and work*. Cambridge: Cambridge University Press.

Miller, T. (2017). *Making Sense of Parenthood: Caring, gender and family lives*. Cambridge: Cambridge University Press.

Miller, T. (2023). *Motherhood: Contemporary transitions and generational change*. Cambridge: Cambridge University Press.

Morgan, D. H. J. (2011). *Rethinking Family Practices*. Basingstoke: Palgrave Macmillan.

Morgan, D. L., Ataie, J., Carder, P. & Hoffman, K. (2013). Introducing dyadic interviews as a method for collecting qualitative data. *Qualitative Health Research*, 23(9), 1276–84. https://doi.org/10.1177/1049732313501889.

Morton, K. (2019). Cost of childcare forcing parents to quit their jobs. *Nursery World*, 29 October. https://www.nurseryworld.co.uk/news/article/cost-of-childcare-forcing-parents-to-quit-their-jobs (accessed 11 April 2024).

Moss, P. & Deven, F. (2015). Leave policies in challenging times: Reviewing the decade 2004–2014. *Community, Work & Family*, 18(2), 137–44. https://doi.org/10.1080/13668803.2015.1021094

Nadim, M. (2016). Undermining the male breadwinner ideal? Understandings of women's paid work among second-generation immigrants in Norway. *Sociology*, 50(1), 109–24. http://dx.doi.org/10.1177/0038038514560259.

Neal, S. & Murji, K. (2015). Sociologies of everyday life: Editors' introduction to the special issue. *Sociology*, 49(5), 811–19. https://doi.org/10.1177/0038038515602160.

Nussbaum, M. C. (1997). Capabilities and human rights. *Fordham Law Review*, 66(2), 273–300.

Oakley, A. (1974). *The Sociology of Housework*. Oxford: Basil Blackwell.

Oakley, A. (1980). *Women Confined: Towards a sociology of childbirth*. New York: Schocken Books.

Oakley, A. (1998). A brief history of gender. In A. Oakley & J. Mitchell (eds), *Who's Afraid of Feminism? Seeing through the backlash*, pp. 29–55. New York: New Press.

Oakley, A. (2018 [1979]). *From Here to Maternity: Becoming a mother*, reissue. Bristol: Policy Press.

O'Brien, M. (2009). Fathers, parental leave policies, and infant quality of life: International perspectives and policy impact. *Annals of the American Academy of Political and Social Science*, 624(1), 190–213. https://doi.org/10.1177/0002716209334349.

O'Brien, M., Aldrich, M., Connolly, S., Cook, R. & Speight, S. (2017). *Inequalities in Access to Paid Maternity and Paternity Leave and Flexible Work: Report*. https://www.researchgate.net/profile/Rose-Cook/publication/326463910_Inequalities_in_access_to_paid_maternity_leave_paternity_leave_and_flexible_work/links/5b4f54f7aca27217ffa1e5e6/Inequalities-in-access-to-paid-maternity-leave-paternity-leave-and-flexible-work.pdf.

O'Brien, M., Brandth, B. & Kvande, E. (2007). Fathers, work and family life: Global perspectives and new insights. *Community, Work and Family*, 10(4), 375–86. https://doi.org/10.1080/13668800701574971.

O'Brien, M. & Koslowski, A. (2017). United Kingdom country note. In S. Blum, A. Koslowski & P. Moss (eds), *International Review of Leave Policies and Research 2017*, pp. 414–26. International Network on Leave Policies and Research.

O'Brien, M. & Twamley, K. (2017). Fathers taking leave alone in the UK: a gift exchange between mother and father? In M. O'Brien & K. Wall (eds), *Comparative Perspectives on Work–Life Balance and Gender Equality: Fathers on leave alone*, pp. 163–81. Cham: Springer Open.

O'Brien, M. & Uzunalioglu, M. (2022). Parenting leave policies and a global social policy agenda. In I. Dobrotić, S. Blum & A. Koslowski (eds), *Research Handbook on Leave Policy: Parenting and social inequalities in a global perspective*, pp. 67–81. Cheltenham: Edward Elgar Publishing.

O'Brien, M. & Wall, K. (2017). *Comparative Perspectives on Work–Life Balance and Gender Equality: Fathers on leave alone*. Cham: Springer Open.

OECD (Organization for Economic Cooperation and Development) (2017). *OECD Labour Force Statistics 2016*. Paris: OECD Publishing. https://doi.org/10.1787/oecd_lfs-2016-en.

OECD (Organization for Economic Cooperation and Development) (n.d.). Net childcare costs for parents using childcare facilities. https://stats.oecd.org/Index.aspx?DataSetCode=NCC (accessed 24 June 2024).

Oláh, L. S. and Gähler, M. (2014). Gender equality perceptions: Division of paid and unpaid work, and partnership dissolution in Sweden, *Social Forces, 93*(2), 571–594. https://doi.org/10.1093/sf/sou066.

Olsen, W., Gash, V., Kim, S. & Zhang, M. (2018). The gender pay gap in the UK: Evidence from the UKHLS. Research Report Number DFE-RR804. London: Department for Education, Government Equalities Office. https://assets.publishing.service.gov.uk/media/5af4261440f0b622dae8dd44/Gender_pay_gap_in_the_UK_evidence_from_the_UKHLS.pdf (accessed 11 April 2024).

ONS (Office for National Statistics) (2016). Trends in self-employment in the UK: 2001 to 2015. https://www.ons.gov.uk/employmentandlabourmarket/peopleinwork/employmentandemployeetypes/articles/trendsinselfemploymentintheuk/2001to2015.

ONS (Office for National Statistics) (2018a). Gender pay gap in the UK: 2018. https://www.ons.gov.uk/employmentandlabourmarket/peopleinwork/earningsandworkinghours/bulletins/genderpaygapintheuk/2018 (accessed 24 June 2024).

ONS (Office for National Statistics) (2018b). Families and the labour market, England: 2018. https://www.ons.gov.uk/employmentandlabourmarket/peopleinwork/employmentandemployeetypes/articles/familiesandthelabourmarketengland/2018 (accessed 24 June 2024).

ONS (Office for National Statistics) (2021). Families and the labour market, UK: 2021. https://www.ons.gov.uk/employmentandlabourmarket/peopleinwork/employmentandemployeetypes/articles/familiesandthelabourmarketengland/2021 (accessed 11 April 2024).

Orgad, S. (2019). *Heading Home: Motherhood, work, and the failed promise of equality*. New York: Columbia University Press.

Orloff, A. S. (2009). Should feminists aim for gender symmetry? Why the dual-earner/dual-carer model may not be every feminist's utopia. In J. C. Gornick & M. K. Meyers (eds), *Gender Equality: Transforming family divisions of labor*, pp. 129–60. London: Verso.

Patterson, L. & Forbes, K. (2012). 'Doing gender' in the imagined futures of young New Zealanders. *Young, 20*(2), 119–36. https://doi.org/10.1177/110330881202000201.

Petts, R. J. (2022). *Father Involvement and Gender Equality in the United States: Contemporary norms and barriers*. Abingdon: Routledge.

Petts, R. J., Kaufman, G. & Mize, T. D. (2023). Parental leave-taking and perceptions of workers as good parents. *Journal of Marriage and Family, 85*(1), 261–79. https://doi.org/10.1111/jomf.12875.

Petts, R. J. & Knoester, C. (2020). Are parental relationships improved if fathers take time off of work after the birth of a child? *Social Forces, 98*(3), 1223–56. https://doi.org/10.1093/sf/soz014.

Petts, R. J., Mize, T. D. & Kaufman, G. (2022). Organizational policies, workplace culture, and perceived job commitment of mothers and fathers who take parental leave. *Social Science Research, 103*, art. no. 102651. http://dx.doi.org/10.1016/j.ssresearch.2021.102651.

Petts, R., Mize, T. D. & Kaufman, G. (2024). Does taking parental leave make you a more likeable worker? Evidence from a survey experiment. *Community, Work and Family*, 1–25. https://doi.org/10.1080/13668803.2024.2321124.

Phạm, Q. N. (2013). Enduring bonds: Politics and life outside freedom as autonomy. *Alternatives, 38*(1), 29–48. http://dx.doi.org/10.1177/0304375412465676.

Povinelli, E. A. (2011). *Economies of Abandonment: Social belonging and endurance in late liberalism*. Durham, NC: Duke University Press.

Prattes, R. (2022). Caring masculinities and race: On racialized workers and 'new fathers'. *Men and Masculinities, 25*(5), 721–42. https://doi.org/10.1177/1097184X211065024.

Qureshi, K. & Metlo, Z. (2021). A British South Asian Muslim relational negotiation of divorce: Uncoupling beyond the couple. *Families, Relationships and Societies, 10*(1), 153–68. https://doi.org/10.1332/204674320X16003573168697.

Ranson, G. (2012). Men, paid employment and family responsibilities: Conceptualizing the 'working father'. *Gender, Work and Organization, 19*(6), 741–61. https://doi.org/10.1111/j.1468-0432.2011.00549.x.

Ranson, G. (2013). Who's (really) in charge? Mothers and executive responsibility in 'non-traditional' families. *Families, Relationships and Societies, 2*(1), 79–95. http://dx.doi.org/10.1332/204674313X664725.

Rehel, E. M. (2014). When Dad stays home too: Paternity leave, gender, and parenting. *Gender and Society, 28*(1), 110–32. https://doi.org/10.1177/0891243213503900.

Reich, N. (2011). Predictors of fathers' use of parental leave in Germany. *Population Review*, 50(2). https://doi.org/10.1353/prv.2011.0011.

Reich-Stiebert, N., Froehlich, L. & Voltmer, J.-B. (2023). Gendered mental labor: A systematic literature review on the cognitive dimension of unpaid work within the household and childcare. *Sex Roles*, 88, 475–94. https://doi.org/10.1007/s11199-023-01362-0.

Rizzo, K. M., Schiffrin, H. H. & Liss, M. (2013). Insight into the parenthood paradox: Mental health outcomes of intensive mothering. *Journal of Child and Family Studies*, 22, 614–20. https://doi.org/10.1007/s10826-012-9615-z.

Roberts, S. & Prattes, R. (2023). Caring masculinities in theory and practice: Reiterating the relevance and clarifying the capaciousness of the concept. *Sociological Research Online*, 1–11. https://doi.org/10.1177/13607804231205978.

Romero-Balsas, P., Muntanyola-Saura, D. & Rogero-García, J. (2013). Decision-making factors within paternity and parental leaves: Why Spanish fathers take time off from work. *Gender, Work and Organization*, 20(6), 678–91. https://doi.org/10.1111/gwao.12004.

Roseneil, S. & Ketokivi, K. (2016). Relational persons and relational processes: Developing the notion of relationality for the sociology of personal life. *Sociology*, 50(1), 143–59. https://doi.org/10.1177/0038038514561295.

Ross, C. E. (1987). The division of labor at home. *Social Forces*, 65(3), 816–33. https://doi.org/10.1093/sf/65.3.816.

Ruddick, S. (1995). *Maternal Thinking: Toward a politics of peace*. Boston: Beacon Press.

Samtleben, C., Bringmann, J., Bünning, M. & Hipp, L. (2019). What helps and what hinders? Exploring the role of workplace characteristics for parental leave use and its career consequences. *Social Sciences*, 8(10), art. no. 270. https://doi.org/10.3390/socsci8100270.

Sandelowski, M. (1994). The use of quotes in qualitative research. *Research in Nursing and Health*, 17(6), 479–82. https://doi.org/10.1002/nur.4770170611.

Schmidt, E.-M. (2018). Breadwinning as care? The meaning of paid work in mothers' and fathers' constructions of parenting. *Community, Work and Family*, 21(4), 445–62. https://doi.org/10.1080/13668803.2017.1318112.

Schmidt, E.-M., Décieux, F., Zartler, U. & Schnor, C. (2023). What makes a good mother? Two decades of research reflecting social norms of motherhood. *Journal of Family Theory and Review*, 15(1), 57–77. https://doi.org/10.1111/jftr.12488.

Schmidt, E.-M., Rieder, I., Zartler, U., Schadler, C. & Richter, R. (2015). Parental constructions of masculinity at the transition to parenthood: The division of parental leave among Austrian couples. *International Review of Sociology*, 25(3), 373–86. https://doi.org/10.1080/03906701.2015.1078532.

Schmidt, E.-M., Zartler, U. & Vogl, S. (2019). Swimming against the tide? Austrian couples' non-normative work-care arrangements in a traditional environment. In D. Grunow & M. Evertsson (eds), *New Parents in Europe: Work-care practices, gender norms and family policies*, pp. 108–27. Cheltenham: Edward Elgar Publishing.

Schober, P. S. (2013). Gender equality and outsourcing of domestic work, childbearing, and relationship stability among British couples. *Journal of Family Issues*, 34(1), 25–52. https://doi.org/10.1177/0192513X11433691%0A.

Schober, P. S. (2014). Parental leave and domestic work of mothers and fathers: A longitudinal study of two reforms in West Germany. *Journal of Social Policy*, 43(2), 351–72. https://doi.org/10.1017/S0047279413000809.

Schwartz, P. (1994). *Love between Equals: How peer marriage really works*. New York: Free Press.

Sevilla, A. & Smith, S. (2020). Baby steps: The gender division of childcare during the COVID-19 pandemic. *Oxford Review of Economic Policy*, 36(Supplement_1), S169–S186. https://doi.org/10.1093/oxrep/graa027.

Seward, R. R., Yeatts, D. E., Zottarelli, L. K. & Fletcher, R. G. (2006). Fathers taking parental leave and their involvement with children: An exploratory study. *Community, Work and Family*, 9(1), 1–9. https://doi.org/10.1080/13668800500421093.

Shirani, F. & Henwood, K. (2011). Continuity and change in a qualitative longitudinal study of fatherhood: Relevance without responsibility. *International Journal of Social Research Methodology*, 14(1), 17–29. https://doi.org/10.1080/13645571003690876.

Shirani, F., Henwood, K. & Coltart, C. (2012a). 'Why aren't you at work?': Negotiating economic models of fathering identity. *Fathering*, 10(3), 274–90.

Shirani, F., Henwood, K. & Coltart, C. (2012b). Meeting the challenges of intensive parenting culture: Gender, risk management and the moral parent. *Sociology*, *46*(1), 25–40. https://doi.org/10.1177/0038038511416169.

Smart, C. (2007). *Personal Life: New directions in sociological thinking*. Cambridge: Polity.

Smart, C. (2011). Relationality and socio-cultural theories of family life. In R. Jallinoja & E. Widmer (eds.), *Families and Kinship in Contemporary Europe: Rules and practices of relatedness*, pp. 13–28. Basingstoke: Palgrave Macmillan.

Somers, M. R. (1994). The narrative constitution of identity: A relational and network approach. *Theory and Society*, *23*(5), 605–49. https://doi.org/10.1007/BF00992905.

Stovell, C. (2021). Can't share? Won't share? Examining work-family decision making processes at the transition to parenthood. PhD thesis, Lancaster University.

Strathern, M. (1992). *After Nature: English kinship in the late twentieth century*. Cambridge: Cambridge University Press.

Sullivan, O. (2013). What do we learn about gender by analyzing housework separately from child care? Some considerations from time-use evidence. *Journal of Family Theory and Review*, *5*(2), 72–84. https://doi.org/10.1111/jftr.12007.

Sullivan, O. (2019). Gender inequality in work–family balance. *Nature Human Behaviour*, *3*(3), 201–3. http://dx.doi.org/10.1038/s41562-019-0536-3.

Sullivan, T. A. (2014). Greedy institutions, overwork, and work–life balance. *Sociological Inquiry*, *84*(1), 1–15. https://doi.org/10.1111/soin.12029.

Tichenor, V. J. (2005). Maintaining men's dominance: Negotiating identity and power when she earns more. *Sex Roles 53*(3/4), August 2005. https://doi.org/10.1007/s11199-005-5678-2.

Tolich, M. (2004). Internal confidentiality: When confidentiality assurances fail relational informants. *Qualitative Sociology*, *27*(1), 101–6. http://dx.doi.org/10.1023/B:QUAS.0000015546.20441.4a.

Topping, A. (2022). Universal preschool funding needed in England, says report. *The Guardian*, 22 September. https://www.theguardian.com/lifeandstyle/2022/sep/22/universal-preschool-funding-england-childcare (accessed 11 April 2024).

Townsend, N. W. (2002). *The Package Deal: Marriage, work and fatherhood in men's lives*. Philadelphia: Temple University Press.

TUC (2017). Better jobs for mums and dads. https://www.tuc.org.uk/research-analysis/reports/better-jobs-mums-and-dads (accessed 11 April 2024).

Twamley, K. (2012). Gender relations among Indian couples in the UK and India: Ideals of equality and realities of inequality. *Sociological Research Online*, *17*(4), 103–13. https://doi.org/10.5153/sro.2756.

Twamley, K. (2014). *Love, Marriage and Intimacy among Gujarati Indians: A suitable match*. Basingstoke: Palgrave Macmillan.

Twamley, K. (2019). 'Cold intimacies' in parents' negotiations of work–family practices and parental leave? *Sociological Review*, *67*(5), 1137–53. https://doi.org/10.1177/0038026118815427.

Twamley, K. (2021). 'She has mellowed me into the idea of SPL': Unpacking relational resources in UK couples' discussions of Shared Parental Leave take-up. *Families, Relationships and Societies*, *10*(1), 67–82. https://doi.org/10.1332/204674320X15986394583380.

Twamley, K., Doucet, A. & Schmidt, E.-M. (2021). Introduction to special issue: Relationality in family and intimate practices. *Families, Relationships and Societies*, *10*(1), 3–10. http://dx.doi.org/10.1332/204674321X16111601166128.

Twamley, K. & Faircloth, C. (2023). Understanding 'gender equality': First-time parent couples' practices and perspectives on working and caring post-parenthood. *Sociological Research Online*, Online First. https://doi.org/10.1177/13607804231198619.

Twamley, K., Faircloth, C. & Iqbal, H. (2023). COVID labour: Making a 'livable' life under lockdown. *Sociological Review*, *71*(1), 85–104. https://doi.org/10.1177/00380261221138203.

Twamley, K., Iqbal, H. & Faircloth, C. (eds.) (2023). *Family in the Time of Covid: International perspectives*. London: UCL Press.

Twamley, K. & Schober, P. (2019). Shared parental leave: Exploring variations in attitudes, eligibility, knowledge and take-up intentions of expectant mothers in London. *Journal of Social Policy*, *48*(2), 387–407. https://doi.org/10.1017/S0047279418000557.

Tyler, I. (2007). The selfish feminist: Public images of women's liberation. *Australian Feminist Studies*, *22*(53), 173–90. https://doi.org/10.1080/08164640701361758.

Uzunalioglu, M. & Twamley, K. (2023). Access to and experiences of parental and associated leaves for UK university staff: A case study. Paper presented at the Accommodating Diversity in the Workplace Conference, 19–20 June, University of Reading.

Uzunalioglu, M., Valentova, M., O'Brien, M. & Genevois, A.-S. (2021). When does expanded eligibility translate into increased take-up? An examination of parental leave policy in Luxembourg. *Social Inclusion*, 9(2), 350–63. https://doi.org/10.17645/si.v9i2.3787.

Valentova, M. (2011). Anticipated parental leave take up in Luxembourg. *Social Policy and Society*, 10(2), 123–38. https://doi.org/10.1017/S1474746410000485.

Van Hooff, J. H. (2011). Rationalising inequality: Heterosexual couples' explanations and justifications for the division of housework along traditionally gendered lines. *Journal of Gender Studies*, 20(1), 19–30. https://doi.org/10.1080/09589236.2011.542016.

Wall, G. (2013). 'Putting family first': Shifting discourses of motherhood and childhood in representations of mothers' employment and child care. *Women's Studies International Forum*, 40(September–October), 162–71. https://doi.org/10.1016/j.wsif.2013.07.006.

Wall, K. & O'Brien, M. (2017). Discussion and conclusions. In M. O'Brien & K. Wall (eds), *Comparative Perspectives on Work–Life Balance and Gender Equality: Fathers on leave alone*, pp. 257–66. Cham: Springer Open.

Walthery, P. & Chung, H. (2021). Sharing of childcare and well-being outcomes: An empirical analysis. Second report: quantitative analysis of the 2014/15 UK time use study. UK Cabinet Office. https://assets.publishing.service.gov.uk/government/uploads/system/uploads/attachment_data/file/957550/Sharing_of_childcare_and_well-being_outcomes__an_empirical_analysis__1_.pdf (accessed 11 April 2024).

Wardlow, H. & Hirsch, J. S. (2006). Introduction. In J. S. Hirsch & H. Wardlow (eds), *Modern Loves: The anthropology of romantic courtship & companionate marriage*, 1–33. Ann Arbor: University of Michigan Press.

Williams, J. C. (2012). *Reshaping the Work-Family Debate: Why men and class matter*. Cambridge, MA: Harvard University Press.

Williams, J. C., Blair-Loy, M. & Berdahl, J. L. (2013). Cultural schemas, social class, and the flexibility stigma. *Journal of Social Issues*, 69(2), 209–34. https://doi.org/10.1111/josi.12012.

Wishart, R., Dunatchik, A., Speight, S. & Mayer, M. (2018). Changing patterns in parental time use in the UK. London: National Centre for Social Research.

Wojnicka, K. (2022). What's masculinity got to do with it? The COVID-19 pandemic, men and care. *European Journal of Women's Studies*, 29(1_suppl), 27S–42S. https://doi.org/10.1177/13505068221076322.

Wolf, J. (2011). *Is Breast Best? Taking on the breastfeeding experts and the new high stakes of motherhood*. New York: New York University Press.

Wong, J. S. (2023). *Equal Partners? How dual-professional couples make career, relationship, and family decisions*. Oakland: University of California Press.

Wood, J., Marynissen, L. & Van Gasse, D. (2023). When is it about the money? Relative wages and fathers' parental leave decisions. *Population Research and Policy Review*, 42(6), art. no. 93. https://doi.org/10.1007/s11113-023-09837-4.

Wynn, A. T. & Rao, A. H. (2020). Failures of flexibility: How perceived control motivates the individualization of work–life conflict. *ILR Review*, 73(1), 61–90. https://doi.org/10.1177/0019793919848426.

Yarwood, G. A. (2011). The pick and mix of fathering identities. *Fathering*, 9(2), 150–68. http://dx.doi.org/10.3149/fth.0902.150.

Yarwood, G. A. & Locke, A. (2016). Work, parenting and gender: The care–work negotiations of three couple relationships in the UK. *Community, Work and Family*, 19(3), 362–77. http://dx.doi.org/https://doi.org/10.1080/13668803.2015.1047441.

Yavorsky, J. E., Kamp Dush, C. M. & Schoppe-Sullivan, S. J. (2015). The production of inequality: The gender division of labor across the transition to parenthood. *Journal of Marriage and Family*, 77(3), 662–79. https://doi.org/10.1111%2Fjomf.12189.

Yerkes, M. (2009). Part-time work in the Dutch welfare state: The ideal combination of work and care? *Policy & Politics* 37(4): 535–552. https://doi.org/10.1332/030557309X435510.

Index

additional paternity leave (APL) 1, 2, 32
agency
    lack of 137, 149
    relational 27, 219, 226
    researching 221
anxiety
    about being solely responsible for care 90, 97, 205, 218
    of child 170
    about 'correct parenting' 14, 24, 80–1, 90, 93, 102, 206
    about finances 51, 99, 149, 201
    inequalities in experiencing 25, 95
    about job precarity 187, 201
    about taking SPL 55, 111–12, 212
austerity 216

bottle feeding 86–7, 122, 124, 155, 182
    see also formula feed
breadwinning
    as care 161, 175, 206–7
    gendered 173, 201, 206–8, 211–12
    meaning 136
    struggles 201, 207
    'universal breadwinner' 195
breastfeeding
    deterrent to SPL 103
    enabled by SPL 119
    inhibiting shared caring 86, 103,
    national recommendations 87
    as representative of 'good motherhood' 84, 126–7, 206
    struggles 24, 81, 91, 105

career
    acceleration 135, 164, 191
    break 99
    compromising of 33, 39, 48, 109, 165, 185, 215
    difficulties of combining with motherhood 40, 171, 192, 196
    factors in choosing a 33, 51, 202
    low aspirations for 64–5, 75, 187, 192, 201
    meaningless 164
    as a means to an end 175, 190
    oriented or ambitious 65, 69, 161, 190, 211
    prioritizing the man's 140, 148, 165, 167, 170, 199, 203
    repercussions feared due to leave 9, 13, 25, 35–6, 38, 40–1, 51, 57, 61, 66, 200, 202
caring masculinities see masculinities
childcare, formal
    costs 99, 138, 140–1, 151, 215
    reluctance to use 41, 139–40,
childhood development 40–1, 92, 102, 173, 197, 205
class see social class
cognitive labour 8, 73, 92, 123, 153, 157, 159, 164, 176
    see also mental load
cold intimacy 45–51, 70, 209
compressed hours 38–9, 181, 187
couple interviews (methods) 6, 16–17, 20
COVID-19 pandemic 8, 216
cost of living 186–7
    crisis 11, 216

daddy bonus see fatherhood bonus
daddy quota of leave, 13, 218
    see also individual entitlement to leave
Dermott, Esther 14, 42, 102, 206, 208, 228
diary elicitation 20, 22, 78
discrimination 70, 196, 202
    see also gender discrimination
displaying family 163, 190, 203, 214
displaying intimacy or couple intimacy 44, 69, 203, 214
Doucet, Andrea 2, 4, 8–9, 15, 17, 21, 51, 97, 114, 116, 146, 153, 158–9, 175, 177, 185, 195, 197, 199, 203, 207, 210, 216, 221–2, 228

emotional labour see emotion work
emotion work 3, 61, 107
enhanced leave pay 12–13, 32, 74, 76, 83, 98, 219
ethical considerations 22
ethnicity 16, 217

Faircloth, Charlotte 9, 14, 20, 35, 41–2, 47, 50, 69, 81, 93, 125–6, 153, 196, 206–7, 209, 215, 229
family practices 101, 166, 203, 213
fatherhood bonus 165, 201
fatherhood forfeit 13
fathers as mothers' 'help' 80, 87, 95–6, 138, 142
feeling redundant 124–5

INDEX   239

feminism
    as cold 49, 209
    as selfish 50
    choice 209
    feminist advice books 195
    feminist care literature 2, 166
    feminist scholarship and men 185
    identifying as a feminist 17, 69–70, 210
    post-feminism 47
    repudiating 17, 47–8, 213
financial difficulties *see* anxiety
Finch, Janet 163, 190, 203, 229
flexible working
    enabling shared parenting 25–6, 176, 187, 192, 219
    impacting on leave 98, 186
    leading to longer work hours 98
    penalised for 8, 13, 75, 199
    taking up 37, 39, 82, 149
    to reduce nursery hours 151
    see also part-time work
Folbre, Nancy 123, 166, 229
formula feed 84, 122, 136, 206

gatekeeping
    collaborative 45, 210
    maternal 34, 45, 56, 75, 120, 210
    paternal 45, 210
gender discrimination 70, 196, 202
gender equality
    fairness 46–7, 50, 69, 89, 145, 196, 209
    symmetry 24, 47, 69, 72, 76, 163, 185, 195–6, 198, 209, 214–15
gender pay gap 6, 8, 32, 196
Goldin, Claudia 8, 23, 36, 165, 185, 196, 199, 202–3, 215, 230
grandparents 4, 216
gratitude
    economy of 143, 162
    to employers 37, 98–9, 200
    to partner/spouse 87–8, 91, 144–5
greedy work *see* Goldin, Claudia
greedy parenting 40–2, 205, 219
guilt 79, 88, 91, 94, 108, 124

household portrait 17–19, 20, 22, 46, 97
housework different to care work 4

ideal worker norm 23, 36–8, 195, 199, 201, 216
individual entitlement to leave 15, 218
    see also daddy quota
individual interviews 10, 17, 20, 22, 54, 129
individual responsibility
    for care 37, 205
    for gender equality 209
individualism 49
intersectionality 217
intimacy
    and equality ideal 3, 24, 51, 76, 158, 208, 209
    between parent and child 4, 7, 80, 85, 128
    practices of 7, 23, 27
    sharing leave beneficial for 184
    see also cold intimacy *and* displaying intimacy
intimate fatherhood 42, 51, 102, 162, 208

intimate negotiations 27, 208

job insecurity *see* job precarity
job precarity 1, 36–7, 51, 101, 186, 187, 201, 215
job promotion 58, 109, 135, 153, 164–5, 203
job security 64, 99, 201

learning to care
    fathers 26, 69, 85, 112, 116, 128, 198
    mothers 84, 90–5, 102, 116, 205
    together 71–2, 186
leisure
    gendered differences in access to 93
    lacking time for 142, 195
    monitoring participation in 69
    see also me-time
listening guide 21, 221–2
longitudinal research 6, 11, 15, 21
love as natural 49, 73
love labour 84, 232

masculinities
    caring 10, 196, 207, 229
    hegemonic 10, 45, 212
    and work norms 25, 61, 185, 195, 199, 203
maternity leave
    as rite of passage 50, 204
    career penalty due to 25, 35, 99, 135
    duration of 7, 11, 31–2
    remuneration 11, 99, 101, 210
    see also enhanced leave pay
mental health 198
mental load 9, 26, 73, 97, 123, 137, 153, 159–61, 168, 171, 176, 192, 198
    see also cognitive labour
'me time' 69, 93, 95
Miller, Tina 14, 41–2, 45, 69, 102, 206, 208, 210, 233
moral pressures around parenthood 40–1
    see also breastfeeding
moral responsibilities, gendered 26, 42, 61, 69, 92, 114, 135–6, 150, 158, 162–3, 166, 176, 190, 211
motherhood penalty 202–3
mother's instinct 174–5
mother as naturally better carer 13, 151, 174, 183
multimodal diaries 20
mutual dependence 166

nagging 73, 157, 210
narrative research 21, 221
neoliberalism 11, 13
Nordic countries 10, 13, 41
nursery care *see* childcare, formal

Oakley, Ann 4, 6, 48, 101, 166, 233
organisational support for parental leave 32, 38

parental advice
    consuming 4, 102, 204
    gendered differences in taking 92, 93
parental leave eligibility 2, 12, 15–16, 31, 51, 218
parenting culture studies 93

part-time work
    for childcare 191
    difficulties 151
    inhibits career progression 153, 164, 219
    norm for mothers 8, 13, 132, 191, 203
    not possible 148
    plans 139, 169
    supporting mother's 34, 109, 214
    see also flexible working
paternity leave
    definition of 7, 197
    duration of 120, 127, 193, 218
    eligibility for 216
    not taking 36–7, 198, 200
    remuneration during 11–12, 32
    take-up of 31–2
    working during 186, 200

recruitment of participants 15–16, 218
relational agency *see* agency
relationality
    and caring masculinities 10
    and family life 210
    in gendered divisions of labour 2, 45, 54, 146, 170, 173
    and parental leave decisions 1, 3, 15, 24, 50–1, 55, 200, 208
    in research 3–5, 7, 21, 30, 221–2
relational resources 56
relationship work 6, 24, 78, 86, 102, 108, 123, 141, 175, 212
resentment between parents 22, 71, 106–7, 142, 215
role specialisation (gender, 35–6, 99, 141, 144, 146, 149, 151, 165, 190, 192

sexism 47
    see also gender discrimination
shared parental leave (SPL)
    eligibility for 12, 16, 216, 218
    take-up rates 2
social class 139, 161, 207
sociology of everyday life 6, 78
stay-at-home father 64–5, 127, 173, 175, 195, 211
stay-at-home mother 137, 139, 140, 150

teenagers, parenting of 169
temporality, child-centred 10, 114
time-use surveys 8, 73, 130, 206
twins, being a parent of 40, 144

work colleagues
    keeping up with 37
    learning from experiences of 192
    negotiations about SPL with 4, 15, 27
    promoting SPL to 62
    supportive about SPL 38, 57, 146, 200
    taking SPL 44
    unsupportive about SPL, 58, 61–4, 159, 204, 210
working from home 82, 132, 157–8, 170, 188
work–life balance 36, 65, 172, 187